Stories My Father Never Finished Telling Me

Living with the Armenian Legacy of Loss and Silence

Douglas Kalajian

ISBN: 0615979025
ISBN 13: 9780615979021
Library of Congress Control Number: 2014904447
LCCN Imprint Name: 8220 Press, Boynton Beach, FL

For Mandy

CONTENTS

NOTE

There's no perfect way to spell Armenian words with English letters. The Armenian alphabet was created in the fifth century with thirty-six letters and has since expanded. Many sounds have no English equivalent. While scholars use a number of transliteration systems, all are imperfect, and I'm no scholar. So I've simply tried my best to mimic the pronunciations I recall from my childhood, particularly the names of foods. Names of people are more problematic. The English spelling of Armenian names, first and last, is often a product of the limited imaginations of immigration officials. I've tried to use the spellings found on documents or provided by relatives, which is why some common names are spelled differently throughout the book.

TUMBLING THROUGH LIFE

I was born in midair. All Armenians are born in midair.

We come to life screaming from the fall, not from the doctor's slapping our backsides. The wind rushing past forces air into our lungs. It is impossible to breathe and impossible not to. We are more alive than other people because we are always tumbling toward death, and we know it.

Some of us know it sooner than others.

I was eight years old when I got my first inkling. I'm sure it was autumn 1960 because we'd just moved into an old house at the crest of a hill in Ridgefield, New Jersey. My parents were busy scraping and painting the living room walls. I was playing with my toy cars in the narrow, chilly front porch that had been closed in with yellow clapboards but not insulated. The whole place smelled of turpentine and plaster dust.

I remember my father calling me, shouting at me to be careful—*goddamit!*—not to step in the mess of spattered drop cloths and shattered plaster in my path. Of course, I stumbled right into it. Dad just shook his head and went back to setting up our portable TV on the dining room table, twisting the rabbit-ear antenna until a black-and-white picture emerged from the snow and static. It was a channel I usually avoided, a sort of pre-PBS called Educational Television. A professor was talking about Armenians.

Nobody on TV ever talked about Armenians.

"This is great!"

"Be quiet," my father said. "Just listen."

The professor pointed to a map and explained where the Armenians lived before they were forced from their homes and marched into the desert.

1

He talked about massacres on a vast scale. He described things I'd never imagined, but nothing was as awful as what I saw right in our dining room.

My father was crying.

I started to cry, too, not because of what I heard but because of what that man on television did to my father. Dad ran out of the room and I ran to my mother.

"Why is Daddy crying?"

"Don't ever ask him about what happened," Mom said. "It's too sad."

"What's too sad?" I asked.

"They killed his mother," she said.

"Who killed his mother?"

"The Turks."

"What Turks? What happened?"

"Never mind," she said. "Just don't ever ask."

This is how it was handed to me, the Armenian legacy of loss and silence. Who wants such a thing, especially at that age? How could anyone know what to do with it? I'm past sixty now and I'm still not sure, so I carry it everywhere, pulled close and wrapped tight in both arms. It is a strange thing to grow up carrying such a fat, invisible weight. It makes other people wonder about you, about why you're walking around all hunched over and grimacing.

The purposeful and systematic slaughter of a million and a half Armenians from 1915 to 1922 was widely reported and well known in America. But that knowledge faded along with most the world's outrage and sympathy as survivors like my father shielded their pain with silence. They thought they were shielding us, too. Once a year on a damp day in April, the old people prayed and whispered about the massacres, but mostly among themselves. The one lasting lesson Armenians drew from six hundred years of Turkish rule was: Keep quiet.

How is it that the Jews learned nothing of the sort?

I met many Holocaust survivors in my work as a journalist. I've sat with them, eaten with them, listened to their stories. You don't have to ask twice. They'll show you their tattoos and their scars. They'll tell you about the neighbors who turned on them, and the ones who tried to help. About the trains, the camps, the gas chambers. The polished brass hooks where the Germans so carefully hung the clothing of the soon-to-be-dead. The rows and rows of shoes, perfectly arranged by size. Ask how they can tell such stories to strangers and every one will give you the same answer: "So it never happens again." It is as if, by talking about the unimaginable, they are vaccinating the world against another outbreak of genocidal insanity. Why didn't this occur to the Armenians sooner, when the survivors were young enough to shout?

It's only in the past few years that Armenians have started to talk out loud and in public about the Genocide. Much of that talk has been generated by children of the survivors, and the children of those children. Universal recognition of the Genocide has become the most powerful binding force among Armenians in America, and this drive has gathered momentum as the one hundredth anniversary of the Genocide has drawn near. The survivors themselves are nearly all dead, but a few smart people had the good sense and courage to ask the old folks one last time to speak into a microphone, or at least speak slowly while they took notes. I have read transcripts. I know a hundred stories, maybe a thousand. There are a million more, or should be, but there is only one story that could have stopped my fall, and it is too late for me to hear it.

My father is long gone.

I never violated my mother's order, not directly, but I did occasionally try to nudge my father into speaking about his family or his childhood or his life before or after the cataclysm. He rarely gave more than a brief reply to a question. More often, he didn't reply at all. He would elaborate only on his own terms, in his own way, at his own pace. He spoke briefly and cryptically about the tragedy he'd witnessed. The stories he told me about Armenia were mostly about things that happened long ago.

Once in a while, when I was very lucky and got his attention just as he was settling down to read, he'd tell me stories about kings and about fools, about battles won and lost, about heroes who weren't very heroic and ordinary men who were. The Armenia he described was a place of unfathomable beauty and endless tragedy, invaded and eviscerated time and again. Yet every so often, once in five hundred years or a thousand, the Armenians would conjure up the strength and courage to repel the intruders, rebuild their country, and reignite their culture. Each time, they would be fooled into thinking: We are safe now, at last. And then, in a terrible instant, they found themselves falling again.

Who wouldn't get dizzy from all this? Who wouldn't be frightened?

I learned to listen carefully, even when I wanted to watch TV or play with my toys. When my father decided he was done, no matter whether the story was just beginning or in the middle or almost at the end, he stopped talking and returned to his books—and there was no bringing him back. It is my lasting memory of him, sitting in that chair, reading night after night. It was the only time he wore glasses, even when he was old.

Many of the old people were like my father in this way, editing their life stories or simply avoiding all talk of the time and place where they lost so much. I encountered this time and again as I asked friends and relatives to share their memories. Gloria Allum, daughter of my father's Uncle Mihran Toutounjian, was born into a community of survivors in New Jersey before the Second World War but heard almost nothing about our family's lives in the old country.

"Growing up, my sister and I never heard much about the past," she said. "When people visited and they were talking about the massacre, there were tears, and conversation stopped when my sister and I were present."

Many immigrants and their children and even their children's children feel pain, especially those whose roots are in a place where pain and the anger it breeds are passed through the generations. If it doesn't kill them, the anger may become their salvation. It propels them here, sustains them through hard times, and fuels their drive to succeed. That much is true of the Armenians. But by the second generation, most immigrant groups let go of the anger. It is their gift to America, a touchstone that reminds the rest of us how lucky we are. The Armenians brought more anger to this country than most but fell short on their contribution. They held onto their anger because it's all they had to remind them of a homeland that vanished.

This is where I came into the picture. We children and grandchildren of the Armenians who found refuge in America in the last century were handed this anger along with the secrets and sadness. It is what keeps us falling. If I could let it go, if we could all let it go, maybe we could embrace our history and our culture without fear, without bitterness, without fighting among ourselves. It's starting to feel like urgent business, even though it began when I was too young to realize any of it.

I first started tinkering with an ethno-memoir when I was a young man who, like all young men, thought he knew everything. My idea was to write a paean to the glories of growing up Armenian in America. I knew it was glorious to be Armenian because it was impossible to read the stories of William Saroyan and come to any other conclusion. I still have a faded photocopy of a 1975 *New York Times* interview with Saroyan in which the great

Armenian-American author gave this advice: "I'm trying to tell people, if you want to do things, get ready and do them. You get to be a writer by getting ready. Create a rich, immediate, usable past that compels you to write."

I took Saroyan's advice to heart even though I was too young to have done anything worth remembering, much less writing about. I began creating a rich, immediate, and usable past by sweeping other people's writing into a pile. I stuffed news clips and essays and historical pamphlets into a manila envelope that eventually became as creased as an elephant's ear before it burst. One envelope led to another until I had a big box full of envelopes, and then a shelf full of boxes.

Somehow, I felt I'd know when I had enough material to write a book. But while I was collecting these scraps, I was also living my own life, which complicated things. My Armenian experience turned out to be far less glorious and a lot more challenging than I expected as a young man. Looking back at that experience and writing about it honestly proved even more challenging than living through it.

For years now, on the many nights when I can't sleep, I get out of bed and sit in Dad's rocking chair. It has been reupholstered three or four times, but the gracefully curved and lacquered arms with their carved goose heads are the same. I run my hands over them and picture my father sitting there, looking as he did when he died, still paratrooper trim at seventy-seven. His hair was still black except for a gentle, distinguished brush of gray at each temple, and still full except for a pronounced cock's peak up front and a palm-sized bald patch at the rear, which he never acknowledged.

He was a handsome man in his youth, and he lost nothing but vitality to old age. His cheeks never sank, nor his eyes. His eyebrows didn't sprout into Fuller brushes. His skin didn't peel or rust or erupt into a cabbage patch of old-man bumps. Dad still had a way of carrying himself that was not quite Army upright but close enough that he seemed taller than five-foot-six, and he walked straight and sure-footed even when he was old. You sensed he knew where he was going, even if he didn't. I think about him, about all the reading and thinking he did in that chair, about how tired he must have been when he sat down and how much he had on his mind. I take one of his books or a photo album off the shelf and I look for pieces of the puzzle that was his life and my heritage.

This is not a mystic quest. I have not been searching for the meaning of life, or even for the meaning of my father's life. I just wanted to know a little more about him and about his family, and about my mother and her family. I wanted to know about these Armenians and their long, difficult journey. I hoped that if I learned enough about them, I might uncover a clue to why I cry when I hear songs sung in a language I cannot understand. Or why I get so angry about things I can do nothing about because they happened long before I was born. Or why I sit up night after night thinking about people I never met and never will meet because they are long dead.

I still have more questions than answers, but I've sifted through enough scraps and memories to tell three stories so tightly bound that I can't separate them and won't even try: The story of the Armenians, the story of my father—at least, as much as I know—and my own story. It's time to write it all down for my daughter and her generation. Maybe they can figure out what to do with the unbearable weight of history. Maybe they can figure out how to put it down and stop the fall without losing all the wonderful and glittering parts of our inheritance.

I am not a historian, and this is not a book of facts and dates and sober analysis. This is a story told by a man born in midair whose only hope for a good night's sleep is to close his fingers around the frayed cord of history and tug with all his might.

LIFE AMONG THE
KETCHUP EATERS

My first inkling that we were different from most other people didn't come from my father's stories about Armenians but from my mother's observations about the Americans. She made them a constant cultural reference point throughout my childhood, distinct from us and the people we knew best.

The subject often came up at the table. I made the mistake of asking for ketchup once because I'd seen it on TV. "We don't use ketchup in this house," Mom said. "The Americans need ketchup because their food has no taste." The Americans ate meat with no seasonings, not even onions, she explained. "They don't know any better," she said. But I did know better, so I had no excuse ever to ask for ketchup. I had no excuse for lots of things American kids got away with. Talking back, for example. I tried that once, too. "Did you learn that from the Americans?" my mother asked. The mere suggestion stung me. The Americans, I learned, lacked proper respect for family, for teachers, and even for the government. That's why American kids got in trouble and became juvenile delinquents—and it was their parents' fault, make no mistake. Their parents let them get away with murder, or its equivalent. Some American kids even called their parents by their first names. Is there a worse crime? The Americans let their kids stay up late and watch weird TV shows like *The Twilight Zone* and then wondered why the kids had nightmares. The Americans let their kids drink Coca-Cola and then wondered why they got tummy aches. The Americans let their kids listen to that rock 'n' roll and then wondered why the kids acted crazy.

Mom said none of this in anger. Like eating ketchup, these were crimes of ignorance, not malice. She liked the Americans, even admired them. They were smart people and good workers. They'd built a wonderful country—the best in the world, she'd say with certainty, although she had no first-hand basis for comparison. The reason my mother knew so much about Americans is that she was one of them. She was so American that she didn't even use the word *odar*, as other Armenians called anyone who didn't belong to our tribe. She was born in Massachusetts and never set foot outside the United States, but my mother didn't grow up like an American. Her father and mother were Armenian immigrants, lucky people who escaped to America before the Genocide.

My mother grew up speaking Armenian in a house where everyone spoke Armenian. Her parents named her Zavart, which means "glad." No one at the hospital bothered to ask how to spell it. Someone simply typed the name Martha on her birth certificate. When my mother turned five, her father asked an American waitress at the restaurant where he worked to take her to school. The waitress registered her as Sylvia. That's the name that stuck. As an adult, she always signed her name Sylvia Z. Kalajian. It was a perfect compromise for someone who had to straddle the worlds of her immigrant parents and her American friends. There's nothing remarkable about that experience. It is the way of all first-generation Americans. She was still straddling when I, her only child, came along a few weeks before her fortieth birthday.

Instinctively, my mother trained me to straddle, too, but it was years before I realized it. I believed my father when he told me I was an American, period, just like him. He didn't talk about the Americans the way my mother did, although I suspect he agreed with her observations. He always spoke about America in the first person plural. This was *our* country, and *we* were Americans above all. He understood America better than my mother did, maybe better than I ever will, because he wasn't born here. I knew this because my mother told me he was born in Armenia. I didn't hear it from him. He hated the word *immigrant*, probably because he'd heard it used as something other than a compliment when he first arrived, but he loved the idea that an immigrant could become an American without an asterisk. An American is an American, he insisted, no matter where he was born. This was more than a matter of law, it was part of the American culture and what truly sets this country apart.

I found out much later that America wasn't his first choice. When it became impossible to remain where he was born, he found refuge in Greece. He thought about moving on to Egypt, or France. Coming to America was not quite serendipitous, but it was certainly a fortunate turn of events. "If I'd gone to those other places, I'd always be an outsider," he said. "You might become a citizen, but you can't become a Frenchman or an Arab. Here, I'm an American."

What a marvelous discovery for a man whose country vanished nearly six hundred years before he was born. He could become an American so he did, but he never melted. He never lost his language or his culture, never forgot his history, never changed his name or tried to hide his origin. He never doubted that he could be completely Armenian and completely American at once and without conflict. He was unwilling to risk any ambiguity where I was concerned, however. He insisted I have an unmistakably American name, Douglas, after Gen. Douglas MacArthur. I did get an Armenian middle name—Haroutyun (meaning "resurrection"), honoring both my grandfathers—but only for baptismal purposes. It was Anglicized to Harry, the American nickname both grandpas adopted, on my birth certificate. I didn't think much about any of this until I went out into the world of ketchup eaters and children who stayed up late and called their parents by their first names. Like most kids, I had no real concept of country. When my father's point of origin finally started to sink in, I thought it was pretty interesting. The more I thought about it, the more I wanted to know how my father's life as a boy was different from mine. I was probably eleven or twelve when I asked him for the first time, "Dad, will you take me to Armenia to see where you were born?"

He didn't say yes or no.

"I've never been to Armenia," he said, and he turned away.

I couldn't understand. I knew my mother wasn't wrong. It didn't occur to me when I asked my father to take me to Armenia that I had accidentally broached the forbidden subject. I didn't realize I was asking him to take me to see where his mother was murdered, to a place where there were no good memories. He deflected me with a technicality, one he repeated over the years each time I asked the same question. According to any wall map or atlas or encyclopedia, he was right. He had never been to a country called Armenia because there was no such place, unless you counted the sliver of Caucuses called the Armenian Soviet Socialist Republic. That didn't count at our house. The only Armenia my father ever spoke about was a long-ago country, an almost mythical place. He talked about that Armenia and he told me to listen closely because otherwise I'd never know it existed.

"You won't learn about Armenia in school," he said. "You won't read about it in American books. No one will make a movie about it. No one who isn't Armenian will ever be interested in our story." He didn't say this angrily or sadly. "It's the way it is. The world doesn't care about us. If you want to know our history, you have to learn it on your own."

He was right, as usual. I don't think I ever heard the word "Armenia" in my American-school classroom. My teachers couldn't find time for a single lesson about our history of triumph and tragedy. We studied long-dead Egyptians and Romans and even the occasional Chinese emperor, but not Dikran the Great, whose empire reached from the Mediterranean to the Caspian Sea in the century before Christ. We learned about the wonders of Babylon and Assyria, which came and went long ago, but we learned nothing about the wonders of Armenia, which came back to life time and again. King Dikran's empire was dismantled by the Romans, but nearly one thousand years later, Armenia's culture was once again ascendant. Literature, music, and art all flourished in the medieval Armenian kingdom of Ani at a time when most Europeans were living with their farm animals in straw huts. The late David Marshall Lang, professor of Caucasian studies at the University of London, called the domed cathedral at Ani a masterpiece of world architecture. It was designed by an Armenian architect named Trdat, whose brilliance was so widely recognized that he was commissioned to restore the Byzantine cathedral of Hagia Sophia in Constantinople. Millions of travelers from around the world have since looked up in awe at the glittering, 180-foot-high dome at the church-turned-mosque-turned-museum in what is now Istanbul, stunned by its beauty and amazed that an engineer working more than one thousand years ago without a computer or even a slide rule could figure out how to hold something so broad and massive in place all this time. No one tells them the genius was not a Greek or a Turk but an Armenian, and that what they are really marveling at is the triumph of the Armenian spirit.

I know these things because my father taught me the lessons my teachers ignored. I read the books he gave me, and I learned to listen carefully when he explained them. "Someday," my mother said, "you'll think back and realize how smart your father was." I knew it even then, although I spent far more time beside my mother in pursuit of silly pleasures. Most nights, Mom and I would watch television together. She liked comedies: *I Love Lucy. The Beverly Hillbillies. Ozzie and Harriet.* Mom wanted to laugh, but she'd settle for a smile. "Life is sad enough," she'd say. "I don't want to watch anything sad." I wasn't sure what she meant. Life didn't seem very sad to me, but I never argued. I understand now that the tragedy of the Armenians was too close, too suffocating, too threatening. It did not end when they came to America because they brought more than anger and pain with them. They brought a psychology of torment, doubt, guilt, and regret. Looking back, I can see the corrosive effects in my mother's two brothers, both smart and literate men who aspired to little. Neither ever married, owned a car, or bought a home. They lived and died quietly. For six hundred years, the Armenians lived that way because they had to. They were not second-class citizens, because they were not citizens at all. They were subjects. My mother and I were born free Americans, subject to nothing but our choices. We chose *My Three Sons.*

Mom and I watched our silly shows while my father sat in the same room, reading. He had headphones so he could listen to Chopin while we giggled. He didn't hesitate to let us know he could hear us. My father would sit in his rocking chair that was upholstered in gray cloth embroidered with a big, stylized, maroon "K," but he didn't rock. He sat very still, peering into his books. He read almost nothing but history and philosophy. He said he'd read enough stories when he was young, but I suspect there was more to it. I have some of his books on my shelf now: Plutarch, Herodotus, Carlyle, Gibbon. There were Armenian authors, too, but those books are long gone. My father had no faith that I'd ever be able to read them, and he didn't want what was in them to be lost. So when he was too tired to read any more, he packed them up and sent them to the country he insisted he'd never seen and didn't exist. He did leave me some Armenian history books that were written in English, but most of the books he left behind were broader historical and philosophical inquiries—books about the origin of man, the origin of civilization, the origin of language, the origin of religion. I suspect he inherited the instinct to retrace the steps of the species from his forebears.

The Armenians have never really been certain where they came from. In the classic view, which held until well into the twentieth century, the Armenians just sort of bubbled up from this ingredient and that, like a science-lab accident. Armeno-Phrygians migrated south and east from Thrace in the north of Greece and crossed into Asia Minor, where they melded with the disintegrating Hittite empire and then, after a half-millennium of fermentation, the Armeno-Phrygian-Hittites rose up and flowed east again until they merged with the native peoples in the lands around Mount Ararat—Urartu—somewhere around 500 BC. Even the Urartuans were considered relative newcomers to the region, which was thought to have been uninhabited until perhaps 10,000 BC. The west-to-east progression was always underscored in the history books. The Armenians were understood to be an essentially Western people who absorbed and elevated lesser cultures.

This view has shifted significantly over the past century as archeologists have dug up more evidence. The people of Urartu and the surrounding kingdoms of the Nairi turned out to be older and much more advanced than anyone suspected. Shell carvings, stone tools, and human teeth make it clear that someone was wandering around the neighborhood five hundred thousand or even one million years ago. The progress that proto-Armenians made from stone to copper and bronze tools and even to carts with wheels lags behind no other civilization in Europe or North Africa, including Egypt. Armenologists today consider the Armenians an essentially indigenous people who absorbed the newcomers from the West, not the other way around.

Wherever the Armenians came from, we know for sure that they should be long gone. The Armenians must be the most trampled people on earth— invaded, subjugated, exploited, and simply beaten down time after time after time. There is no logic to their continued existence, none at all. Where are the Sumerians? The Phoenicians? Yes, I know the world is full of other peoples who lost their lands long ago but kept their identity. Chaldeans, Assyrians, and maybe a hundred more across Asia. But how many were pursued as relentlessly as the Armenians were? How many were slaughtered century after century? How many had enemies who tried so earnestly and enthusiastically to erase them from the Earth?

Of course, you think of the Jews. The analogy is powerful and fascinating, but it is not exact. You know what happened to the Jews. You probably don't know what happened to the Armenians. The Nazis paid for their crimes, too late and not enough, but the verdict was rendered. Germany still pays, but no one pays the Armenians. My father was right: The world does not care about us. It didn't make him angry, but it makes me angry—not just at the world, but at the Armenians. The world is a big, cold place. It doesn't really care about any people unless it has to. The Armenians have never been able to make that happen. Maybe we've just been too busy trying to survive.

Maybe we just haven't told our story often enough or loud enough or well enough.

Mostly we tell it to ourselves, but even many Armenians have never heard it. Or they've heard everything but the most important part, the part about their own families. It was true for a lot of kids who grew up in America, the children or grandchildren of survivors. For all my father told me about Armenia's past, the Genocide was the one subject he couldn't talk about or even listen to someone else talk about. Sometimes he'd start and then just get up and walk out of the room. Other times, he'd change the subject. But he told me a little now and then, mostly when he didn't have time to think first, when something made him angry or sad or brought back some feeling I could never understand.

He would say a few sentences, or maybe just a few words, and then he would stop. That happened sometimes even when the subject wasn't impossibly sad. By the time I was born, my father was forty years old, and he had traveled the world back when that was much harder and much less common than it is now. He'd crossed mountains on foot and deserts on a camel. He'd shivered from cold while trying to sleep in the snow and shivered with malarial fever in the tropics. I never got the full story about any of it.

I know this was my father's way of dealing with pain, but I also suspect Dad was purposely blurring the borders of his own memories to obscure the seams between his harsh, early life as a Near Eastern refugee and his new and cherished identity as an American businessman and proud veteran. It was almost demanded by his ideal of becoming and remaining perfectly American and perfectly Armenian at once and indivisibly. It is an ideal I admire and still try to live up to, even though I'm not sure that balance is attainable. In any case, it's awfully hard. It might have been easier if my father hadn't blurred that line so much that I still can't see it. It might have been easier still if he'd told me what was really on his mind.

Someone who is much more observant than I once wrote that Armenians always start stories in the middle. They assume you know so-and-so, or where such a place is, or that you remember who had the little store by the mill alongside the bridge on the road to the next village. My mother was like that. She'd be talking about Mrs. Hampartzoumian and I'd ask, "Who in the world is Mrs. Hampartzoumian?" And she'd say, "You remember. She lived upstairs from the Simsarians."

"When was this?" I'd ask.

"Oh," she'd say, "it was in Union City around 1932," and we'd both burst out laughing because that was twenty years before I was born.

My father at least started from a logical point, if not exactly the beginning. Putting things in order was up to me. He'd tell me something once and expect me to remember it in case he came back to it. He never sat me down and said, "Let me tell you about my time in the Army." Instead, something would trip his memory about his days on Corregidor just before the Second World War and he'd tell me an anecdote about firing the 12-inch mortars of the 59th Coast Artillery or about playing golf for the first time in his life out of sheer boredom.

This is how my father offered whatever he did about his life, in small and jagged bits. It was a long time before I realized they were parts to a puzzle and by the time I caught on, many of the parts were lost. I learned to listen quietly because if I interrupted or asked for details, he'd change the subject. Or he'd just announce that the story was over, a decision that was not open to appeal. Asking him to tell me a story was almost always futile. I learned that when I was seven or eight years old, when my mother told me my father once went to China. "You should ask him about it," she said. So I did. It didn't help my quest that I interrupted his evening reading. My father shot up out of his chair, slammed down his book and said, "Goddamit. I never went to China. Why do you ask such a stupid thing?"

I went running to my mother, who laughed. She said he just didn't want to tell me. She told me to ask him again another time, so I waited a few months and tried again, but I got the same response. This went on for years, only he'd get a little less angry each time I asked. By the time I was an adult, this became something of a running gag between us. I'd say, "Dad, are you ever going to admit you went to China?" He'd flip the back of his hand my way, but I knew he wasn't telling me the truth, because my mother remembered it. She said that during the Depression, Dad signed on to a merchant ship and off he went. She had no idea where, exactly, or what he did when he got there, but he told her he went to China and that was all. "You know your father," she said, and we both laughed.

Except that I didn't really know my father, not as well as I wanted to. I wanted to know about China. I wanted to know about Armenia. I wanted to know every place he'd been and everything he'd seen, but he never gave me the chance. My mother had an interesting theory about Dad's reluctance to tell me about his life: He didn't want me to go off on some crazy, dangerous adventure just to be like him. I think she was right, but that should have passed when I got older. He couldn't think I'd abandon my family and run off to China, could he?

We knew he'd learned to keep his secrets when he was a boy because they were too awful to share—maybe too awful to think about. So I could be persistent about something like China and we'd both laugh about it, but I had to be circumspect about the most important stories of all, stories about his mother and his father and his lost country. It was a maddeningly delicate balance. When I heard a clue, I'd seize the opening but never too directly or boldly or obviously. Remember *Concentration,* that TV game show where the clues were revealed but then turned over again, so you had to remember where and what they were?

That's how my life-long conversation with my father went. Years would pass between pieces of the puzzle, and he'd rarely offer me any help recalling them, much less fitting them together. I'd try and try, and mostly fail. Then, out of the blue, he'd tell me something that changed the way I thought everything fit.

In the end, I think he wanted to tell me more, but it was too late to change. He probably told me more during the last year of his life than he had in all the years before, or it may just seem that way because he told me at least a few stories that illuminated the rest. Most likely it was because we spent more time together, just the two of us, once my mother was gone. I know that losing her also jarred loose the memories of all the other losses and traumas of his life—and along with them came others that were no less fascinating to me because I'd never imagined them.

My father and I went to a tropical plant show in Florida some time during that last year. He was a horticultural wizard, so I wasn't surprised when he pointed to an exotic flower and recited its Latin name from memory. I checked the plant's marker and, of course, he was right. As we walked away, he shrugged and said he'd only seen that plant once before—in Borneo.

Borneo? I was nearly forty years old, and I'd never hear him mention Borneo.

"Why didn't you ever tell me you went to Borneo?"

"I only went for the weekend," he said, and he kept on walking.

LOST IN THE WORLD

My mother was our family's photo archivist. Mostly this involved stuffing hundreds of black-and-white snapshots into plastic bags, which she'd tape shut and tuck into the lower drawer of her dresser. The ones that meant the most to her—photos of her cousins and aunts and close friends posing on the tenement stoops of Union City, New Jersey, in the 1930s and '40s—were glued into an album that she'd flip through from time to time as I sat by her side.

I don't recall my father joining in, and he had no photo album of his own until much later in life. When they retired, Mom made one for him, and I was surprised to see how many pictures he'd kept hidden away—or more likely, that my mother had kept for him—including photos from his days in the Army and even a couple of snapshots of his own father in America. Until then, the only image of Grandpa Kalajian that I'd ever seen was a gray-toned, three-by-four head shot in a stand-up frame atop Dad's bedroom bureau.

Dad did have one photo from his childhood, which he kept in a thick, cardboard folder in the closed compartment of his book case. He brought it out rarely, once every year or two, walking it slowly to the dining-room table with deliberate care befitting transport of a religious relic. He'd put on his black-frame reading glasses and stare deeply into its features, as if he were trying to find his way back to a distant home on a faded map.

I first saw this picture of my father as a little boy when I was only a bit older than he was when it was taken. It was a curiosity then, a picture of a boy wearing a dress. For years, I saw this as an amusing contradiction: My father, so serious and manly in my mind, is dressed like a girl. He showed no hint of humor about it. "That's how all children were dressed in the old country," he said. Even as a kid, I wanted to ask a thousand questions, but my mother's warning kept nearly all of them from escaping my lips. Whenever I did blurt one out, my father usually parried effectively by snatching up the photo and putting it back in the desk. Sometimes, however, he'd tell me a little bit before he chased me away. Other times, when I was patient enough to sit quietly while he stared, he'd volunteer a little more information. He responded often enough to my questions or my silence to make each emergence of this photo a treasured occasion. In the course of our lives together, this photo became a window through which I could see at least a foggy shadow of my father's childhood. It maddens me now to think that this view might have been clearer and better focused if only I'd been more persistent or smarter about what I asked, but I'm probably being too hard on myself and on my father. I know I should be satisfied with what I did see and learn, although none of it could ever make me happy.

Nishan's family in Diyarbakir/Dikranagerd about 1914. Nishan is the blurred figure lower right. The girl is his Aunt Virginia. Nishan's mother, Hermine, is second from left. Her mother is at the center. The rest are unidentified.

I was so fascinated by the image of my father in the dress that I made nothing of the context. I noticed two people other than my father in the photo because my mother pointed them out. The young, slender, and pretty woman is the boy's mother—my grandmother. My father had a friend crop her image into a separate photo, and he had that one copied again and again. He wrote her name on the back of one copy in pencil: Hermine (Hehr-mee-neh). Otherwise, I'd never have known.

She was seventeen or eighteen when the picture was taken. She was nineteen when she died.

The other person I noticed in the picture was the little girl who really was a little girl: Hermine's much younger sister, my father's Aunt Virginia. I knew her when she was much older. She lived with her husband and children about an hour away from us in Cranford, New Jersey. Aunt Virginia was only about a year older than my father, but she seemed old to me, an old woman who moved slowly and always sounded a little sad. The girl in the picture is beautiful and lively, but not as lively as the little boy. My father obviously would not stand still for the photographer. His face is a blur. I've looked at it a thousand times, comparing it to the face of the father I knew. I can't really make out the features. Not his forehead, not his nose. Not the distinctive mole on his cheek. But I'm sure it's him, and I'm sure he's smiling. At least, I want to believe he is smiling.

I wonder now if this was the last truly happy moment of his childhood.

What I know for certain about his childhood is that Dad had the misfortune of being born within the ancient, musty walls of Diyarbakir, Turkey, in March 1912, as his family and homeland were about to be crushed by the weight of the collapsing Ottoman Empire.

Diyarbakir is a Turkish name meaning both "the city occupied by Arabs of the Bekr tribe" and "the city of copper." But in the hearts of Armenians, it will always be Dikranagerd, the city of Armenia's most glorious king. Historians and archaeologists have been arguing for years about the true site of Dikran the Great's long-ruined capital, but the Armenians of Diyarbakir never doubted that they were Dikran's descendants. The city's fortress wall was all the proof they needed. Since ancient times, the people of Dikranagerd were protected by this wall built to withstand the brute force of history. But no wall could protect the Armenians from the forces closing in at the dawn of the twentieth century, because the enemy was already inside.

For six hundred years, Armenians and Turks and Kurds lived side by side there along the fertile banks of the Tigris River, where watermelons grow as fat as lambs. But neither friendship nor kinship could save the Armenians as the Ottoman Empire imploded. Greece and part of the Balkans had already broken free, and the first of two wars that would wrench the rest of the Balkans from Ottoman hands had just begun. Turks were under siege nearly everywhere in their once-sprawling domain. Now, even their grip on Asia Minor seemed threatened, and they were determined to hold tight.

Diyarbakir in relation to present day Armenia. MAP BY DAVID BLASCO.

I know very little about my father's family before then, except that most had survived the wave of massacres launched in the late 1800s by Abdul Hamid II, the last and bloodiest sultan. A Turkish doctor had stood alongside my father's grandfather on the roof of the Kalajian home, warding off the attackers during the siege of 1895. It's not an uncommon story. In Dikranagerd and other cities and villages, Muslims and Christians lived separate but inseparable lives. An artisan like my great-grandfather would have been comfortable doing business with any of them. The harsh realities of their small world wouldn't have given him any choice.

I know almost nothing about my great-grandfather, not even his first name. A generation or two earlier there might have been no one in the family named Kalajian. The familiar, modern protocol of Armenian surnames ending in *ian* or *yan*—meaning "the son of," or "of the family"—was loosely applied until being formalized in the nineteenth century for the convenience of Turkish tax collectors. Occupations became the basis for many names, and the Turkish authorities often used Turkish roots. The family name Kalajian was based on a Turkish adaptation of the Greek word for solderer or pot maker, *kalaji*. The village *kalaji* could be relied on to keep copper cookware shining, and its tin lining smooth and intact. Great-Grandpa Kalajian was a kalaji on a grand scale, a true coppersmith. The family's main forge was in Dikranagerd, famous through the centuries for its abundant stores of copper, and there were smaller shops in the surrounding villages. Each son got his own shop when he came of age. My father had at least two shadowy memories of the family forge: the great, yawning bellows and the brilliant, withering flame.

Armenians have worked in copper as long as any people on Earth, and with so much practice, an Armenian smith is expected to be a true artist. An everyday pan or ladle traces a delicate form and dazzles the eye. Such skill was well-rewarded. In the context of that time and place, our family was prosperous: They had a good house, and they never went hungry. A king could hardly ask for more.

What more could there be? A comparably well-off American family of the day had plenty more: plumbing, electric lights, a telephone, a Model T. Such things would have seemed like sorcery to the Armenians of Dikranagerd, whose day-to-day life had hardly changed since the Middle Ages. My father might as well have been born in 1612 or 1412 or 1212. Water flowed down from the mountains in ancient, open aqueducts caked with leaves and aerated by the death dance of drowning bugs. Asses and goats still splashed their waste over stones laid before the Roman legions marched through. Women still rose before dawn to stoke the hearth and bake the daily bread. It was almost as though Dikranagerd had been sealed off from the rest of the planet, and in a sense it had been, along with the rest of historic Armenia.

When Armenia was the gateway to Asia, Dikranagerd was the gateway to Armenia. Armies of Greeks, Romans, Persians, and Arabs all found their way to its gates and took their turns atop the parapets. The Armenians were a constant presence throughout the centuries, enduring each occupation with certainty that it would pass. Regardless of whose flag flew from the towers, a stream of traders, travelers, and Crusaders passed through the great walls, and each left something of value behind, including all the spices of the East and the secrets of the world's cooks. The local language was spiced, too, with the aftertaste of many tongues.

The Turks, however, left nothing behind because they never left. When the Turks came, the caravans stopped. The Turks were interested in plunder, not trade. Columbus wasn't merely looking for a shorter route to the East, he was looking for a detour around the Turks. Europe set out to sea and left the Armenians high and dry, but not all Armenians sat still. Waves of Armenian refugees headed for more peaceful shores rather than submit to Turkish dominion. It wasn't until I started thinking about this book that I realized my grandfather became one of them soon after my father was born.

Grandpa is the obvious missing figure in the Kalajian family photo, an absence my father explained with his usual shrug: "He was gone by then." I guessed that meant he'd gone with the rest of the Armenian men who were drafted at the start of the First World War. Armenians formed the Ottoman Army's slave-labor corps. Many were starved or worked to death, or shot. The few who survived could not come home because their homes were gone, along with their families. This fit what I knew about my grandfather. "He came back to Dikranagerd too late," my father said. But how late? A day? A year? No matter. Most of the people Grandpa knew were dead when he got there, and he had every reason to believe my father was dead, too. Haroutyun Kalajian made his way to America alone and in mourning. You can see it in his eyes in each of the handful of photographs that survive. He didn't leave much else. I have his faded US citizenship papers, his still-crisp passport (used only once), and his gold pocket watch encased in a yellowed and cracked plastic dome.

I can see my grandfather but I cannot hear him, which is a great loss. For years, my father searched in vain through old Armenian phonograph records for the sound of his father's voice. Grandpa was a singer from a family of singers who all believed their voices were God's gift. They sang in church, they sang at parties, but they would not sing for money. My father said every Armenian in Dikranagerd knew Grandpa's voice and knew the instant they heard it that this was a special occasion—a wedding, a funeral, a celebration. It was no different when he came to America, except once. An Armenian coaxed Grandpa and a few other musicians to board a train for Coney Island. When they got there, a man gave them each a Turkish costume complete with a fez, one of those Turkish hats that looks like an upside-down Starbucks cup with a tassel on top. "Authentic Turkish musicians, ladies and gentlemen," the announcer shouted. They played their songs while a belly dancer shimmied. None of them ever went back. After that, Grandpa sang only in the narrow living rooms of cold-water tenements, and in the parks where the Armenians went to roast their kebab.

Harry Kalajian taps out a rhythm as he sings songs
of misery with other Armenian men.

I found the most telling picture of Grandpa in the album Mom put together for my father: He is sitting at a picnic bench under a tree with other Armenian men. They are probably in New Jersey, and it is certainly the 1920s. Grandpa is playing the *daf*, an Armenian tambourine. You can see the clear, unlabeled bottles of *arak* liquor on the sun-dappled table. You can see the hole in the sole of one man's up-raised shoe. They are all wearing white dress shirts and ties. It might be Sunday after church or Saturday after work, but you can tell from their faces that this is not a happy day. There are no happy days. These men are drinking and singing on a beautiful day in the park, but they are all sad. They are singing about their lost country, their lost wives, their lost children.

They survived, and they are miserable.

How my grandfather survived was a mystery to me until I'd run all the permutations of his name that I could think of through census and immigration records long after my father was gone. I was surprised to discover that Grandpa arrived in New York in May 1913, aboard the steamship *Roma* by way of Marseille, France. This was two years before the onset of the Genocide. By then, it didn't take a mystic to sense what lay ahead for the Armenians in their native land. Armenians and Turks had briefly but enthusiastically embraced in 1908, when the Young Turks, with the help of Armenian revolutionaries, shoved the sultan aside and unfurled a constitution that promised to protect the rights of minorities. The Armenians wanted to believe. Even the revolutionaries disarmed and joined the new government, but soon a new wave of persecution followed.

Now I know that Grandpa was among the many Armenian men who made a desperate leap alone to America, where even a poor immigrant could make a safe place for his wife and child to follow. Grandpa Kalajian crossed both sea and the centuries to reach the world of Model Ts, telephones, and electric lights. He was twenty-eight years old. His wife was left in the dark to wait and pray and pose with her baby in front of a photographer's tattered backdrop. Grandpa must have written or somehow sent word: "I am here, you will come soon." She must have sent him the photo, maybe with the next lonely emigrant from Dikranagerd, as proof that all was still well and their son was growing strong. It is the only way this picture could have survived.

Grandpa may have been dazzled by the wonders of this new age, but it's unlikely he experienced them firsthand. He must have found work in one of the many American factories fueled by a steady stream of immigrant labor. He could live in a gas-lit boardinghouse for one dollar a week, sleeping on the floor in a room packed with other Armenian men, eating beans and dry bread to save his pennies. He had no need for a day off. I imagine him, dog-tired, sitting on a stoop in Boston or New York or Union City, staring at the photograph and singing to his far-off family.

What I know for sure now is that whatever he was doing, wherever he lived, he was far from his homeland when the first ominous reports of massacres began to appear in the American press. Not that he could read the American press, but the Armenians had their own papers, and there were fresh waves of Armenian refugees bringing tales of new oppression and fears of much worse to come.

What could Grandpa do? What could anyone do?

The great city walls that withstood so many siege engines through the centuries had no chance to repel the one that took aim at Dikranagerd in the sulfurous summer of 1915. The Turks inside the city flung the gates open in welcome. Soldiers marched in and joined police in rousting the Armenians who remained: the old men and the women and children. The Armenians were assured that they would return when it was safe, but most knew better, and they all prepared in their own way. Some sewed coins into their hems or buried rings in their bread so they could bribe their tormentors. Many prayed to Jesus for salvation. Some prayed to Allah for the first time, hoping their prayers would at least be answered by Turks if not by God.

What happened in Dikranagerd happened in Kharpert, Van, Marash, and every other village or city where Armenians lived under Turkish rule. The Armenians were ordered to march, and most did. The ones who refused were slaughtered on the spot. Armenians were hacked to death in their homes or in the streets in view of their children and neighbors. Some ran, but not to get away. They ran to church. They chose to die in God's kingdom, not the sultan's. Turks burned Armenians alive as they knelt in prayer.

The Armenians who obeyed the orders to leave were marched hundreds of miles toward the Syrian desert. It might as well have been a thousand miles, or a million. There is no secret about what happened next, not only because some of these stubborn Armenians lived to tell but because there were other witnesses. American and European missionaries watched in torment, unable to help. A few who tried to help disappeared. German officers attached to Turkish units observed the massacres in fascination.

Everyone in America knew what was happening, too—at least, everyone who read a newspaper, and that was nearly everyone in those days. If it happened today, the Armenian Genocide would be seen live and in color on TV news. In 1915, the depth and extraordinary cruelty of the campaign shocked readers of the *New York Times*. The report published August 18 was typical:

ARMENIANS ARE SENT
TO PERISH IN DESERT
The roads and the Euphrates are strewn with corpses of exiles, and those who survive are doomed to certain death since they will find neither house, work nor food in the desert. It is a plan to exterminate the whole Armenian people.

The American government knew even more, and knew it sooner. Henry Morgenthau, US ambassador at Constantinople, repeatedly cabled reports to the State Department in Washington and even confronted Turkish authorities.

"Persecution of Armenians assuming unprecedented proportions," he wrote July 10, 1915. Morgenthau asked Washington what he could do to help. The State Department's reply on July 15 concluded, "The Department can offer no additional suggestions relative to this most difficult situation. . . ."

The Armenians caught in this most difficult situation found themselves robbed, raped, and murdered along the march. These tired, thirsty, and defenseless people were set upon time and again by brigands and brutes who stole their possessions, their lives, and their loved ones. The *Times* report of December 12 quotes a German missionary: "In Harput and Mezre the people have had to endure terrible tortures, such as their eyebrows being pulled off, their breasts cut off, their nails pulled out, their feet cut off; or they hammer nails into them, just as they do with horses. The soldiers then cry: 'Now, let your Christ help you!'"

Armenian children, the lucky ones, were snatched from the arms of dying mothers to become servants or slaves. Mothers who could not bear the thought of their daughters becoming Turkish wives, much less concubines, drowned their babies in rivers or flung them over cliffs. Others who could not bear the thought of their children dying begged or bribed their captors to take them.

My father was one of these children.

Sometime in that awful year, a Turk murdered my father's mother. I don't know if it happened on the street in front of their home or on the road to Syria. I just know it happened, and that my father was there. But no Turk snatched him away; his grandmother did. She pulled the little boy in a dress from the arms of her dying daughter and gave him to a Kurd, the chief of a tiny tribe. She could not have hoped to see her grandson again. She could hope for nothing except that he might live.

Grandpa, a long way off in America, could know only that unthinkable things were happening in his homeland. It must have tortured him. There was nowhere to write, no agency where he could make an inquiry, no place to file a petition or even beg for help. All he could do was wait. He waited until the First World War was over, three long years, and made his way back. He must have borrowed nickels from every friend and relative he could find. Somehow, he forged a path through the postwar chaos and finally reached Dikranagerd.

Miraculously, he found survivors. Armenians were coming back to their homeland, although their homes were gone. Some believed America and

Europe would keep their promises to protect them. Instead, the survivors returned to find their homes occupied, their businesses confiscated, their fields tilled by Turks and Kurds. And still, they stayed to start over, as Armenians had done so many times after so many other disasters. These troubles, they believed, would pass, as trouble always did.

They were right, but only for a while. There were no massacres now because the Europeans were still around and still watching, if not very closely. There was still international outrage, and there were inquiries. Promises were being made, but they were also being broken. In the east, where the Russians had retreated from the region they'd ruled, Armenians weren't waiting to be given their freedom. They were fighting the advancing Turks. But in Dikranagerd and other cities and villages where Turks remained in control, the Armenians returned to a familiar, tenuous existence. It was understood that questions should be left unasked. No international agency bothered to compile a list of missing property, much less missing people. What was gone was best forgotten, unless you had come back across the globe like Haroutyun Kalajian and what was gone were your wife and son.

When my father told me that Grandpa had returned "too late," he supplied a few other details. Grandpa found his sister's husband, who told him what he knew and helped him find out more. I know that my father's grandmother, the one who saved him, survived the massacres and eventually came to America, but I don't know if she'd made her way back to Dikranagerd by the time Grandpa got there. I don't know if he knew his son had been snatched away, but he was convinced his wife and son were both dead. His brother-in-law knew it wasn't safe to keep asking questions. Both men left the city and went up into the hills, where Grandpa mourned for his family the only way he knew. He sang the ancient hymns and dirges all through the night. His voice carried down to the city, and everyone knew who it was.

Not all the Armenians who survived had relied on luck. Some were traitors who turned against other Armenians. One of them heard Grandpa's voice and led the Turks into the hills to find him. Grandpa and Uncle were dragged back to the city and locked up. That night, one of Uncle's sons sneaked into the jail. He either beat or killed the jailer and opened the cell door. Sometime later, he encountered the traitor and killed him, too. Grandpa headed back to the hills and kept going, back to America.

I know he was living in Chelsea, Massachusetts, in 1918, because he registered for the draft. Armenians had been drawn to the factory and mill towns near Boston, where shoe factories were numerous and always eager to take on fresh immigrant labor. Grandpa found work at the Millar and Wolfer Shoe Company. He was still there two years later when he answered the US census: Haroutyun Kalajian, single white male, was living in a boarding-house full of Armenian shoe workers. Another Haroutyun, who eventually became my other grandfather, lived nearby in the same town. The census form for Haroutyun Bichakjian lists a wife and six children, including my mother-to-be. His occupation: boardinghouse cook.

The two Haroutyuns may have been distantly related by blood or mar-riage—I will never know for sure—but they were clearly animated by the common yearning to better their circumstances. They cooked up an idea over the next few years to quit working for others and open a restaurant. They saved as much as they could until the right opportunity came along. An Armenian friend told them about a restaurant they could buy in New Jersey, where there were lots of other Armenians. They took a train ride to see the place. It was overflowing with customers, a guaranteed moneymaker. They bought it, quit their jobs, and moved to New Jersey as quickly as they could.

The deal turned out to be a typical immigrant hustle. The Armenian who led them to the place had been paid by the owner, as had the customers. The place was no gold mine, just a storefront hash house. The two Haroutyuns, their pockets empty, were starting all over in another strange place when Grandpa Kalajian got the miraculous news from the old country: His son was alive.

FOUND BUT NOT SAVED

I read a story by the Armenian writer Aram Haigaz in a tattered copy of the *Armenian Review* magazine my father left behind. The main characters are two Armenian boys swept up by a tribe of Kurds during the Genocide, an experience shared by the writer and my father.

The boys in the story were brought to a mountain village and put to work as shepherds. The tribe was really just an extended family, and the village was more like what we'd call a ranch: a main house, some shacks for the hands, and a few utility buildings for storage or baking or housing the animals. The boys were watched over by a son of the tribal chief and were treated well. They were fed, clothed, and housed in exchange for their work. They were expected to work equally hard at becoming good Kurds and good Muslims.

In time, they were told, they would forget all about their former lives as infidels—*giavours*, as the Turks called them—the sooner the better. They would forget their vulgar language and customs. They would forget their families. Most important, they would forget their religion. Allah had shown them great favor by saving them, and they were obligated to devote themselves to Him.

One day, their overseer told them excitedly that he was marrying an Armenian girl, another orphan snatched up during a massacre. He was certain she'd become a perfect Muslim wife, but she was still adjusting. He asked the boys to come to his home and speak with her in Armenian and help her understand how wonderful her new life would be. The boys did as they were told, and the girl was so happy to have their company that they were invited back several more times. Then, suddenly, the overseer turned cold.

28

He told them he'd heard enough Armenian talk and that it was time to forget such nonsense. With that, the visits stopped.

For months after, he talked about the marvelous progress of his wife's conversion. She became an example for all Armenians to follow. She did indeed become a perfect Muslim wife, faithful not only to her husband but to Allah. No native-born Kurd ever prayed with such piety, he insisted. Then one day, the overseer appeared grief-stricken. His perfect Muslim wife had died suddenly of fever. She was praying to Allah right until the end, but the fever made her delirious. Just before she died, she touched her right hand to her forehead and said something he couldn't understand. He thought it was gibberish, but perhaps it was Armenian. He repeated her words and asked the boys if they understood.

"Hanoon hor . . ."

They understood perfectly: "In the name of the father . . ."

The perfect Muslim wife was trying to cross herself. She had forgotten nothing, least of all that she was an Armenian Christian. Of course, she was old enough to be married, probably at least in her teens. How much would a younger child forget? My father, for instance.

I don't know what he remembered as an adult about his life as a Kurd, much less his life before that, except that he had no bad memories of the family that took him in. They gave him a Kurdish name, but I don't know what it was or even whether he remembered it. He learned to speak their language. He prayed to Allah. When he was old enough, he tended sheep, just like the boys in the story. His adoptive father, the chief, was kind, and my father got along with the other children. And then, as in the story, there was a sudden death. The chief died and the little tribe fell apart. My father was seven or eight years old. His adoptive mother sent him down the mountain, alone, and told him to go back to Diyarbakir.

So he returned to a city he no longer remembered, this time not as a toddler in a dress but as a bigger boy in Kurdish robes, alone in the world. He remembered walking the streets when he found himself surrounded by a gang of older boys. What did they imagine they could rob from a poor little Kurd? They were beating him when a Turkish policeman pulled him free. The boys scattered. The policeman asked where he lived. He answered honestly: "Nowhere." If my father had been found wandering the streets of Dickens's London, he'd have been sent to a draconian orphanage and fed thin gruel until he was old enough to be apprenticed to a smith or a carpenter. But there were no orphanages for lost Kurds in Dikranagerd circa 1919, nothing so generous as free meals and vocational training. This explains why my father enjoyed reading *Oliver Twist* and laughed when Oliver begged for a second helping. He should have been happy to get even one!

But little Mustafa or Mohammed or whatever my father called himself was not unlucky. Instead of leaving him to wander, the policeman led the boy into the local bathhouse and gave him to the owner. Can you imagine a policeman finding a homeless orphan and simply giving him to someone who might need help? The bathhouse man decided the boy could be useful cleaning up and running errands. He could sleep on the floor and eat whatever scraps the customers left. So he did, for days—maybe weeks. He might have grown up sleeping on the floor of the Turkish bath if he hadn't wandered outside one day and indulged himself in a simple and foolish act of childishness: He picked up a rock and threw it at a passing boy. The boy fell down, cried, and ran away.

Soon after he came running back with his older sister, who grabbed the little Kurd and said he was going to learn a lesson. The girl pulled him through the street to her house so her mother could beat him. The mother was about to do just that when an older woman put out her hand, clenched the boy's chin, and pulled him close. She stared at the mole on his cheek.

"Nishan!"

He had no idea what she meant, nor that she was his grandmother. He tried to run away, but the younger women held him back while the old woman brought out a picture of a family standing in front of a traveling photographer's cloth backdrop. She pointed to her dead daughter.

The boy began to cry.

The next two years were the closest my father came to living a normal childhood. He became Nishan again. He went to church and sang, as his father did. He adopted a pet quail. Sometimes he even went to school, when there was a school to go to. But for the Armenians in Dikranagerd, life would never be normal again. Armenians in what is now eastern Turkey and present-day Armenia won their freedom in 1918 but lost it again by 1920. They were crushed by the Communist Russians and the once-again emboldened Turks. The Europeans were gone, no longer interested in the Armenians. The leaders who had plunged Turkey into war and genocide—Taalat, Enver, and Djemal—were in exile. They were paying the price not for what they did to the Armenians but for being on the losing side of the Great War. For the Armenians in the interior, life was worse than it was before the war. Everything they'd owned or built was gone. So were most of the Armenians. Nothing in logic would draw them back to this place, except that it was the only place they knew—the place that had been theirs for three thousand years.

My father's place now was with his cousins, Yervant and Hagop, who became his older brothers. Their mother was his father's sister, Hormeeg, a Kalajian by birth and now Deriklian by marriage. My father spoke more lovingly about his aunt than anyone else in his life except my mother. She not only took him in, she saved his life at least twice more. Once, he was kicked in the groin by a mule, and the wound became infected. This was long before antibiotics. His aunt boiled herbs and his cousins held him down while she poured the scalding mixture on the infection. He passed out from the pain. When he woke the next day, the infection was gone. Another time, he was feverish and so congested he couldn't breathe. Again, his aunt knew which herbs to boil, and she made a tent where he could breathe the vapor as she poured the mixture over hot rocks. She stayed up with him through the night. The next morning, he was breathing fine.

If only Auntie could work these miracles against human pestilence. The real threat to the family and to all the Armenians left in the Old World was Mustafa Kemal, who did not look like a threat at all. He did not even look like a Turk. Kemal, who later adopted the name Ataturk—meaning "father of Turks"—looked like a European diplomat, or perhaps an American executive, at least when he presented himself to the Western world. He wore suits and neckties instead of pantaloons and a fez. His coxcomb hair was razor sharp. He had piercing blue eyes that glimmered beneath brows plucked neat as a Hollywood starlet's.

Kemal emerged soon after the Ottoman defeat as postwar leader of the Young Turks—or, perhaps, the Younger Turks, the old ones having fled. Nearly everyone expected some sort of Allied reckoning for the Armenian massacres, even though the word *genocide* hadn't been coined and the very concepts of human rights and international law were in their infancy. The persecution of the Armenians, so brazen and outrageous, helped nurture these new ideas. The Western powers formed a war-crimes commission that condemned the Armenian massacres as a violation of the "laws of humanity." World opinion was so powerful, so insistent that even the first postwar Turkish government responded by investigating the persecution of

Armenians and identifying many of the perpetrators. Former leaders were tried, some in their absence, and found guilty. Turkey even signed the Treaty of Sevres, recognizing Armenia's independence and agreeing to respect its borders.

In the chorus of calls for justice for the Armenians, one of the clearest and strongest voices belonged to the president of the United States. Woodrow Wilson insisted on including a free and secure Armenia in his Fourteen Points for a lasting world peace. He even signed his name on a map restoring the historic Armenian provinces of Ottoman Turkey to their rightful heirs. America's Little Ally, as he called Armenia, could not be left to the wolves.

Few presidents victorious in war have faded from power as quickly and completely as Wilson. Weakened by illness, his lame-duck status, and the rising tide of Republican isolationism, the idealistic Democrat who rallied so many to Armenia's side was now a comic figure widely caricatured as Quixote with a top hat and glasses. On the surface, America was simply in no mood to take on such an expensive and potentially entangling obligation. Not far beneath the surface was oil. The Ottoman defeat in 1918 touched off a commercial sandstorm throughout the Middle East as American, British, and French oil companies scrambled to stake their claims in the oil-rich regions the Turks had occupied and where the Turks still held considerable influence. Who doubted that there might also be an ocean of oil beneath all of Asia Minor? A submissive but stable Turkey run by someone who understood the lure of profit might be the greatest treasure of all.

Then as now, oil blurred everything when the West looked east. Even the crystalline clarity of the long-suffering Armenians' moral claims began to fog. Now there were new, loud assertions that perhaps all that was exaggerated, or that war made such a mess that it was impossible to tell who suffered most or who was at fault. The rise of Kemal, the Western-style dandy, made the prospect of an oil-rich Turkey more tantalizing. He was a man of Western ideas but not Western ideals, a revolutionary who aimed to recast Turkey in a modern European mold with none of the messy complications of true democracy. He roused the defeated Turks with nationalistic fervor, much as Hitler would soon rouse the defeated Germans. It wasn't the superior military might of the Allies that had defeated them, he insisted, but the treachery and subversion of their old enemy within—the giavours.

The Sevres treaty bound Constantinople to guarantees of autonomy for Greeks and Armenians, but Kemal's new government renounced all treaties.

Kemal - Smyrna

By 1922, his army was in control. Kemal showed his disdain for European meddling when he led his forces into the historically Greek port city of Smyrna in what is now southwestern Turkey that September. Even at the height of the Genocide, Turks had shown restraint in Constantinople and other ports open to the world's gaze. Kemal, however, relished the spotlight. That night, when the Greeks and Armenians and Assyrians were all locked away, Turkish soldiers set fire to their homes. Smyrna smoldered for days, a signal fire of unspeakable horror and unmistakable meaning that flashed across the Mediterranean. More than one hundred thousand Greeks perished along with perhaps thirty thousand Armenians and other Christians. The French, the English, and the Americans all saw what happened. They all protested, denounced, condemned, and expressed their deepest sympathies. But they did nothing to help, and they did nothing to stop Kemal from trampling the Armenians along his march.

Luckily for the Armenians, the Western peoples did not abandon them even if the Western governments did. Americans and Europeans responded to this new crisis by donating to religious charities and social agencies, such as the Near East Relief Committee, that took on the enormous task of transporting nearly the entire remaining Christian population of Turkey as refugees. Even then, most Western countries refused to provide the needed refuge. God Bless Greece! Desperately poor and under siege, Greece could clearly not afford to take on the burden, but it did. Greece opened its ports not only to Greek refugees but to Armenians, and it sent ships to carry them all. Kemal made the task harder by blocking the Armenians' path and launching new massacres. Refugees fled north to the Black Sea or south through the Syrian desert, where they'd been driven before, in hopes of reaching Beirut.

My father was ten years old when he began yet another life, this time as an Armenian refugee. By now, the family had sent word to his father in America that Nishan was alive, but there was no way to reach out for him. If Nishan could get to Greece, perhaps it would be easier for his father to find him and bring him to America. Nishan left Dikranagerd with his uncle, aunt, cousins, and other refugees for the last time in fall 1922. Their caravan headed west, toward trouble, but they would cut south into Syria after they crossed the Euphrates. As soon as they reached the river, my father heard gunfire.

"There were bandits shooting at us," he said.

As he told me this, Dad smiled.

33

"It's like something out of Kipling. I was really being shot at by bandits!"

A man fell off his horse and tumbled into the river, bleeding. Horses bucked. But the defenders rallied and chased the bandits away. My father was carried across by his cousin Yervant. I know this because Yervant told his daughter, who told me. If he had been alone, he might have drowned in the panic. When the caravan reached the desert, they traded their horses to Arabs for camels. My father found this amusing, too, although maybe not at the time. "Imagine me on a camel riding through the desert," he said. Somewhere in Syria, my father left his cousins behind and continued by caravan to Beirut, where he boarded a Greek ship with the other lost children. I don't know how long it took to reach Greece, or where they landed. My father never described the ship or the journey from that point on. I understood why when I came across Esther Pohl Lovejoy's memoir *Certain Samaritans* published by Macmillan in 1933. She was an American doctor who witnessed the burning of Smyrna and treated refugees in Turkey and in Greece. She saw the caravans and the ships, and what she saw sickened her.

Refugees, she wrote, "crowded aboard freight ships expecting to land somewhere in Greece. But the quarantine stations were glutted on account of these hordes arriving with pestilential diseases, and a halt had been called while ships were on the sea. Dante, himself, could not have imagined the horrors of these floating Hells, packed with children, short of food and water, with typhus fever and smallpox raging in their holds, and no place on the face of the earth to land."

My father said nothing about any of this until just before he died. We were in church for a memorial on the anniversary of my mother's death. When the priest started to chant, my father started to cry. I put my arm around him, but he couldn't stop. He got up and walked outside. I didn't follow because I assumed he wanted to be alone. I also assumed he was crying over my mother, but I was wrong. The priest's chant carried his mind back nearly seventy years to the refugee camp in Greece where he finally landed. Everyone was hungry, and most were sick. Bread was handed out once a day. My father got in line the first day but never got his bread. "Somebody pushed me out of the way and took it," he said. It happened again the next day, and the next. He apparently had survived the Turks only to starve in a refugee camp in Greece. He said he felt no panic, no fear.

"People were dying. I was going to die, too. There was nothing I could do."

All around, families were wailing over lost children or lost parents. Death was no less familiar than disease and starvation, but this was different. They had no priest. These refugees were burying their dead in a foreign land without prayers for their resurrection. What could be worse?

My father was watching a family bury its dead when he spontaneously began to sing the hymn for the dead, just as he'd sung it in church in Dikranagerd. "This family was so thankful someone was there to pray that they shared their bread with me," he said. That kept him alive for another day. That day, he didn't bother getting in line. He went looking for a burial.

"I sang the hymns each time someone died, and families gave me bread. If I was lucky, I got an olive, too."

It was my father's great fortune, and mine, that people kept dying until he reached the next port.

STRANDED ON AN ISLAND IN AMERICA

My father spoke Greek whenever he met a Greek in a shop or restaurant. As a kid, I figured it was natural. I knew people spoke more than one language where he came from, and I assumed Greek was one of them.

I don't know when I was finally set straight, but one day I asked how he picked it up. Dad offered little information.

"I grew up in Greece," he said.

"I thought you grew up in Armenia?"

I realized my error immediately and shifted to another question before he could cut me off. "Where did you grow up in Greece?"

"On Corfu, when I was in the orphanage," he said, and that was all. The definite article in the phrase "when I was in the orphanage" was an effective rhetorical device. It implied that I was supposed to know this already, even though it came as a complete surprise. Dad used this technique a lot. It caused me to pause just long enough to think while he moved on. Question time was at an end, and so was my knowledge of Dad's life in Greece until I was much older.

The subject came up from time to time, but he never entertained questions. I was puzzled for years about why he'd be stuck in an orphanage. I wondered why his father didn't just send him a ticket to the United States. I might as well have wondered why his father didn't charter a yacht. I think it must have pleased my father to know that my life in America was so far removed from the poverty and desperation he'd grown up with that I couldn't quite grasp the bleak reality of his world.

Our most illuminating conversation about the orphanage occurred about thirty years after Dad first mentioned it. It began the way our adult conversations usually did, with my father's signal that he was ready to relax. "Let's have a drink," he'd say. When I heard that for the first time, I felt I'd joined his special club of adult company. The drink was almost always scotch over ice with a splash of water. One of the most useful bits of advice my father gave me was never to drink cheap whiskey, but it's a waste of twelve-year-old Chivas Regal if you add a mixer. We usually settled on Dewar's White Label.

Even a drink or two rarely dislodged deep thoughts, but it usually got my father talking about something. I didn't care if he wanted to talk about garden pests or Lyndon Johnson or the Yankees. Hearing my father's voice, knowing he wanted to share his thoughts with me, made me happy. I still feel his presence when I have a few sips of scotch before supper.

The orphanage conversation occurred one night in Florida when my father and I went to dinner. We each ordered Dewar's on the rocks—Dad always added the water himself—and settled into our talk. He ordered steak. I ordered lobster.

"Don't order that," he said. "Eat real meat. We can afford it."

I didn't want meat. I wanted lobster, and I told him so. Besides, lobster cost more than steak. What was he talking about?

"I hate those things," he said.

I'd never seen him eat lobster or clams or most other shellfish, but I didn't know he hated the stuff. I asked how that came about. "It was at the orphanage," he said. And just like that, my father began telling me a story I'd never heard before. He started by repeating a few things he'd mentioned over the years in scattered references: Soon after landing in Greece, he was evacuated from the refugee camp and taken to an orphanage for Armenians on the island of Corfu. He never described the place other than to say it had a library and he read as many of the books as he could. Until that night at dinner, he'd told me just one story, which he repeated: One day he was called out of class and told he'd been picked to become a priest. He'd leave the next day for a seminary. As he prepared to leave, his teacher pulled him aside. He said, "That's not the life for you." My father trusted his teacher, so he stayed. Another boy took his place. If my father had gone to the seminary, I'd never have been born. The boy who took his place later became a priest at a parish in New Jersey. He was the priest who baptized me.

"I was always hungry in the orphanage," my father said as we waited for dinner. "We'd go down to the beach to look for food."

He and his pals would dive off the rocks and scoop up whatever they could carry, mostly shellfish. Then they'd build a fire and toss it all in. It tasted good at first. "But after a while, you get sick of it. I promised myself that if I could ever afford real meat, I'd never eat that goddam fish again."

My father lived in the orphanage on Corfu from age ten until he was nearly sixteen. When he was old enough to work, he was apprenticed to a man with a greenhouse. I don't know if it was on the grounds or nearby, but the owner had relatives who owned a greenhouse in Massachusetts. My father loved working with plants and learned quickly and well. The owner promised that if my father ever went to America, he could work in the family greenhouse there.

During his first few years in the orphanage, my father thought he'd be leaving for America soon. A relief agency had contacted his father and told him to send money to help feed the boy until he could save enough to send for him. By now, my two grandfathers were struggling to eke out a living from their storefront lunchroom. Grandpa Kalajian sent money every month, but the people who ran the orphanage told my father he was poor and that he was lucky to get any food at all. My father wrote letters begging his father to send for him, but he rarely got a reply. One day he was sent to deliver a message to one of the orphanage officials. He went into the superintendent's quarters where the adults were eating. The table was overflowing with food. There were men in suits, and even priests. No one offered him anything.

He decided that if these people were so selfish, they were probably liars, too. They might even be the kind of men who'd throw away a boy's letters. He decided to write one more letter. This time, he hopped over the wall and mailed it from town. He told his father to send for him quickly or he'd leave. When Grandpa got the letter, he got all the cousins and uncles and friends together. They bought my father a first-class ticket from Greece to New York on the SS *Edison*. Grandpa enlisted the help of an Armenian charity to be sure the ticket reached his son.

The ticket arrived as my father was trying to decide whether to set off for France or Egypt. He said goodbye to his greenhouse master, who kept his word by giving him a letter of introduction to his family in Massachusetts. A kind man from the Armenian charity made sure my father got to the boat. "Too bad your family is so poor," the man said. "You have to go in steerage."

My father had no idea what that meant until he took his place in the fetid bottom of the ship with the poorest, most ragged refugees. The nice man from the charity had traded in his first-class ticket for a pauper's passage. The man pocketed the profit and left my father alone in a jostling crowd once again.

I can't imagine he had any real notion of what might lie ahead, although he was certainly better informed than his father had been about the changing world. Corfu wasn't quite Paris or even Athens, but neither was it the dark side of the moon. There was plenty of conversation among the orphanage staff and visiting business and charity workers for eager young ears to absorb. I'm also certain Dad snatched up stray newspapers to read along with all those books.

Still, the America he read about must have been hard to picture. Even Americans themselves were dazzled by the pace of change. Movies had barely started to talk when the newspapers reported that some genius figured out how to make pictures not only move but fly through the air into something called a television. Crazier still, Henry Ford was reinventing the car. His Model T, quivering symbol of America's limitless mobility and industrial genius, gave way to the smooth and sleek 1928 Model A. Meanwhile, band leader Fletcher Henderson was rescoring the soundtrack to the Jazz Age with increasingly sophisticated and danceable arrangements that previewed the Big Band Era.

Henderson and his Dixie Stompers, including sax genius Coleman Hawkins, spent April 6, 1928, in the Harmony Records studio in New York City recording such can't-sit-down hits as *Oh Baby!* and *I'm Feeling Devilish (Oh by Golly Oh)*. Ford had sailed across the Atlantic to get a first-hand look at his English factories. He responded eagerly to questions from reporters by predicting that Herbert Hoover would be elected president and that America would remain a paragon of prosperity.

My Dad and Henry must have crossed sea-lanes somewhere in mid-Atlantic. The *Edison* sailed into New York Harbor that same day, April 6, but Mayor Jimmy Walker and the city's press corps must not have gotten word that Dad was coming. I got a hint of his less-than-regal greeting in his new country when I asked him if he wanted to visit Ellis Island with me. I'd seen so many movies where teary-eyed immigrants break into song after getting their first glimpse of the Statue of Liberty that I thought such a visit might stir enough good memories to open a dialogue. I was correct in guessing he'd passed through the echoing halls of America's greatest immigrant portal, but I was wrong about the reason, and I was flat-out loopy in thinking he'd be nostalgic about it. "I hated that place," he said. "I couldn't wait to get out of there." When I pressed him, he added only that he'd been forced to stay overnight, but his father showed up the next day to take him home. I assumed there had been a mix-up about his arrival date, but I was wrong again.

What I didn't realize when I stepped blithely into yet another conversational swamp is that Dad had good reason to be angry. He did not belong at Ellis Island, which was mostly reserved for steerage passengers. Immigrants with first- and second-class tickets were processed on ship as routinely as most travelers today pass through customs. In fact, Dad did not need to be scrutinized like a foreigner anywhere because legally he was already an American. By law at the time, minors became citizens when their fathers were naturalized, and his father had become an American citizen the year before. If the Armenian thief hadn't stolen Dad's ticket, he'd have strolled down a shaded gangplank onto a West Side dock like an Astor or a Roosevelt. That's very likely where my grandfather was waiting in vain, wondering how his boy could have gotten lost in the middle of the Atlantic Ocean.

Nishan and his father after they met in America in 1928.

It's a wonder Grandpa found him at all after a journey more than twice as long and far more tortuous than the typical three-week passage on a crowded, creaking steamer like the *Edison*, which was built in 1896. All Dad ever told me about the timing of his trip was that he sailed in February 1928. I assumed that meant he landed later that month or sometime in early March. But long after he died, I read and reread the yellowed identification papers he carried from Greece. Nishan "Kalaidjian," born 1912 in "Dikranagard" was granted passage from Athens on February 20, 1928.

The alternate spelling of the family name was the key to locating the record of his arrival in New York on Friday, April 6. Nishan was recorded as being detained by the vigilant Inspector Travis, who suspected him of being "LPC," and added the note, "Visa?" As an American citizen, Dad needed no visa, but it was unlikely he could explain that in a language Inspector Travis understood. "LPC" was shorthand for "likely public charge," the catchall designation for foreigners with no money and no family or friends to vouch for them. The onus was on the suspected LPC to prove himself otherwise. To fail in that regard meant incarceration with thieves, anarchists, and other undesirables until they could all be shipped back to where they came from.

Ship arrivals were important news back then, and the *New York Times* noted the *Edison's* arrival that day along with the date it sailed from the Port of Piraeus, Greece: March 19. Where had Dad and the ship lingered since Feb 20? Maybe they were stuck in port with a broken steam valve, or awaiting inspection or—who knows? Who knows what he ate on board or where he slept, or whether he slept at all while listening to the night-long hacking of tubercular refugees, clutching his slim purse against the threat of pickpockets and thugs. Who knows whether there was any heat as the ship sliced through the frigid North Atlantic, or if he would gladly forego heat for one breath of fresh air up on deck?

All I know for sure is that Dad held on to his dignity and determination and endured a final night of noisy anxiety in the cavernous detention chambers of Ellis Island, listening to the cries of the hopeless, until his father somehow found him there the next day and brought him to a home he'd never seen. Father and son truly met for the first time that day in New York Harbor. I don't know if they hugged or kissed or cried. I don't know anything about their conversation except this: My father proudly showed Grandpa his letter of introduction from the greenhouse owner. He'd come to America with a real skill and the prospect of a job.

Grandpa tore the letter to pieces.

"I didn't bring you all the way to America to become a gardener," he said.

Neither of them ever mentioned it again.

Memories of New Jersey
before I was born

My mother told me lots of stories about the old days. I'm sure she left out a few details, because she freely admitted that there were things she didn't want to talk about.

Her aversions weren't nearly as severe as my father's, thank goodness. Mostly they reflected her generation's sense of propriety: Some things just weren't nice, she'd say. So Mom steered clear of anything salacious or even vaguely dishonorable, especially where her family was concerned. She didn't say that no one gambled or drank to excess or cheated on his or her spouse. She just didn't talk about it. She also avoided one important subject altogether: The word *cancer* never came out of her mouth. This left some pretty big gaps in my knowledge of our family's health and occasionally caused me to be blindsided by the deaths of close relatives I never knew to be ill because Mom just didn't want to bring it up.

Just about every other subject was fair game, including my father. I think she wanted me to know much more than he ever shared because she hoped it would help me understand him. Mom eventually told me everything she knew about my father's early life. Unfortunately, that wasn't really much at all. What Mom knew best about my father's life began the day they met in April 1928, a week or so after his sixteenth birthday and a few weeks before hers. It was Dad's second full day in America. Grandpa Kalajian took his son to the apartment of his friend and business partner, Harry Bichakjian, and said, "Play with these children while I go to work." There were two boys and two girls in the Bichakjian household. At fifteen, my mother was the oldest, as her half-sister, Mary, was already married. Mom was forced to quit school a year earlier when her mother died so she could take over as housekeeper, cook, and surrogate mother. She told me she took one look at my father as he walked in the door and said out loud, "Just what I need around here, another foreigner."

The Kalajians and the Bichakjians lived just a few blocks apart on Central Avenue, the spine of Union City's Armenian community. The bustling little city just across the Hudson River from lower Manhattan must have looked mighty strange to my father with its towering tenements and crowded trolley cars, but it sounded a lot like home. The Armenian community had already grown strong enough to build Holy Cross Church more than twenty years earlier. Immigrants from Dad's native Dikranagerd were numerous, including many who had recently drifted down from Massachusetts when the shoe factories began closing. The Armenians had plenty of familiar neighbors, too, as there were so many Syrians, Greeks, and Assyrians all around them that the neighborhood was known as the Dardanelles.

I should have paid closer attention to my mother's reminiscences about Union City because they revealed so much about the Armenian-immigrant experience in twentieth-century America. What interested me far more, however, was that Mom's stories previewed my own experience—and really, my existence. The round-about journeys of the Bichakjians and the Kalajians set the circumstances of my birth not so many years later. I was born less than two miles from the cold-water flat where my parents met.

I enjoyed these stories because I could picture the setting. When I was a boy, Mom and I often rode the Public Service bus from North Bergen, where we lived, to the shopping district in Union City. Along the way, Mom would point at soot-smudged store windows or faded-brick apartment buildings and say, "That's where . . ." And a story would follow, about this uncle's store or that cousin's house or the winter of the great blizzard or the election when the Democrats gave everyone five dollars—a fortune!—to vote for Franklin Roosevelt. Thank goodness no one had invented the shopping mall, or I might never have heard half of it.

Mom assured me that most of what I saw hadn't changed much over the years, but circumstances certainly had. For the Armenians of the 1920s and '30s, tenement life in Union City was like tenement life anywhere: crowded, noisy, broiling in summer and freezing in winter. For thirty dollars or so every month, each family got a set of railroad rooms. That meant the rooms lined up in a row, with no connecting hall. You just walked from one room to the next, as if moving from one rail car to another. There was no central heat on Central Avenue. Everyone gathered around the coal stove in the kitchen. There was no bathtub either. The kids could bathe in the kitchen sink or in a tub on the floor. The adults went to the *paghnik*, the Turkish bath. Bathing was a community event—the men went one night, the women the next. They ate there, drank there, smoked there, sang there. You went out to take a bath and likely came home the next day. A mere seven days later, you'd go bathe again.

The Armenians of Union City didn't need cars because they didn't need to go anywhere. Everything came to them, or at least was close by. Men in wagons brought ice, milk, bread, and vegetables. If they needed to go to a store, they could walk because it was just downstairs or at the corner or, at most, around the block. The one store all the Armenians knew well was Uncle's grocery store.

Uncle who? His name was one of the many missing details in Mom's stories, but not because of censorship or even because I wasn't paying attention. Armenians don't call uncles or aunts by their first names. There are enough words in Armenian to identify each one by relationship: father's brother, mother's sister. An adjective or two takes care of multiple siblings. Even in-law uncles and aunts are covered. If I knew all those words, and their Dikranagerdtsi variations, I might begin to puzzle out who was who in all my parents' stories, which might make no difference in the story's entertainment value but would give me great satisfaction. For now, I'll take my satisfaction from having figured out that the grocery store belonged to Uncle Hagop Nalbandian. The Nalbandians were my mother's family on her mother's side. She and my father both told me this story, which is probably my favorite of all their memories from Union City because it says so much about those times and those people:

Uncle Hagop had a big cast-iron potful of *gouvedge* percolating away on top of the coal stove all winter long. Don't worry about how to pronounce it—just imagine eggplant, squash, okra, onions, and other veggies, all simmering in a lamb-and-tomato broth thick as syrup and pungent as gin. You could smell the seasonings halfway down the block, sharp and sweet at the same time: garlic, coriander, allspice. The real treat was always down deep. Swimming below a glistening layer of bubbling fat were fist-sized chunks of lamb bones—necks and joints—that surrendered soft, sweet meat as they melted down. You know gouvedge is done when you can suck every last trace of meat off the bone, and then you suck the bone itself because inside is the nectar of all true Dikranagerdtsi lamb eaters, *dzoodz*, or what the Americans who so foolishly discard it call marrow.

Mom said Uncle made one pot of gouvedge at the first sign of frost and that was it for the winter. Instead of starting fresh, he'd simply replenish it every day with more vegetables and meat, and he'd even provide a loaf of fresh bread. Everyone who came into the store went straight to the stove, broke off a piece of bread, and dipped it into the pot. All Armenians are cooks, so they all had asbestos-like hands that worked as well as any ladle or fork, but some hands were more asbestos-like than others, or their owners were simply more daring. The most daring got the best stuff from the bottom of the pot, the really tender meat and the vegetables that had marinated overnight or perhaps for days. The timid got bread and sauce. No matter how deeply, everyone's hands went into the gouvedge, and no one ever complained about that, much less died from hand poisoning (as far as anyone knows).

What does this tell you about Armenians? Perhaps that they didn't believe in the germ theory? No. It tells you that Armenians, at least the Armenians of my parents' generation, took eating personally. The Armenians certainly didn't invent the concept of eating as an act of intimacy—breaking bread is an ancient testament to friendship—but these desperately poor people understood how precious and fragile sustenance can be. They were cursed by fate and the kindness of strangers to be known throughout the Western world as the Starving Armenians, personified by gaunt faces of dying children on Near East Relief posters. They were less concerned with the image than with the reality. They were still poor, but they had landed in a God-blessed place where even poor people could eat their fill if they worked like dogs, assuming they were lucky enough to find work. The ones who weren't so lucky could always find a mouthful of bread and dzoodz at Uncle's store and a hundred others like it in the factory towns of Paterson, New Jersey; Providence, Rhode Island; Worcester, Massachusetts, and wherever else Armenians made their new homes. Sharing what little they had was more than an act of kindness or courtesy, or even of sacrifice or obligation. It was a familial bond. And of all the things Armenians might fear in their hearts and souls—Turks, Communists, earthquakes, starvation—the sweat and soil of their brother's fingers hardly seemed daunting.

The Nalbandian clan's exploits provided many other lasting memories for both of my parents that became so familiar through repetition that they now seem to be my own. They are my memories of New Jersey from before I was born. One of the clearest is of Uncle Ray gliding along the narrow city streets in his Packard, a car that seemed as long as a city block and that probably cost as much. Technically, it wasn't his Packard, and just as technically, he wasn't actually Uncle Ray. He was Uncle Aram Nalbandian, youngest brother of Hagop. I think Mom was the only one in the family who called him Ray, a childhood nickname.

Uncle Ray was one of the few Armenians back then who didn't own a shop or work in a factory. He worked at a car dealership selling Packards, which were among the most powerful, stylish, and expensive cars in the world. One of the benefits was that he got to drive a demonstrator, which made a big impression on all the Armenians. Imagine driving a car that cost more than anyone you knew would ever earn in a lifetime?

I know Mom didn't dream this because an artist from Union City named Ashod Pinajian drew a very clever cartoon depicting an Armenian outing in the early 1930s. It features many of the names I heard in stories from that era, with little blurbs and caricatures that captured their most notable traits: the barber, the cigar smoker, the news reporter. Uncle Ray is shown cruising into view in a flashy convertible. The blurb says, "Nalband—Packard Salesman."

The Nalbands were great *kef* makers, which very roughly translates as party people. Uncle Charlie was the greatest of all. He played the *kanoon*, an Armenian zither. When the music carried him, he'd jump up and swing from the chandelier, which dangled from a thin cord. Somehow, Uncle Charlie swung along with the music without pulling the ceiling down.

The men all smoked heavily throughout the day, but they smoked even more at night when they made kef, as though each cigarette were a little steam engine that replenished the energy they'd spent during the long, hard workday. The women and children rolled the cigarettes while the men played. They had to be fast but flawless. The punishment for a sloppy job was not exactly shame but something close. "Her spit is no good," the men would say, and it was never forgotten. A generation later, my mother could still remember the names of the women whose spit was no good. I wouldn't repeat the names here even if I remembered them. After all this time, they deserve forgiveness.

As soon as winter passed, the Armenians poured out of their railroad rooms and into city parks, carrying their *shishes* to roast kebab and their lute-like *ouds* to make kef. My father remembered the first neighborhood picnic after he came to America. He told me about it one night near the end of his life during one of our scotch-stimulated discussions. He remembered a merry-go-round in the park. Not an elaborate, electrical, musical, bobbing-horse merry-go-round. Just one of those squeaking, rickety, sit-down-and-push merry-go-rounds that kids propel with their feet—the more kids, the merrier.

Uncle Aram Nalbandian got plenty of attention driving a Packard to Armenian gatherings in Union City, N.J. during the Depression.

"I got on the merry-go-round with the little kids, seven or eight years old. I was sixteen, but I stayed on it all day, going round and round."

He paused.

"It was the first time I'd ever really played like a kid. I didn't want to stop."

Dad's dalliance with childhood didn't last through many more afternoons. He accepted his new country's promise of a free public education, but his interest evaporated two weeks later when an American kid picked a fight with him. He was happy to oblige. He ended up in the principal's office, and Mom's brother Mike was called in to translate. It wasn't necessary, as Dad had already decided to move on. What he moved on to is unclear, as the entire family saga goes out of focus for the next few years.

At this juncture, Mom's stories lost more detail as she edited out the sad effects of her father's physical decline from heart disease, which dictated that he stop working. That meant Mom had to start. As best I can tell, she was seventeen when she went to work in a dry-cleaning factory. This did not relieve her of household duties, and the combination must have guaranteed exhaustion. My father also faced a sudden change in domestic circumstances when Grandpa Kalajian decided to marry again. He sailed to France in June 1929 and returned with a bride. Dad always spoke fondly and respectfully of his stepmother, and he clearly was in no hurry to leave home. Eventually, he also found work at a dry-cleaning plant, driving the delivery truck.

Back in the 1920s, dry cleaning was incredibly hazardous as well as debilitating. Most individual stores didn't have cleaning machines. They sent the work to enormous cleaning factories, where clothes were dipped in vats of fuming, flammable petrochemicals. The dripping clothes were hung downwind of giant fans that were also supposed to suck the fumes away from the workers. That worked, except for the fumes they'd already inhaled while standing over the vats. Sometimes the sparks from the fans set the fumes on fire. Sometimes the boilers exploded. Either way, people died.

Working in a cleaning factory was not what most Americans would consider a good job, even during the Depression. Most people preferred to sell apples or dig ditches or go on the dole. Like most immigrants, Armenians couldn't be choosy. Dry cleaning was to Armenian immigrants what scrub work was to the Irish and Poles or tomato picking was and still is to many Mexicans. Why do so many Americans complain about immigrants taking jobs that no American would dream of doing? Dry cleaning was so nasty, though, that I'm not sure anyone complained about the Armenians.

I'm not sure where they started out, but I know Mom and Dad worked in the same factory for a while before he moved on to learn much more about the business from his mother's brother. In 1930, Uncle Mihran Toutounjian opened a cleaning store in Cranford, New Jersey, about an hour south of Union City. Moving there kept my father in familiar and loving company. Close by was Uncle Mihran's sister, Aunt Virginia, the little girl in the picture from Dikranagerd. With her was her mother, Sogomon, the grandmother who had snatched my father from his dying mother's arms. How did she survive? That's another lost story.

Looking back from my too-comfortable perch in the future, it seems impossible that the turmoil in my father's life didn't end at this point. After so many devastating losses, he now had a real family and real work with solid prospects for the future. Why didn't he settle down? Of course, I know that no one's prospects seemed very solid in 1930, least of all a young immigrant's. But I think there was something more at work. I think my father was deeply unsettled. I'm convinced he'd been displaced so violently and so often that he'd been conditioned to feel unsafe and unsure. The result was a powerful urge to keep moving.

What little he told me about this time was delivered in short bursts that he never connected to each other. Once when we were on vacation at the Jersey Shore, my mother decided I needed a haircut and asked Dad to take me to a barber. "I'll cut it myself," he said, and suddenly I was sitting in a straight-back chair draped in a bed sheet as my father snip-snipped around my ears. This is how I found out that he'd gone to barber school in New York City, where he and the other students practiced on hobos. His hair-cutting career ended when he nearly cut a guy's ear off and decided he didn't like mopping up blood. He was proud of having passed the course, however, and kept his barber scissors. I still have them.

Another time when we were in a restaurant, he spotted soft-shell crab on the menu. He told me he'd eaten plenty of it when he was a short-order cook during the Depression. The boss told him he could eat the ones he burned, so he kept burning crabs until he was full. He soon lost his taste for soft-shell crabs, burned or otherwise, and quit the job.

Years later, when I first expressed an interest in newspaper work, he told me that he'd seen a newsroom or two when he was an errand boy for a photoengraving shop. He liked the job because it carried him all over New York City, to offices and factories as well as magazines and newspapers. He encountered interesting characters and contraptions everywhere he went. Once he walked in during an early demonstration of television as a roomful of men gaped at the wobbling, soundless image of two prizefighters pummeling each other. Between errands, he sat on a bench waiting his turn with the other boys, some of whom were well past boyhood. He remembered sitting next to a man who said he'd been to college. For that man, born in an America so recently soaring with energy and enthusiasm, the Depression was aptly named. But my father remembered thinking, "What a great country! I already have a college man's job."

Perspective is everything, isn't it? My father, taught to expect so little from the world, was thankful for every reward, including the most meager paycheck. I think he bounced between jobs not only because he was restless but because he could, and that was thrilling. In the old country, you did what you were born to do, or what you were ordered to do. In America, you could be a barber one day and a cook the next and an errand boy the day after that. It was as though a man could live many lives. He liked some jobs better than others, but the only one he hated was the one he was most thankful for, the valet job his father's friend Vartan Aslanian had gotten him. It was a good job in a classy place, the Hotel Park Lane, where many wealthy and interesting people not only stayed but lived.

Most of the hotel's residents were pleasant, and many were generous. He didn't mind picking up dirty clothes or delivering fresh ones and laying them out for rich people. But he hated the idea of sticking his hand out for a tip. A free man set his own price, or at least agreed to a fair wage before he set to work. In the world he knew best, only beggars put their hands out.

The figure who made the greatest impression during my father's short stint at the Park Lane was a retiree who lived nearby and passed the hotel each day on his morning walk. Herbert Hoover, the very recent former president of the United States, was distinguished not only by his tailored clothes but by his bearing and his unfailing good humor. He smiled and said hello to the doormen and other workers along his route, and they all wished him well. My father was struck by the contradiction between the humanity he observed in Hoover and the dour portrait presented in the newspapers and, later, in history books. He was even more deeply impressed by the polite and even friendly reaction of the everyday workers Hoover exchanged greetings with, most of whom had certainly voted against him and blamed him for the Depression. Where else on Earth could an overthrown leader walk so casually and easily without fear among the people he'd formerly ruled? Certainly not in any place my father had lived.

I have no idea how many other jobs my father managed to wring out of the depressed economy. I gather he moved between Union City and Cranford more than a time or two. What I know for sure is that in 1934, he joined the United States Army, which must have made perfect sense. Now he not only had a country, he had a country to serve.

For the next two years, Dad patrolled the Panama Canal Zone. He never said much about it except that it was hot, but I found a number of snapshots in his album that show him looking quite proud in the honorable role of professional soldier. The images of Dad and his buddies wearing putties and broad-brim hats reflect the First World War rather than the Second, which was still years off. In one shot, my very dignified father is swinging from a jungle vine like Tarzan. In another, he's taking deadly aim with a Springfield rifle, the sling pulled tight against his shoulder and his right elbow cocked high and held out in the classic stance. He looks very much like a trained killer, which by then he was.

Dad sent at least one picture back to New Jersey with an inscription. The photo shows him standing shirtless in the midday heat. The message reads: "It is sun-shine here. How is the snow there?"

He sent it to my mother.

A DOG WITH TWO NAMES

Dad re-enlisted in 1939, after deciding he liked Army life better than driving a delivery van or frying crabs. At least, that's my guess. He never told me much about the inter-Army period of his life, and there are no photos from that time. If that's when he went to China, he didn't take a camera, or he threw the pictures away. I'd believe either version.

This time around, the Army shipped him to a place even farther from home than Panama. He was assigned to the 59th Coast Artillery on the island of Corregidor in the Philippines. That's where he adopted a homeless mutt with floppy beagle ears and stubby bulldog legs. Dad named him Recoil, after the thunderous jounce of the mortars on Battery Geary, where he was a pit commander.

I know the name because the photo album my mother set up for Dad had newfangled plastic sleeves instead of the old stick-on pages. When I pulled out the dog photo to get a closer look, I spotted his name written on the back. I also pulled out the photo next to it, which was identical except for the name Ex-calibre. It didn't strike me as odd that he'd give his dog two names because he gave himself a new name whenever the mood struck him. He was Nishan, of course, and Nish for short, or Nick to his Greek friends as well as to the 1930 census taker. He startled me one day late in his life by introducing himself to a friend of mine as 'Shan. When I asked him why, he shrugged, "Why not?"

I spotted the dog photos not long before Dad died and I asked him about his pet's alternate name, which I assumed was another bit of armament-related whimsy. It was, but it also had a deeper meaning. "You've never heard of Excalibur, King Arthur's sword?" he asked. Of course I had, but not as a dog's name. "The sword was at Arthur's right hand, the companion that never failed him," Dad said. "Now do you understand?"

I don't remember ever seeing my father pet a dog, so it was hard to understand such deep affection for one. My mother told me we once had a dog, but I was too young then to remember it. Mom, who gave no hint of tolerance for pets, admitted she doted on Skippy, a purebred cocker spaniel, even cooking it dinner instead of buying dog food. My arrival clearly brought out the jealousy in Dad's pampered pet, and Skippy made the mistake of growling at my crib.

My discovery of Recoil/Ex-calibre was fortunate as well as entertaining. My dog questions didn't result in the usual lightning-like change of topic. Dad seemed willing to tell me more about his time in the Philippines, and the reason became clear as we talked: He wanted to share some lessons he learned, including a few that made him sad and others that made him angry.

The dog was one of his few pleasant diversions on the island at the mouth of Manila Bay. The troops called the island The Rock because that's what it was, a craggy boulder used as an anchor for giant artillery emplacements that were installed when the United States occupied the Philippines nearly a half century before. Army life on Corregidor was as stark and monotonous as the island's nickname implies. Dad and his crew spent the first part of each day firing artillery shells into the sea while training native troops to take over their soon-to-be-independent nation's defense. The rest of the day was spent rounding up the raw troops who scattered far and wide with each blast.

After two years of boredom as intense as the tropical heat, Dad and his pal Virgil Johnson came up with an unlikely escape plan: they applied for transfers to a new branch of the Army called the Airborne. If they were accepted, they'd be trained to jump out of airplanes. I doubt Dad had ever flown in a plane, much less considered jumping out of one until then. "We just wanted to get off that rock," he said. "I didn't think about jumping." Really, why bother? The vast majority of volunteers were rejected out of hand, and most of the rest failed to meet the Airborne's exceptional fitness standards. Many more washed out during training, while others froze the first time they stepped to the plane's open cargo door and looked down.

Dad and Virgil got lucky. Each received an enthusiastic recommendation from their commanding officer and their transfers came through in late

October 1941. Soon after, they shipped out for the mainland with a stop-over in Hawaii. Their ship was approaching California on Dec. 7 when the Japanese attacked Pearl Harbor. Japanese planes bombed the Philippines hours later, followed by an invasion force.

The outbreak of war resulted in a short detour, as Dad and Virgil were held up in California while the Army there assessed its coast artillery needs. But they were soon moved along and they passed every test, including the most important one. "When I got to the door, I looked down and I felt fine," Dad said. "So I jumped." He jumped again and again, as America prepared to enter combat while figuring out how best to use its new airborne cabability. Meanwhile, Dad got a tour of bases in Georgia, North Carolina and Louisiana. As a wily sergeant, he was often able to wangle a long weekend's pass along with enough rationed gasoline to reach New Jersey. He and Mom were married on one such visit in October 1942.

Nishan, weariing his paratrooper boots, married Sylvia in 1942. Sylvia's brother John is at center, next to their sister Ann. Cousin Peter Doramajian is at right.

Virgil got into combat first, as Dad got sidelined when his chute tangled in a tree during night maneuvers. He cut his lines and dropped like a stone, injuring his legs. He was left behind when his buddies shipped out, and he was eventually transferred to the walking infantry. He arrived in Europe in December 1944, just in time for America's bloodiest engagement of the European war, the Battle of the Bulge. He found himself firing a cannon again—this time at Germans, who kept firing back. He marched across the Elbe River with the 331st Infantry on the drive to Berlin, only to march back again when they were ordered to let the Russians go first.

When the war ended in 1945, Dad had been in the Army so long he was nearly half-way to a military pension. He thought about making the Army his career but he thought more about Mom and starting a family. I asked if he regretted not sticking with the Army and he didn't hesitate to say he did not. But he clearly had mixed feelings and talked from time to time in what-ifs. He rarely talked about the war but he talked often about the Army and his pals, although even then he was as stingy with details as he was when he talk-ed about the rest of his life. And as always, anecdotes were often provoked by seemingly unrelated topics. For example, I dislodged an important piece of his Army story when I told him I'd decided on a career in newspapers.

"It was a goddam newspaper editor who got me blackballed from the paratroopers."

This editor-turned-officer summoned him one day and asked questions about his Armenian political leanings. He asked if my father had any fascist sympathies. Dad resisted the urge to punch the guy, although I'm not sure how. Armenian Communists were spreading the calumny that Armenians who opposed them were pro-Nazi, and America's alliance with Stalinist Russia was now making Communists seem like reasonable people. This was a case of reverse McCarthyism long before McCarthy. Dad told the offi-cer the truth, that he belonged to a party dedicated to liberating Armenia from the Communists as well as the Turks. He stressed that he was also an American patriot willing to fight any enemy. Nothing more was said, but he was transferred to the marching infantry soon after without explanation.

Dad did sometimes share a few tidbits after getting in touch with Virgil and a few other Army buddies over the years. Virgil stayed with the para-troops and jumped into Normandy, where he was captured. He spent the rest of the war in a German prison camp. At that, he was luckier than many of the men they'd left behind in the Philippines. The gallant defenders of

Corregidor ran out of food, ammunition and hope on May 6, 1942. The Japanese did not accept their surrender graciously. Dad later learned that his closest friend was beheaded in a prison camp. I did not dare buy a Honda while Dad was alive.

Dad's anger at the Japanese intensified after a chance meeting with a veteran of Corregidor back in the early 1980s. The man detailed the loss of old friends in horrific circumstances. Dad told me almost nothing about the conversation beyond those general terms, except to recount an afterthought: "I told him I always wondered what happened to my dog."

Without a doubt, the man said, Dad's steadfast companion met the same fate as every other dog on the island after the rations ran out. "We ate them all."

MY LESS TURBULENT WORLD

Dad sent enough of his wartime pay home to Mom to get them out of the cleaning factories and into their own shop after his discharge. They rented a store and opened Merit Cleaners, 446 61st Street, in West New York, New Jersey.

I don't have to guess at my father's joy in finally settling down to marriage and a business of his own. He left a clue on the stationery he ordered, a rare public display of his sense of humor that produced another twist on his name: "N. Merit Kalajian, prop."

A few years later, they bought a three-story building on Hudson Boulevard in North Bergen, New Jersey. It was the sort of place you see in older cities: a storefront with apartments stacked on top, jammed in the middle of a block of identical twenty-foot-wide, tan-brick buildings all squeezed together in a solid row. Our block was a model of urban efficiency before anyone thought to call it that. We had a drugstore, a beauty parlor, a candy store, a paint store, an eye doctor, and even a Plymouth dealer. Best of all, there was a grocery store just across the boulevard—and I mean grocery store, not supermarket.

This is where I debuted in 1952. Mom, Dad, Uncle Mike, and I shared five rooms and one bath right over the store. This arrangement lasted until I graduated from my crib to sharing a bed with my uncle. After one night of my relentless tossing and kicking, Uncle Mike set out to look for an apartment.

Dad had everything he needed in our second-floor sanctuary. He had a living room for his reading chair and lamp, plus enough wall space for his bookshelves. Out back was a little yard where he planted roses and a cherry tree. Mom got everything she needed, too: a dining room to serve company dinner, and a kitchen to cook it in. Both my folks were spared any commute. Mom got a generation's head start on multitasking by running up and down the stairs between the store and our apartment so she could simultaneously execute work and domestic duties. Her child-care arrangement was not only pure genius, it was extra comfy for me: When I grew too big for my baby carriage, she tossed me into a canvas laundry hamper next to her sewing machine. Years later, Mom rolled her eyes at the thought. "You poor kid," she said. "You were in there with all those germs from all those dirty clothes." It must have been the equivalent of a good vaccination because I don't seem to have suffered.

Sylvia and Nish enjoying life in their little kitchen
above the cleaning store in the 1950s.

Daily life at our house did not start at first light, as it had in Dikranagerd. It started earlier. My parents set their ivory-colored clock radio every night, more out of habit than need. My father, whose internal clock was forever set to Army time, jumped out of bed by 5:30 a.m. most days, except on Sunday. On Sunday he was up by five because he hated to waste his only day off.

Mom and Dad worked in the cleaning store six days a week without fail, except for two weeks in July when they closed for vacation. They never got to take a day off to go to the beach or a ball game. They couldn't come in late when they had to run errands. They couldn't leave early when they were exhausted—and even as a kid, I knew they were exhausted a lot.

Dry cleaning is not the heaviest work, but it's draining because a cleaning store is hot. The boiler's always on full blast, even in summer, pumping steam through the pressing machine and the puffers, which were perforated pipes that mimicked the shapes of arms and heads and knees—a row of hissing, stainless-steel prosthetic limbs that leaked steam. My father would work the pressing machine, which looked like a giant, elongated waffle iron with a top that swung down and locked in place. He'd blast creases into suits and pants while my mother used the puffers to coax the wrinkles out of shirts and blouses and delicate skirts.

Good pressers have a rhythm, and my father was a very good presser. He'd pick a pair of pants out of a hamper with one hand and smooth them flat across the ironing-board bottom surface of the pressing machine with the other. Then his free hand would swing up and pull the top of the pressing machine down while he stepped on a pedal that locked it in place. One blast, two blasts—each garment got exactly what it needed. He'd unlock the top, swing it up, flip the pants like a flapjack, swing the top down, lock it again, blast it again. Then, *whoosh*, the pants were off the board and on a hanger and another pair was already in the air.

My mother would be a few feet away at the puffers, slipping sleeves over the one shaped like a loaf of French bread. She worked fast, too, because she had to. She also did the sewing, sorted the dirty clothes, hung up the clean ones, and waited on customers. My father did, too, but Mom liked chatting with people much more than Dad did, and the customers liked chatting with her. When the chime signaled that the front door had opened, my mother dropped her puffing or sewing or sorting and rushed up to the counter. She never failed to smile. She greeted every customer by name. She asked about their children, she listened to stories about their jobs and houses and hobbies and vacations. She fetched their clean clothes and tagged the dirty ones. She made change and thanked them for coming and rushed back into the rising heat.

Sometimes, she was in too much of a rush. She did her sewing at an old-fashioned, coal-black Singer, a heavy-duty industrial machine bolted to a lacquered-wood table. It had a big electric motor that looked strong enough to pull a train. Her hands kept pace with the motor, as quick and sure as Rubinstein playing Chopin. Her fingers and the stuttering needle were always in perfect rhythm, except once when the needle went straight through her left thumb. She sewed and puffed and sorted and tagged one-handed for weeks, but she never stopped, because she couldn't. She couldn't stop when she'd bump into one of the puffers and burn an arm so badly it would become infected. She couldn't stop when she had the flu. She barely stopped when she had me. Two days later, I went downstairs to work with her for the first time.

My mother went right back to work, but my father hadn't stopped. Each of them could do everything the other could do, if not quite as well. My father could sew but he hated it. My mother could clean clothes and often ran the machine, but spot removing was my father's specialty. He learned it from master spotters before the war. It's an art—really part chemistry, part muscle. He could identify a stain in an instant. He had bottles of solvents, scrapers that looked like tongue depressors (and probably were), and a steam hose. He'd lay the garment on the spotting table, size up the stain, and spritz on just the right combination of chemicals. He knew just when to work the stain hard and when to use the most delicate touch. He had a genius for the work. It's what drew customers who could afford the best clothes—hand-tailored silks and linens, the sort of clothing they couldn't trust to just anyone and that even rich people couldn't simply throw away because it got soiled.

I used to watch my father from a distance. The stuff he used smelled awful. He told me to stay back or it would ruin my lungs. It ruined his. He always insisted he'd done everything he could to keep the store well-ventilated. We had fans and ducts and a closed system of pipes to cycle the fluid and fumes between the machines to the reclaiming still. By the time I was born, dry cleaning meant a good spin in something called perchloroethylene. Perc is one of those miracle chemicals we used to thank God and America for back when average folks really believed in better living through chemistry. It was certainly a big leap from carbon tetrachloride, which itself was a big leap from naphtha and kerosene. The whole atmosphere was certainly better than life in the cleaning factories where Armenians worked during the Depression. It was still one tough way to make a living, but I never heard a complaint from either of my folks.

Once we were upstairs, we felt as far from the store as from Chelsea or Dikranagerd. Mom went straight to the kitchen and Dad headed for his rocking chair, but I wasn't left out. I have proof in faded, '50s Kodak color that my father used to bounce me on his knee. I spent a lot of time there and in his lap or wrapped in his arms until I was too old to pick up. Even then, Dad never discouraged my presence unless I was intent on making noise while he tried to listen to Fulton Lewis Jr.'s radio commentary each night at seven. But he was never interested in idle chat, and I didn't know how to make serious conversation about the things my father was interested in, such as history or politics. I certainly couldn't interrupt his reading, and there was hardly a moment when he wasn't reading, unless he was sleeping, driving, or pressing someone's suit. Dad even read throughout his coffee breaks. The little table in the back room of our cleaning store was covered with his books, magazines, and newspapers, and there were piles more underneath.

Some of his reading material was in impenetrable Armenian, like the *Hairenik Daily* newspaper from Boston, but I started nosing my way through the English papers and magazines almost from the time I learned to read. I loved that. Reading alongside my father, or at least reading the same words my father had just read, made me feel closer to him even if I couldn't always understand what I was reading. It also made me a slightly odd kid. I'm pretty sure I was the only regular reader of *U.S. News and World Report* in my third-grade class. At times, though, my attention flickered while reading yet another analysis of the Nixon-Kennedy tiff over Quemoy and Matsu. Then I'd turn on *Howdy Doody* a bit too loud, with predictable result. "Tell him to turn that down," my father would shout. It didn't matter if I was within arm's reach while my mother was at the other end of the house; my father invariably made his complaint known through her. I can't be sure, but I suspect he just never wanted to be the bad guy.

I don't know if my father was ever beaten as a child by Turks or Kurds or the people who ran the orphanage. If so, he never mentioned it, but he was certainly beaten down by a cruel world. I know that his harrowing childhood experiences made him resolve to be a kind, protective parent because he told me so. Once when I knew I'd done something worthy of a scolding or worse, I confessed and asked him not to hit me. "Have I ever hit you?" he asked. No, he never had, and he promised me then that he never would. Nor would he ever send me to bed without supper, because he knew what it was like for a boy to go without supper. Looking back, I can't think of a single time in all my childhood when my father punished me in any way for anything at all, except by expressing his disapproval. No beating could have hurt worse.

When Dad called on my mother to keep me quiet, her solution was to call me into the kitchen. Often, she didn't have to call. I'd run there whenever I smelled butter and onions on the stove, which is how all Armenians meals start. Mom never discouraged me from spending time at her side while she cooked. I think she liked the company, but she also made a point of explaining what she was doing, even when I was too young to understand. Watching Mom was like watching my very own Armenian Food Network. She showed me how to chop, mix, sauté, and simmer before I could add, subtract, multiply, or divide. "You have to know how to cook to be independent," she said. I wasn't sure why I'd want to be. "Because I won't always be around," she explained. I know now that she was thinking of her own mother, who died young and left her in the kitchen alone.

Not only can I picture Mom's kitchen, I can still smell every crowded inch of it: a plate of freshly chopped parsley on the table, a pot of braising lamb on the stove, a bowl of chopped walnuts mixed with sugar and cinnamon on the short shelf next to the sink. Preparing so much food in so little space made every meal a juggling act—something always had to be up in the air—but Mom never dropped a thing. She loved her little kitchen. "I can reach everything," she'd say. "Why would I want to walk farther?" Her four-burner stove was no wider than the yardstick she used to hem dresses. The refrigerator was just inches away, to the right. She really could reach in for any ingredient she needed. She never complained about not having enough counter space even though there was no counter at all. All of the mixing, chopping, seasoning, and battering had to be done at our very 1950s kitchen table with its steel legs and red Formica top. The color was worn clean through in the corner where Mom clamped the meat grinder to the tabletop. She did not trust the butcher to grind meat as lean or as finely as she wanted, so she cranked and cranked at the long iron handle as I sat and watched the wiggling red worms of chopped lamb squiggle their way down into the mixing bowl. When I was older, cranking became my job, although Mom always insisted on feeding in the meat because she worried I'd feed in a finger.

Mom never complained nor even hinted that all this cooking was a burden. She'd been cooking for a crowd since she was fourteen, when she took over the household chores after her mother died, and she always said it was no more trouble than cooking for two. Mom always made enough to feed at least twice as many guests as she'd invited ("You never know who's going to drop in"), and these were Armenian servings, which meant it was probably four times what most hosts would consider generous. No matter how many were coming, she prepared at least two main courses because not everybody likes everything. Often, that meant one more-or-less American dish, like a roast beef, and one Armenian dish, like *kufte*, which I'll explain in a moment.

Each main dish was accompanied by the appropriate range of side dishes, which meant Mom always made two complete dinners. The roast beef came with mashed potatoes—the real thing, of course—and brown gravy, never from a mix or a can. The kufte—well, give me another moment—came with Armenian salad, which is a lot like an American salad except everything is cut very small and it's brimming with diced green onion and parsley. Plus she always served the mandatory kufte accompaniment, fresh *madzoon*, which is what Armenians call yogurt. Mom always made her own, which is easy enough if you know the tricks. The ingredients are milk and yogurt. That's the first trick: You have to have yogurt to make more yogurt. Every Armenian house used to have a big bowl of madzoon in the icebox, with a small bowl of the same madzoon by its side, preserved as a starter for the next batch. Woe to anyone who ate the starter! Everyone knew that all madzoon was not the same, even though no chemist could possibly tell the difference. Mom knew whose to borrow and whose to avoid, although this was delicate business best dealt with in whispers. To reject someone's madzoon is a terrific insult.

Mom's madzoon, like everything she made, was fabulous. Of course she started with whole milk, which was the only kind I remember back then. The milk went into a heavy pot to be heated until exactly the moment before the milk boiled. The moment before—not a few moments before, and God forbid not a moment after or the milk would be burnt and ruined. When you've made madzoon a few thousand times, as Mom had, you don't have to squint to see the thousand tiny bubbles form on the surface or stick your nose into the pot to see the quivering white mass begin to rise. You just sense it and lift the pot off the fire exactly then and pour its hot, thick, frothy contents into a bowl with an equal amount of cold milk. Then you stir in maybe a half cup of old madzoon slightly diluted with more milk. Finally, you cover the bowl with a dish and then wrap the whole thing in a big bath towel or some other insulation. Mom's favorite was a very old, very tattered, yellow-and-brown-striped bathrobe of Dad's. It was so old, even when I was little, that I never remember it being a bathrobe. It was always the madzoon robe. The point of the wrapping was to keep the heat in so the culture could do whatever cultures do in the heat and dark of a madzoon bowl while sitting on the stove top overnight. Mom swore nothing worked as well as the madzoon robe, and it worked every time.

By morning, magically, the bowl of milk had always turned into a bowl of madzoon, but it wasn't nearly ready to eat. After Mom unwrapped it, she placed a clean, folded cheesecloth on top of the madzoon, covered the bowl with foil, and put it in the refrigerator. Another day would have to pass before the madzoon was ready for unveiling. While the madzoon was chilling and setting, the cheesecloth drew moisture out and left the madzoon below thicker and creamier than anything you can buy in the store. It was as thick as ice cream but as light and easy to scoop as whipped topping. I was always standing by, waiting for the first taste: cold and sweet, not sugar sweet but cream sweet. I can feel it coating my tongue and then my throat, sliding down easily at first and then teasing me with a sudden tartness.

Tasting the madzoon only made me all the more eager for the kufte, which could be described as stuffed Armenian meatballs. Picture a palm-sized flying saucer made of ground lamb—flat on the bottom, round on top. It's always palm-sized because the cook's slightly cupped hand forms the mold that shapes the kufte shell.

The lamb for the shell has to be superlean and ground three times, so it's malleable. You mix it in a bowl with seasonings and blend in a handful of the smallest-size bulgur—cracked wheat, once known in America to no one but health-food fans but now familiar to many as the soft-but-sandy stuff in tabouleh salads. Now you wet your hand—not too wet, but wet enough—and scoop out a ball of the shell mixture. Poke a hole three-quarters of the way through with your opposite thumb, then keep your thumb in there while you start spinning the ball in your hand so you can widen the hole and flatten the meat. Picture a lump of clay on a potter's wheel and you get the idea. If you're good—and you'll get that way only after you've made enough kufte to feed King Dikran's army—you'll have a yawning handful of lamb almost thin enough to read through.

Now you're halfway done.

You hold the shell mixture in one hand and spoon some stuffing into the middle of it with the other hand. Did I mention that it takes a day to make the stuffing? At least it's simple: chopped onions, chopped parsley, chopped lamb, and whole pine nuts, all sautéed in plenty of butter. Season well and chill overnight. The mixture coagulates inside all that butter and fat into a sort of lamb-and-onion Jell-O. Scoop it out, place it in the middle of the open shell, then wet your shaping hand so you can knead the hole closed and complete the saucer shape. Now you're really done, except for cooking the kufte. Some people fry it and others bake it, but Mom preferred boiling. You drop the flying saucers of lamb into the water and wait until they rise to the top, like ravioli. Serve immediately, if not sooner. Put a boiling-hot kufte in a bowl and plop a dollop of icy-cold madzoon on top. Then the real fun begins. When you stick your fork in—splat! Out squirts all the now-melted fat, which, of course, is where the flavor comes from.

What makes kufte sensational is the sensation of biting into so many flavors and textures and temperatures at once: sweet, savory, hot, cold, chewy, slippery. And all of it just makes perfect sense together. What makes kufte a sensational dish for company is that it's so damned hard to make. To serve someone kufte is to say, "You are special. You are worth the effort."

This was true of every meal Mom served, not just the centerpiece dishes but the entire menu, which always included a variety of desserts, including *paklava* and her thick, crispy Dikranagerdtsi bread called *lavash*. Her knock-out specialty was apricot pie, perfectly tart and sweet with a light, golden crust. There is nothing more Armenian than apricot pie because there is nothing more Armenian than the apricot. You can look it up in the encyclopedia, under *prunus Armenicus*.

And this was true not only of the meals Mom served to company. It was true of the meals she served to my father and me every day. The only difference was that we got only one main dish, which was no real sacrifice. Who wants roast beef when you can have *tass kebab* (braised lamb in tomato sauce) or *moodfooneh* (lamb stew with turnips) or *dolma* (eggplants, peppers, and other vegetables stuffed with lamb and rice)? If this was poor people's food—and it was, way back when—I'd hate to have been rich and missed out. Even when meat was dear, back in Uncle Nalband's day, no one went hungry, because there was always plenty of bulgur pilaf, which is like rice pilaf with bulgur in place of rice. Like all filling grains, bulgur expands in water—and keeps on expanding in your stomach. Eat your fill of bulgur and you'll stay full for a long time. You may end up waddling home, or flying. A scientific study of bulgur and the Armenian diet could point the way to unlocking vast new stores of nitrogen and methane.

Most of Mom's Armenian dishes would be unfamiliar to Americans, but they would not seem terribly odd. Meat, vegetables, tomatoes—the essentials are hardly exotic. We traditionally prefer lamb to beef because cows keep falling backward when you try to herd them up a mountain. What's common to nearly every culture except America's is that Armenians eat the entire animal, and that results in some dishes that would make the average American flee in terror. One of my father's favorite dishes was *chuckle-muckle*, heart and lung stuffed with rice and ground lamb. Another dish that was wildly popular among Dikranagerdtsis was *mahkoo havgeets*—battered and fried lamb's testicles. (No, they don't taste like chicken.) My wife tells a story about one of her father's many little practical jokes. He invited a buddy home for dinner and fed him a big plate of mahkoo havgeets, which the guy apparently mistook for extremely tender and sweet veal cutlets. After they ate, her father told him the truth. The poor man lurched from the table. Luckily, he reached his destination just in time.

Of all the dishes resulting from the use-everything imperative, my favorite was *patcha*, which says a lot about what a weird kid I was. Patcha is a soup made from lamb's feet, tongue, intestines, and various other bits and pieces. In the old country, and in some homes here, those pieces included the lamb's head, complete with eyeballs. I like to think of patcha as the soup that looks back at you. The first time I had patcha was at the home of the Garjians, Bert Aslanian's parents, when I was probably six or seven years old. The Garjians were phenomenally sweet people who always treated me like one of their grandkids, and I always felt and acted like one, except the day Grandma Garjian announced that the patcha was ready. All the other kids ran away, but I sat right down. My father laughed. "Do you know what patcha is?" I had no idea, but I was hungry. He laughed even harder. "If you get the eyeball, it's good luck," he said. I splashed frantically at the bowl, but found nothing so unsettling, so I ate. Then I asked for more. What a discovery! Patcha is a soup that eats like a roast, not so much because it's full of meat but because the broth itself has a consistency that seems to defy the laws of hydraulics. It's not overly greasy, not if it's properly made, but it's loaded with whatever it is that turns boiled horse hooves into gelatin. You almost feel as though you're chewing the liquid. Stranger still, it feels as though it's chewing back. Your lips stick to your tongue, which sticks to the roof of your mouth. What makes this enjoyable is that the flavor sticks, too. Lamb broth is, by scientific measure, approximately one thousand times tastier than beef broth. It's not just the flavor of the lamb that sticks, it's the crushed garlic and lemon you add to patcha just before eating. I loved the whole concoction instantly, and I said so. Whatever it was that Grandpa Garjian said in Armenian, it was clear that I'd won his praise! My mother, obviously puzzled by my reaction, shook her head. "Well, if you like it, I'll make it," and she did.

From then on, making patcha was an occasional but greatly appreciated ritual at our house. At least, it was appreciated by my father and me. Poor mom had to do the work, boiling up the lamb parts in a super-size pot. Each batch had to be boiled three times. The first two broths, full of fat and flotsam, were discarded. The giant patcha pot was the same one she used every so often to render fat—*yoogh*—which is what she used for frying. Today we worry about saturated fats and transfats. Back then, we worried about nothing except running out of fat. I'm convinced it did less harm than we'd imagine these days because Armenian lamb fat could be heated to incredible temperatures so it never soaked into the food. It just seared, sealed, and almost instantly cooked whatever was lowered into it: sliced potatoes, strips of meat, cubes of eggplant or zucchini dipped in egg and dusted with bread crumbs. How could it hurt people when it actually preserved meat itself? Don't be fooled into thinking the French invented *confit*, the method of preserving duck in a vat of its own fat. Armenians have been preserving lamb in fat for roughly a million years, give or take a few hundred thousand. We call it *kavourma*.

In the old country, making kavourma was one of many methods of keeping meat on the table through the winter, but Mom used to make it all year-round. There was almost always a crock of kavourma in our fridge (or on the back porch in colder months). If you took the cover off, you'd see nothing but a frozen pond of white fat, but dig down and you'd discover salty blossoms of fork-tender lamb that could be easily scooped out—and each came encased in its own frying medium, so there was no need to grease the pan. Better yet, you could fry up some kavourma, leave the fat in the pan, and then fry up a couple of eggs, which would suck up stray bits of salty meat. It was the best breakfast ever, anywhere, and the Armenians who ate kavourma for centuries wouldn't have been remotely interested in our fixation on cholesterol. Poor people facing a murderous mountain winter needed lipids to stay alive, and any people facing so many enemies, human and natural, could not afford the luxury of obsessing over longevity, even if they had known what kavourma was doing to their arteries.

I wonder what it did to mine.

The thought was unnerving until I dug out Mom's only picture of her father, taken when he was probably about sixty. One look at that picture and it's obvious where I got my waistline. He was not a thin man, but what would you expect of a professional chef who cooked everything in lamb fat? I haven't touched the stuff in years, but I could probably wear his pants. I find this oddly comforting. The size of my jeans was clearly dictated by my genes, so I don't fret about being a typically fat, middle-aged American who gets winded walking up a flight of stairs. After all, there's a reason Otis invented the elevator. But I'm not suicidal, so there is no kavourma in our refrigerator.

I have eaten my lifetime's ration of kavourma, and that makes me sad, but not quite sad enough to boil sheep fat.

MAKING A FAMILY

When we were home, Armenians were always around and above us. On the top floor in a two-bedroom apartment identical to ours lived my father's cousins Arax, Doris, and Anne Sarkisian. Their house was our house, as far as I was concerned. I napped there, snacked there, and watched TV there. Anne took me to the Bronx Zoo when I was three years old. I still have the pictures.

A few years later, more cousins moved next door: Onnik and Araksi Dinkjian and their baby daughter, Anahid. I could climb out our kitchen window, walk a few steps across the tar-paper flooring in the air shaft between the buildings, and climb into theirs. One day in 1958 when I was six, Araksi called my mother and told her to send me over to see something amazing on TV: Onnik was singing on *American Bandstand,* a teen dance show that featured the top rock 'n' roll hits of the week.

Today, Onnik is one of the best-known Armenian singers in the world. Then, he was—well, Onnik from next door. He'd made a record with an oud player named Chick Ganimian. The song was *Daddy Lo Lo,* a sort-of '50s hep-cat version of an Armenian song, *Dari Lolo.* Very catchy. I wish I could hum it for you, but take my word. More important, it was very Armenian, even if Onnik was singing English words. Not only were these rock 'n' roll teens grooving to Armenian music, Onnik was leading them in an Armenian dance:

"Daddy Lo Lo, Daddy Lo Lo, Lo Lo
"Hand in hand you dance and kick your toe—oh!"

What's really amazing now is that this didn't seem amazing at all. Why wouldn't Onnik be singing Armenian music on TV? After all, it was the music I heard every day at home.

Onnik and the Sarkisian sisters weren't really my father's cousins in the sense that Americans know the term. But to the scattered Armenian survivors who were forced to knit together new families after the Genocide, cousins and uncles—even fathers, mothers, brothers, and sisters—were simply the people you chose (or who chose you) to love and keep and protect.

Grandpa Kalajian chose Azniv Dinkjian, a good Dikranagerdtsi, as his second wife. He had to go all the way to France to marry her in 1929, the year after my father came to America. At seventeen, my father not only got a new mother but also an extended family within easy reach. When I checked the 1930 census, I found Harry, Azniv, and their son, listed as Nick, living at 487 Central Avenue, Union City, New Jersey, apartment 141. In apartment 140 were Mark and Margaret Sarkisian, Azniv's sister, along with their daughters Alice (Arax), 9; Dorothy (familiar to me as Doris), 5; and Anne, 3. The discovery made me smile. I loved the idea that my father was living next door to the very same cousins who lived directly upstairs from us when I was a boy. I could never share the experience of his early years in the old country, but now I felt that I had shared at least a taste of the fleeting days of his youth in New Jersey.

What I don't know is whether Grandpa's marriage was a product of this proximity. The marriage was certainly arranged, and who better to make such arrangements with than the next-door neighbors? If you couldn't meet the woman you intended to marry beforehand, you'd at least feel reassured if you knew that her sister was a kind, loving mother and a good cook. And a Dikranagerdtsi to boot.

The clan grew again after the war when Azniv's brother Nishan moved from France to the United States with his wife and their adopted children. My father immediately embraced Nishan Dinkjian as his uncle and always called him Diyeh. By the time I came along, Grandpa and Azniv were gone, but Diyeh was firmly embedded in the family landscape. He owned a dry-cleaning store in New York City but lived in Palisades Park, New Jersey, just a few miles from us. He was a jowly but jaunty man about a dozen years older than my father who became as close to a grandfather figure as I would ever know.

Like my father, he was not the sort to play catch or go fishing with. But unlike my father, Diyeh was a storyteller. Unfortunately, he never told stories in a language I understood. I knew he was telling them, though, by his dramatic inflections and theatrical gestures: Diyeh wasn't merely telling stories, he was performing them. And even though I could not understand a word, I enjoyed the performance.

I can picture his home on a steep hill. It was a green-shingled house, newer than ours and with a good-sized lot on both sides and in back where Diyeh planted his vegetable garden. He grew the best tomatoes I have ever tasted, and I can taste them now. I'd follow my father into Diyeh's garden on a hot summer day, and he'd reach down and pick a tomato for me to eat right there. A moment later, sweet tomato juice dribbled down my chin as I ran, tomato in hand, to show my mother. Everything tasted special and different at Diyeh's house, even the water.

Diyeh's wife, Aunt Oghida, served drinks in bright-colored metal tumblers that made my tongue tingle as I sipped. The food looked familiar but it tasted different, too, because Diyeh loved garlic, which my mother used sparingly. He loved fat even more than he loved garlic, and he insisted that none of it be trimmed or skimmed or otherwise diverted from his plate or mouth. When Diyeh came to our house and ate my mother's patcha, the lamb-innards soup that she so painstakingly defatted, she set aside a gravy boat of rendered fat for Diyeh to pour back into his bowl. He ladled it in with gusto, smacking his lips loudly.

Diyeh always commanded full attention and full service. He insisted the coffee table in the living room be as bountiful as the dining-room table, covered with dishes of *mezza*: cheese, nuts, fresh cucumbers and tomato slices, dried meats, and bread. And there was always a bottle of scotch, which had replaced the nuclear-strength raisin liquor called arak as the favored drink of Armenian men in my father's circle. Serving a guest a drink that was poured in another room was an insult. A bottle had to be open and available until it was empty.

Diyeh's house may have been in New Jersey, but it was not really very far removed from Dikranagerd. As in the old country, the men would sit in the backyard or in the living room playing backgammon and drinking. In the old country, they'd have been surrounded by singers and musicians playing ouds and *dumbeg* drums. Here, through the marvel of modern electronics, those very same musicians, long dead, were entertaining them still—and the more the men drank, the more likely they were to join in. Diyeh's reel-to-reel tape machine not only amplified the music, it accentuated the scratches of the old

78s and the drunken-mouse squeak of the stretched-out acetate tape. The women were spared the squealing because they spent the whole time in the kitchen. The kids ignored it because we were busy running uphill and down between Diyeh's yard and the yard of his friend and fellow Dikranagerdtsi George next door. We could run a long way without running into an odar. There were plenty of kids for me to play with, too: Diyeh's grandchildren (Anahid, Ara, Bobby, and Renee); plus the children (Margaret, Mark, and Paul) of his nieces, the two older Sarkisian sisters; and even George's grandson (Raymond).

I was the idiot of the group, the only one who didn't speak Armenian. Bobby, a year or so older than I, was more than fluent. He was downright chatty. He not only conversed easily with the adults, he spoke to me in Armenian—in Dikranagerdtsi, no less. I'd just stare back, but my father was impressed and always complimented not only Bobby but his parents on the fine job they'd done teaching their children the ancestral language. At the time, I was puzzled and a little hurt. Now, it really pisses me off. It was my father, after all, who refused to speak to me in Armenian, claiming he didn't want my English corrupted. Bobby shot his theory all to hell. He grew up to be a successful New York lawyer and administrator of the state commission that reviews judicial conduct. We spent a pleasant evening together a couple of years ago at his Uncle Onnik's house. I can testify that Bob's English is flawless.

Diyeh was an astounding and confounding linguist, speaking Armenian, Turkish, French, and God-knows-what-else all at the same time. He'd always greet me enthusiastically in sort-of English—"Hallo Dougie-boy!'— and then race off into his own alternately melodic and guttural tongue. My father occasionally tried to translate for me but wound up laughing too hard to continue or just shrugged it off by saying, "You can't translate Diyeh." I picked out this much: Diyeh's stories often involved some seemingly routine errand or trip that turned into a fiasco because, in his view, no one else knew how to drive. The joke was that Diyeh was the worst driver in the family, maybe in the United States. He wore out or wrecked more than enough cars to supply a midsize city's taxi fleet.

I was one of those kids who noticed cars and identified every adult by the car he drove as soon as it came into view, but I don't identify Diyeh with any one car because he was always driving something different. He never failed to entertain with his explanation of why the old one blew up, fell apart, or mysteriously crashed—and yet, nothing ever discouraged Diyeh from getting back on the road.

My father's good humor dissipated quickly when Diyeh announced that he was planning to drive to Canada for a vacation. Dad worried that he would get lost, or worse, and tried to talk him out of it. Diyeh dismissed him with the familiar backward flip of the hand that my father always used to dismiss my most annoying questions. My mother translated Diyeh's words. "What are you worried about? I found my way here from Dikranagerd, didn't I?"

The joke turned on me when I got my learner's permit at age seventeen. My father accompanied me once, for about three blocks, before he ordered me to stop and announced that I'd have to find someone else to teach me how to drive. He soon relented, but only partly. He found someone else to teach me: Diyeh. "But Dad," I pleaded, "after all the stories about Diyeh's driving?" My father responded only with his wry smile, which meant I had no choice. I still don't know what he was thinking, but Diyeh showed up at the appointed hour in his latest car, a white 1962 Ford Falcon Futura with red bucket seats, column-shift automatic, and no power steering or brakes. The only words I understood during my entire first driving lessons were "Hallo Dougie-boy." The rest was accomplished with hand signals—essentially, one hand signal, the familiar backward flip. Sometimes it meant go, sometimes it meant turn, and sometimes it meant stop. Diyeh didn't seem too fussy about which was which. He didn't waste any time before urging me into traffic along Bergen Boulevard and then down the hill on Edgewater Avenue. I remember making a comically wide turn across the incoming lane, then staring down and over the hood at the fast-disappearing ground below. I remember thinking, "Oh crap!" I held on and kept going.

We made a loop around Ridgefield, during which I discovered that without power steering, it's best to start turning the wheel before you get to the corner or you'll be too late. The Falcon's brakes demanded even more advance planning, at least a half-block's notice even at around-town speed. But turning the steering wheel and stabbing the brake pedal both provoked far more response than pushing the accelerator pedal, which seemed to produce mostly noise. We were nearing the end of our first lap around town when I found myself waiting to merge with traffic on Route 5, the main north-south truck route that divided Ridgefield from Palisades Park. I stopped and stared at a big rig bearing down on us. Diyeh flipped his hand in the truck's direction, then cursed in Turkish. I wasn't sure if he was cursing at me or the truck. Then he flipped his hand again and looked my way. "Poosh!" he commanded. At least, that's what I heard. I still don't know if he was telling me to push the accelerator pedal or if he was saying something in French or if he really said *aboosh*, which is Armenian for "stupid." I hit the gas. Luckily, maybe miraculously, the truck didn't hit us. We cleared the intersection by inches and made it home.

Diyeh delivered his report to my father in Dikranagerdtsi, but I know it wasn't too critical because they were both laughing. Better yet, Diyeh came back to give me more lessons. I don't think I've ever enjoyed driving so much since. We drove together about a half-dozen times, but it finally became clear to my father that I'd need lessons from someone who not only spoke the language but had some reasonable familiarity with American traffic laws or I'd never pass the driving test. The professional instructor my father hired turned out to be a whole lot less fun.

Diyeh died in 1979, not long after he wrecked his last car. My wife Robyn and I were living in Florida by then, and I was fast losing touch with the people I'd grown up with, including the patchwork of cousins I played with in Diyeh's yard. I've seen most of them only a few times since. We met Margaret and Ara for breakfast a few years ago in Fort Lauderdale when they were both passing through to board an all-Armenian cruise. Margaret flew in with her family from their home in Arizona, and Ara and his family flew down from New Jersey. We'd have gone along on the cruise except that Robyn's school wasn't on break. So we had to settle for a brief reunion at a breakfast buffet in a hotel courtyard on a sunny Sunday morning in February.

What struck me as we talked and caught up on recent events was that none of us are related by blood or genes or anything you could prove in court or a science lab. Margaret is the only one of us actually related to Diyeh because she is the granddaughter of his sister Makhrouhi. Ara is the son of Onnik Dinkjian, Diyeh's adopted son. But we are clearly something more than three people who share childhood memories. Ara is a part of my life even though I rarely see him, because he is a musician and I love his music, no doubt in part because I love Ara. He is a composer and an accomplished oud player who has done more than any politician or writer or social activist to bring Armenians and Turks together. He writes such transcendently beautiful songs that Armenians think they are Armenian and Turks think they are Turkish and Greeks think they are Greek. He has many fans in Turkey and gets big crowds when he performs there. He never hides his identity, and he is adored just the same.

Ara must be a very determined artist, because he is the most modest, retiring guy you could ever meet. It would be impossible to imagine him performing on stage if I hadn't seen it. Margaret may be even more determined than Ara. She and her husband, Artie, adopted Ani, a little girl from Armenia, under circumstances that were beyond daunting. Armenia has not made it easy for Americans, even Armenian-Americans, to adopt its orphans. Scam artists and corrupt politicians have made it that much harder. Margaret and Artie thought they had the adoption settled when the arrangements collapsed and everyone in both countries assured them there was no hope. But they went to Armenia anyway, on their own, and found their daughter and brought her home. She is, by the way, very possibly the most charming and beautiful child in either Armenia or America.

Margaret and Artie gained a daughter, and I gained a cousin. I'm proud of them all because they are such nice people, such warm and decent human beings. They are my cousins because I want them to be. For Armenians, that is truer and more important than anything.

OUR OWN MOUNTAINTOP

By the time I was in school, my once-adventurous father might as well have been under house arrest. His daily commute consisted of walking downstairs in the morning and up again at night. It was Mom who finally insisted on moving somewhere—anywhere—so she'd at least be guaranteed a chance to step outside twice a day.

When I was eight years old, my parents bought a small house in Ridgefield, a town built on a hill as steep as any in San Francisco. I don't know how they found their way to Lot 4, Block P, Bergen County Map No. 500. I sure don't remember a real estate agent coming to the house or any Sunday drives to look at neighborhoods. I just remember my mother telling me we were moving, and then we did. It was October 1960. The house was typical of the neighborhood: wood frame covered by faded-tan asphalt shingles. It had six real rooms plus a skinny front porch that was once open but now enclosed. Even to a kid, the place looked tired, but the real attraction was the long, narrow and slightly crooked property that stretched back more than 250 feet from the street out front. It was mostly downhill but leveled off, more or less, after a steep drop halfway back.

Anyone else might see overgrown weeds, a wooden garage ready to blow over in a stiff wind, and a gravel driveway that would be impossible to climb in winter. My father saw nature, and a chance to sow to his heart's content. He was sufficiently moved to pay $16,500, most of it mortgaged at 6 percent. The house was hand-built by a Swedish immigrant sometime in the 1920s. He was still living there when my folks bought the place from him. He was obviously a man of simple pleasures. He left behind an empty liquor bottle and a snuff tin flanking the lone toilet at the rear of the kitchen. There were no walls around the toilet and no sink near it. On our first weekend in the new house, my father and my Uncle Mike plumbed-in a sink and walled it all off to make an official half bath. With a full bath upstairs, that gave the house a grand bathroom total of 1.5, a Kalajian family record that stood until Robyn and I moved into a two-bath apartment in Florida in 1978.

The Ridgefield house sat on the very crest of the town's signature hill at 529 Bergen Boulevard. This was really an extension of the same boulevard we'd been living on, but the name changed as it stretched into the northern suburbs and it became less of a truck route and more of a mom-and-pop route. Although it was only two miles from the cleaning store, the Ridgefield house seemed much farther away. Ridgefield was a real small town with real houses and yards and streets lined with maple and oak trees. Our house was on the busiest street, but it was set back and shaded. The sloping yard was filled with trees and bushes and wild berries. The slope was so steep that the front of the house was at street level but the rear of the first floor was at least a story high. The wooden back porch outside the kitchen was big enough for a small table. We'd eat dinner there when the weather was warm, looking out at the treetops. "I feel like we moved to the country," my mother said over and over to my father. It made them both smile.

Before winter set in, Dad hired a man to build a greenhouse out of two-by-fours and old wood-framed windows on the south side of the mostly above-ground basement. Nothing fancy, but it made my father happy. He removed a small window from the basement wall and widened the hole with a sledgehammer so he could climb out to the greenhouse. He even had lights installed so he could work at night.

His greenhouse bounty spilled over into the basement across makeshift tabletops of plywood laid over barrels, where a miniforest of cuttings and seedlings sprouted beneath long fluorescent light fixtures that dangled from chains anchored in the rafters. As the plants grew, they were repotted and moved to the next table, so the forest got taller and thicker as you walked from the greenhouse toward the far-side wall. The plants on the rear-most table were lush and strong and often in full bloom. Red geraniums and white begonias mingled with exotic tropical flowers in a dazzling palette. As they grew, Dad's plants filled every windowsill, table, and shelf in the house.

Dad's greenhouse grew into a miniature tropical rain forest a few miles from Times Square, crowded with orchids, rubber plants, and birds of

paradise. Even in midwinter, waist-high trees bowed from the weight of or-
anges and Ponderosa lemons. And always, there was at least one variety of
exotic cherry peppers, hot as nuclear-reactor rods. Dad said he grew them
strictly for their brilliant red color, but I think it was homage to his father.
Grandpa, he said, ate his morning eggs with peppers hotter than anything
my father could stand. It helped that Grandpa anesthetized his stomach first
with a shot of arak.

Some nights, Dad would read for a while and then climb out to the
greenhouse. Other times, he went straight from the dinner table to his nurs-
ery. My father grew plants from seeds and bulbs and cuttings. He cultivated
and he cloned. He didn't mind if I visited, as long as I was quiet. He even
showed me how to repot a seedling, dropping a few pebbles or broken bits
of clay at the bottom of the pot before filling it with soil. I never understood
how a man so impatient with people could be so patient with plants, nurturing them for months as they grew and blossomed. It bored me just to think
about it. I'd watch for a while, then go back to the TV.

The greenhouse was rebuilt several times over the years, expanded and
improved with permanent heat, a misting water spray, and Plexiglas panels
in place of glass. But the sledgehammered basement entry never changed.
Dad was fifty when he started hopping up on that cinder block and hurling
himself through the jagged window hole. He was well along in his seventies
when he huffed and teetered his way in for the last time. He always had the
option of walking outside and entering the greenhouse upright, but I think
he got some special exhilaration from thrusting his head past the soot-soiled
basement wall into the dazzling jungle world he'd created in this most unlikely place.

Our house was always full on weekends, especially Sundays, and this
made my father happy. As cantankerous as he could be, especially when I
tried to talk to him about his life, Dad loved company and he loved a good
time. My mother got up as early on Sunday as she did every other day, only
instead of going to work she cooked. Regardless of whether company had
been invited, Mom insisted on being prepared just in case someone rang the
bell. In the Armenian tradition, there is no excuse to serve anything less
than a feast to anyone who comes to the door. My father's participation was
limited but vital: He'd make time every Saturday to stop at Kocher's butcher
shop to buy meat for the weekend, always the best cuts and in quantities suf-
ficient to feed the Armenian national soccer team.

The prospect of leftovers never deterred him from buying a little extra, and then some more. "A refrigerator should always be full," he'd say, and he'd often peek to make sure it was. Yet he rarely reached in for a snack and ate modestly even at meal time, no matter how hard Mom had worked to make his favorite dishes. After being so hungry for so long as a child, he was satisfied simply to fill his belly and insisted I should be, too. "Eat as much as you want, but don't waste food," he'd tell me. He never wavered. He weighed 135 pounds the day he came home from the Army, and he weighed the same the day he died forty-five years later.

Sunday was not just Mom's cooking day, it was baking day, and that meant it was lavash day. Maybe you've seen the word on a package of flat bread, hard or soft. It's one Armenian tradition that's caught on in this country. You can thank us for sandwich wraps, but don't thank me. My mom's lavash was nothing like that. Mom made Dikranagerdtsi lavash because, like my father, her mother's family was from the city Armenians call Dikranagerd. Everything made in Dikranagerd tastes better than its equivalent in any other part of Armenia, or the world. Mom explained it this way: Armenians cook with their hands, so Dikranagerdtsis must have tastier hands than anyone else. Dikranagerdtsi lavash is richer than other flat breads. It's thick and layered and has a crisp golden crust because it's brushed with butter. You eat it with salty Armenian cheese and strong coffee, which is the only kind an Armenian will serve.

People came to our house to drink Mom's strong coffee and eat her lavash while they listened to my father's music. Dad loved music even though he couldn't read music or play a note. He had a reel-to-reel tape recorder, one of those unwieldy contraptions you see in old movies with two big spinning spools and a ribbon of shiny brown tape running from one to the other. He was the original party-mix king, only his party music was what Armenians called kef music. I'm not sure there's an exact parallel in English, but it's the word the old timers used when they set out to have a good time. You don't do kef or have kef or enjoy kef. You make kef. You make kef by playing the right music and singing along and dancing and eating pistachio nuts and dried lamb sausages and drinking whiskey.

Sometimes company would just listen to music while they talked and ate lavash and drank coffee. Sometimes they came to make kef. No matter, my father had the right music. He loved the classics: Chopin, Beethoven, Tchaikovsky. They were the reason he became a hi-fi fan. He had woofers and tweeters before most people knew what stereo meant. He had a big, gold-colored amplifier called a Harman Kardon that pumped sound to speakers in the living room and dining room. His idea of Sunday wake-up music was the 1812 Overture. I'd jump out of bed believing Napoleon's Army was marching straight through our kitchen.

Depending on his mood and the company, he could segue from Dvorak to the Dorseys, from Glenn Miller to Mitch Miller, from Louis Armstrong to Lou Monte. But when our company was Armenian, as it almost always was, so was the music. At least, it was what I thought of as Armenian music, what people my parents' age called Oriental music. If I'd known more about music or language, I'd have recognized some of it as Greek or Arabic or Turkish. I just knew it wasn't American because it was nothing like any music I heard on the radio or on TV or in stores or anywhere but in the homes of other Armenians.

You know that agonizingly slow, almost eerie music you hear in Chinese restaurants? Imagine it with a thumping dance beat—one, two, three, kick, kick; one, two three, kick, kick. That's not really it, but I think that's what it would sound like to the average American. I think this because one night when I was about twelve, the great storyteller Jean Shepherd was reminiscing on his late-night radio show about watching 1930s movie serials featuring the villain Fu Manchu. The mood music playing behind him was instantly familiar. I heard a howl from the next room where my father was listening to the same show. It started as a howl of laughter, then turned into a howl of disgust and ended with "son of a bitch!" Shepherd's idea of Chinese mood music turned out to be an old recording by Armenian singer Armenag Shahmouradian.

Most Armenian music is actually more Western than Eastern in the sense that you can play it on Western instruments. You'll lose nuance but not the essence. Armenian musicians who came to this country early in the twentieth century were resourceful and clever. They adapted a variety of American instruments to their needs. For example, they learned to tune a violin so it could mimic a *kemanche*, an Armenian fiddle that's balanced on the knee instead of the chin. A variety of reed instruments were substituted for the *duduk* before the clarinet was widely adopted as a suitable if imperfect stand-in.

You can even play Armenian music on a piano, although you'll wear out the black keys much faster than if you stick to rock 'n' roll. You can't play

Turkish music on a piano—at least, I couldn't. I was pretty good at pecking out most songs by ear, a talent my father generally encouraged, but Dad was frustrated by my inability to make any headway with his favorite Turkish songs. Of course, I didn't know they were Turkish songs any more than I knew that I was on a fool's errand hunting for the right notes among a pitifully restrictive Western scale. Western music reflects the values of Western civilization—it is orderly, predictable, precise. Those words do not apply to much of anything east of the Dardanelles.

One instrument common to Armenian and Turkish music is the oud, which looks something like a lute, one of those fat, half-melon stringed instruments you see in movies about King Arthur's court. Except the oud from King Dikran's court has no frets, the musical speed bumps on guitar necks that prevent one note from skidding into the next. Frets keep everything tidy, like the keys on a piano, so that every note sounds the same every time. An oud player has no use for frets because he is engaged in a musical free-for-all. He is not restricted to twelve notes, or twelve thousand. He makes whatever note he needs, whatever note he feels.

My dad's party mix was itself a jamboree of scratchy, old-time recordings that would have fooled Jean Shepherd every time, along with newer stuff played by American-born musicians. It was all lively, jumping, screeching, shouting, hand-clapping, get-up-and-move music. It beckoned the company out of their seats to form a dancing line that snaked from room to room, pinkies linked and held above their heads. Whoever was leading the line waved a white hankie in time with the beat. Everybody would laugh and sing along as they danced.

Commercial recording was in transition in those days from the old 78 rpm records to LPs. Do you remember phonograph records at all? Armenians started preserving their music on 78s when recording was still done acoustically, without microphones. Big companies like Victor and Columbia sent scouts into ethnic neighborhoods to recruit musicians and singers who could turn out records the company could sell back to the same neighborhoods. These records were still around when I was growing up. Every Armenian home in New Jersey had a stack of black-lacquer recordings by Karekin Proodian or Hovsep Shamlian, whose songs are still being recorded by Armenian-American musicians. The music raced along as quickly as the cast-iron needle could trace its path along the grooves, making 78 complete spins every minute. You didn't need to look at the dark-red label or even recognize Shamlian's voice to know whom you were listening to because each of his records began with a man shouting, *SHAM-lee-yahn REH-cord*!

In the late '50s, the next generation of Oriental musicians began releasing slow-spinning, 33-rpm, long playing albums with vastly improved sound quality. Each side of the LP delivered four or five songs before you had to turn it over. There were only a few Oriental LPs around in the late 1950s and early '60s. Everybody we knew had the same ones by a handful of artists: Artie Barsamian, Eddie Kochak, Mohammed El-Bakkar. Some of them had racy album covers with half-naked dancing girls. All of them were well-worn from being played over and over. When a new Oriental LP came out, my father got it before anyone we knew, but he almost always said the same thing when he played it: The old music was better.

This new music was jazzed up, Americanized. The beat was more Latin than Middle Eastern. The instruments were Western, too—even accordions. I guess the musicians got tired of playing the same old thing, or they were trying to be inventive, or maybe they were just trying to please a new audience in the nightclubs where this exotic music was catching on. No matter. The old music, the real Oriental music, was better. So my father gathered up all the old 78s that everyone else wanted to get rid of and copied them on his reel-to-reel tape machine. It wasn't long before he had hours and hours of music no one had heard for years. I heard it over and over and never understood a word.

I knew only that some of these songs made people laugh and some made people dance and a few of them made some people, including my father, very sad. Sometimes when there were only a few visitors left, and only men, my father played the sad music and they would sit and drink in silence. That really threw me. I couldn't understand why anyone wanted to listen to music that made people sad. These days, hearing even the saddest of my father's music makes me happy.

For the first five years of my life, I listened to my father's music and watched the company come and go and believed, in the way kids believe, that this was the way everyone lived. I assumed everyone ate lavash and pistachio nuts and listened to Oriental music and danced in circles. I also assumed all parents spoke Armenian and all kids didn't. It was certainly true of most kids I knew.

We'd all picked up a few words here and there, but only a few of my cousins or the children of my parents' friends could speak more than a sentence or two in Armenian. Most of us couldn't understand our parents' conversations. Over the years, we were at least receptive to the conspiracy theory: They didn't want us to understand so they could talk in secret right in front of us. My parents occasionally exploited that advantage, but they kept their Armenian conversations to a minimum for a practical reason: They spoke different dialects.

Just as she cooked Dikranagerdtsi, my mother spoke Dikranagerdtsi. The dialect is as distinctive as the food, flavored by the words and accents of all the traders and conquerors who marched through over the centuries. Dikranagerdtsis don't just sound different from other Armenians, as a Texan sounds different from a New Yorker. Dikranagerdtsi can be nearly incomprehensible to most other Armenians. Anyone who speaks the dialect risks ridicule among purists and snobs, even those who speak equally impure and vulgar dialects. My mother was reminded of this every time she spoke to one of her aunts or cousins in my father's presence. He'd mimic her and pretend to scold her for not speaking proper Armenian. I'm sure he thought this was very funny. I know she didn't. She never failed to point out the irony: She might speak the language of Dikranagerd, but he was born there. "So don't pretend you're any better," she'd say.

Of course, he didn't think that at all. He was just a stickler for language. He learned proper Western Armenian and refined it by reading. I can't vouch for his Armenian language skill but I can make an educated guess by using his English as a gauge. English was his fifth or sixth language, but it was second in his heart and first in his head. He never acknowledged speaking English with an accent, although he did, but he used the language like a native. Better, in fact, than most. In conversation, he was betrayed as an autodidact only by the occasional mispronunciation or misplaced accent. His grammar and diction were exceptional. Even as an adult and a professional writer, my vocabulary lagged behind his. If I put down the *New York Times* crossword without finishing, he'd pick it up and fill in whatever had stumped me.

From the day I was born, I was his incentive to speak English well and always. He wanted me to hear and learn the language of America and to use it properly, not only as a tool but as a mark. He never wanted anyone to take me for an immigrant's son. Teaching me to speak well was an obligation he adopted and fulfilled. Learning Armenian would have to wait until my English was secure and immune from cross-contamination.

He was certain when the time came that I'd simply learn it, as he'd learned English. I never did, and I know he was disappointed. My failure is easy to explain but difficult to accept, even for me. It's neither excuse nor comfort to say that I'm not alone. Every immigrant family in America loses its language after a generation or two, but it's a peculiarly emotional loss for Armenians. It is more than a little like losing their country again.

My mother's relationship with language was more casual than my father's and in many ways more fun. When he'd correct her Armenian, or occasionally her English, she'd fling the back of her hand in his direction, a very Armenian gesture with no literal meaning but a universal sign of dismissal. She'd say, "You know what I mean, so be quiet." And he would be, unless he heard her trying to teach me Armenian. Then he couldn't help intruding.

"That's not Armenian," he'd say. "That word is Turkish." Or maybe it was slang, or simply mispronounced. Again, he'd get the sweep of her hand. "It was good enough for my mother," she'd say. Who could argue with that?

Even if she wanted to, my mother couldn't filter out her Dikranagerdtsi slang. It was part of her everyday vocabulary, especially in the kitchen. She didn't cook in a pot, she cooked in a *tass*. She didn't make French toast, she made *hatzov dabag*. She didn't make gravy, she made *jeenj*. When we were alone, my mother taught me the Armenian name, at least the Dikranagerdtsi name, for everything in sight. Like most kids, I had little use for verbs as long as I could point. I had a hefty collection of nouns that served no purpose except to amuse my mother's relatives and annoy my father. My father would correct my mother's Armenian, but he rarely corrected mine. He'd just tell me to speak English. He didn't want anything to compromise my great fortune in having been born in America.

I can't say he was wrong, but I wish things had been different. I wish I'd learned Armenian—his Armenian, my mother's Armenian, any Armenian—while I was young enough to digest it as easily as young people do. I know he wanted me to learn and that my failure disappointed him. Why wouldn't it? He learned English as a young adult. Why couldn't I learn Armenian? Of course, he had an advantage in learning all his languages: He had no choice. An immigrant learns to speak or he starves, but an American expects the world to adapt to him. Anyone who heard me speak would have no doubt which side of the cultural fault line I stood on.

The doubts were all mine, and they began early. I don't remember what triggered this, but it was very early in kindergarten when the teacher asked me a question. It was something simple, like what do you like to eat? And I said, turkey with jeenj. Or hatzov dabag. Or lavash. What I remember is the puzzled and, I thought, disapproving look on the teacher's face. I had no idea until that moment that Americans were so ignorant. My mother hadn't warned me that these people could be stumped by a child's vocabulary. The moment passed quickly for the teacher but not for me. I understood instantly that there was something different not only about the Americans but about me.

I was careful about what I said, and I learned to be cautious around the ketchup eaters who laughed as I ate dolma at the lunch table. From that moment on, I was never entirely comfortable in the Americans' world. This is not a small point. I am not an Armenian who happened to be born in America. I am an American whose father was born in Armenia, the almanac be damned. At least I had plenty of company. About the same time I started American school, my parents enrolled me in Sunday school. It was my first real exposure to other Armenian-American kids who weren't my cousins. I couldn't name a soul from my American kindergarten class, but my Sunday school pals made an indelible impression. Aram Aslanian, Greg Nedurian, Bobby Derian, Jimmy and Johnny Bashian, Richie and Kenny Sarajian, Greg Babigian. I could probably name them all, even though I haven't seen most of them in decades.

Most of my new friends didn't speak Armenian any better than I did. When we were old enough to go out together, we listened to rock 'n' roll and we ate hamburgers with ketchup, like the Americans—because, of course, we were Americans. Just like the children of Italian immigrants and Jewish immigrants and Japanese immigrants and Mexican immigrants and all the other immigrants. And like them, we were different from other Americans, the ones with last names that sounded more like first names.

I made friends among these other Americans, good friends, but they were not like my Armenian friends. I never hid my background from the Americans, but I rarely let on how much it meant or how deeply attached I was to my other life. They could hardly guess.

LONG LIVE THE REVOLUTION

Killers came to our house often, wearing suits. Brown, usually, but always dark.

They wore hats, too—felt fedoras with shiny bands, like the hats you see Edmund O'Brien wearing in old movies. They removed their hats like the gentlemen they were, but they kept their jackets on, and when they unbuttoned their jackets before sitting down you could see ties as wide as the Euphrates River.

I didn't think of these men as killers. I thought of them as old men, old friends of my father's. A few, he told me, had been his father's friends. My father always called me into the living room when they arrived, but I had no real part in their visits except to stand and be inspected. Always, one of the men would ask me a question in Armenian, and I would turn to my father, who would explain that I spoke only English. I hated that moment and still do. I hated having to be explained, as though I had some defect or oddity, but at least it was only a moment. Then I was excused and sent to my room. A few moments later, as soon as she'd served the coffee, my mother joined me. Mom and I watched television in my room until it was time for me to go to sleep. She must have sat by my side after that until it was time for the men to leave. To this day, I have no idea what my father and these men talked about, except that it was the secret business of the Dashnaktsutyun—the Armenian Revolutionary Federation—and it looked very serious.

I saw these same old men praying in church and eating shish kebab at Armenian picnics and sitting on folding chairs in the audience at our Sunday school programs, smiling as their grandchildren sang. They didn't look like killers, but I know some of them were because when I was old enough to have an inkling about such things, my father told me. One day he pointed to a man I'd seen in church a thousand times. He was a distinguished man with thick, white hair parted almost in the middle.

"That's Dajad," my father said. "He was a real *fedayee.*"

A real fedayee! This is what Armenians called the revolutionaries of the previous century. Most were long gone, so seeing one was as amazing and thrilling to me as seeing a real cowboy. Of course, that's all my father said. It wasn't until years later, after Dajad was gone, that I read his memoir, *The End of Davo the Traitor.* Davo was an Armenian who betrayed the defenders of Van by telling the Turks where their ammunition was hidden. His end came courtesy of Dajad, who shot him through the head.

Another time, my father pointed to Arshavir Shiragian. He led me to him and told me to shake his hand. "You just shook the hand that killed the Turks," my father said.

What Turks? Of course, he didn't say. The answer came from Arshavir himself, long after he was gone. He'd written a book, *The Legacy,* that told how he survived the Genocide as a teenager in Istanbul, where Armenians were brutalized but not slaughtered en masse. After the war, when he learned the fate of his countrymen, he volunteered to be an instrument of justice.

Under Western pressure, a Turkish military court identified many of the perpetrators of the Armenian massacres and even issued death sentences, but by then the Young Turk leaders had all fled to safety in Europe or deeper into Asia. The world didn't care enough about the Armenians to hunt down their tormentors and call them to justice. A handful of young Dashnaks volunteered to carry out the mission. It was long, hard, and dangerous work. The exiled Turks, living on stolen fortunes, were well-guarded and politically connected in their host countries, already plotting a return to power and, ultimately, the rebirth of an empire that would subsume the fledgling Armenian Republic.

The vilest of all the exiles was Talaat Pasha, former minister of the interior who had given the incendiary signal to begin the extermination of Armenians throughout the provinces. He was gunned down on a Berlin street in 1921 by one of the Armenian avengers, Soghomon Tehlirian, who was captured and beaten by a crowd. Tehlirian was arrested and charged with murder, but he assumed the role of prosecutor rather than defendant. His highly publicized trial exposed the depth and cruelty of the Turkish plot to destroy the Armenians. The German jury was so moved that it found Tehlirian not guilty—an extraordinary turn of events in a country that had done so much to encourage Turkish bloodlust.

Arshavir's assigned targets were less well-known but no less culpable or deserving of execution. I could tell you who they were, but they don't deserve to be remembered by name. Against tremendous odds—he was captured along the way and nearly killed before escaping—Arshavir tracked down and killed three of the Genocide's architects in Rome and Berlin, two with the help of fellow avenger Aram Yerganian. Arshavir was never caught. He made his way to America and settled in New Jersey, where he sold rugs. Most people who met Arshavir had no idea what he'd done, nor that he carried a gun the rest of his life as protection against Turkish assassins. When Arshavir died as an old man of natural causes, he was mourned by Armenians all over the world and hailed as *azgayin heros*, hero of the nation. The hand I shook was severed before he was buried, and it was enshrined in an Armenian museum in France.

Arshavir and Dajad were unusual men who both wrote and spoke about their lives as survivors and patriots. Most of the others offered no more testimony about their experiences than my father did about his, not even to their families. Like my father, Vartan Aslanian left nothing but hints and jagged bits of puzzle.

He died when I was a boy, but I remember him at least vaguely because he was Aram Aslanian's grandfather and also because my father made a point of saying that he was my grandfather's friend. That made him special. He was the man who got my father the job at the Hotel Park Lane back during the Depression, but Vartan was more than just another industrious dry cleaner. He had the vision, or the luck, to buy a few pieces of property that turned out to be valuable. Then he bought more, including a place in Florida. My father got a kick out of that. Imagine an Armenian from New Jersey who took vacations in Florida at a time when most could barely afford to ride the Staten Island Ferry?

I remember Vartan for another reason: He was a real fedayee. I know this because Aram still has a picture of Vartan in uniform, his chest laced with bandoliers. There is nothing written on the picture, and no note anywhere that Aram can find explaining the circumstances. Aram's father, Serak, may have known—or maybe not. He never said anything except that his father fought Turks, and now it's too late to ask for more.

I asked Aram to send me a copy of the photo. The only caption was a question from Aram: "What did he fight for?" We can only guess. It appears from records that Vartan came to America in 1913, when he was twenty-three and single. We know he went back to his native Van to marry and then brought his wife to America—but was this just before the Genocide, or after? Did he fight as a teenager or was he part of the revered Van defense force? We will probably never know, but I promised Aram I would include Vartan in this book because books have their own life.

Someone will read this years from now, after we've all passed on, and they'll know about Vartan Aslanian, Armenian patriot. So Vartan will live on while the Turks he fought are dead and forgotten, which will prove that justice can come from books as well as from bullets.

MARKED FOR LIFE

My parents were married at Holy Cross Armenian Church in Union City, and I was baptized there. Yet I have almost no memory of the place because we rarely stepped through the doors after that although we lived just a few miles away.

Once when I heard some of my mother's relatives talking enthusiastically about the upcoming bazaar or some other special event, I asked if we could go. My father hushed me immediately. Later he gave me an explanation that explained nothing, at least that I could understand. "Don't ever bring up politics in front of company," he said. It took many years, but I eventually understood that politics intrudes almost everywhere among Armenians, even into church socials—even into church itself. I certainly can't explain Armenian politics—I don't think anyone can explain Armenian politics—but I did eventually learn enough to make sense of what my father said that day.

In June 1931, the very tall and dignified Archbishop Levon Tourian stepped off the ocean liner *Britannic* at a New York dock to begin his term as prelate of the Armenian Church in America. That term turned out to be much briefer and nastier than anyone anticipated. Almost everyone in this country was focused on The Depression and hoping for better days ahead, but many Armenians in America remained focused on the past. They were still fighting mad about the tragedy that had driven them from their lands—and having no one else to fight, they often fought among themselves.

The two main political parties, the Dashnaks and Ramgavars, had faulted each other for every unfortunate turn of events over the years. Now the split was growing deeper and the anger rising as the Communist government in Yerevan called on Armenians in the diaspora to embrace Soviet Armenia as their spiritual home. Dashnaks resisted, while Ramgavars and many non-aligned Armenians took a more pragmatic view. Soviet Armenia, they reasoned, was the only Armenia that remained. The church could hardly stay neutral, as it was based in Soviet territory and the hierarchy there was being terrorized.

It was in this volatile atmosphere that the archbishop was called on to speak at Armenian Day festivities at the Chicago World Fair in 1932. As he stepped to the podium, he made what he probably thought was a small, conciliatory gesture toward the Soviet government by insisting that the tri-colored flag of the former Republic of Armenia be replaced by one bearing the Communist hammer and sickle. The crowd roared, but not in a good way. Fistfights broke out, and the fighting spread through Armenian communities across the country.

The furor continued for more than a year, as Dashnaks tried to replace Tourian. The battle over Tourian's tenure ended in a New York City church on Dec. 24, 1933 when someone plunged an eight-inch butcher knife into the archbishop as he walked toward the altar through the crowd. Detectives were at a loss to make sense from the chaos. No one could say whose hand thrust the knife, but nearly everyone in the church was certain who was really behind the tragedy:

SECRET GROUP BLAMED
IN ASSASSINATION CASE
By the Associated Press
New York, Dec. 26—Identification of five prisoners—alleged members of a secret Armenian revolutionary society—as participants in the attack which led to the assassination of Archbishop Leon Tourian was claimed by the district attorney's office Tuesday.

The announcement came as police delved deeper into the activities of Tashnak—a secret society said to have been formed to wrest Armenia from control of the U.S.S.R.

Eventually, nine Dashnaks were convicted of various charges in connection with the murder. Two were sentenced to death, but the sentence was commuted. All of them, and the Dashnak leadership, denied any involvement. They blamed a mystery man who was seen leaving the church but never identified. Most likely, they argued, he was a Communist who murdered the archbishop to discredit the anti-Communist movement.

If so, the scheme worked. The murder of Archbishop Tourian scarred a generation of Armenians in America and deeply affected those to come. Armenians were revolted and shamed by the act and by the gusher of attention that followed. The image of Armenians as good people, as good Americans, had been horribly stained by the archbishop's blood. Across America, on Christmas Day of all days, people who had known Armenians only vaguely but sympathetically as those poor, starving refugees, were shocked by the news. What kind of people kill their priest in church?

I was born nearly two decades after Tourian's murder but I still felt the repercussions. When my father and the other sons of Dashnaks came home from the Second World War, they discovered that Armenian politics hadn't changed but they had. They were no longer content to live in tenements, or in the margins of an immigrant community. They did what other returning vets did: worked hard, got married, had kids, bought homes in the suburbs. But they continued to be bound by everything that made them Armenian. They needed churches, but they were not willing to keep quiet, and they would not bow to any bishop who bowed even ceremonially toward the Kremlin. So, they built their own churches.

In 1956, the ancient See of Cilicia, based in Lebanon, became the seat of a church-in-exile, taking responsibility for a new prelacy in America. Three years later, Sts. Vartanantz in Ridgefield, New Jersey was consecrated under the prelacy's authority. It certainly isn't coincidence that my family moved to Ridgefield the following year. One of the prime attractions of our little house was that our new church was just a block away—and what a beautiful church it was, at least to us.

Sts. Vartanantz had a modern, almost American mien of muted-red brick instead of the quarried stone used in the old country, but you'd know it was an Armenian church the moment you stepped inside, assuming you know Armenian churches. Here's a clue: There is light everywhere in an Armenian church. It glistens from chandeliers, flickers from candles, glints and slants and pierces its way through windows all around. It reflects off white walls and gold chalices and silk robes. It reaches every corner and bathes every congregant. The symbolism is impossible to miss. When you walk into church, even on the darkest day or in the middle of the night, you walk into the light, as the Armenian nation did in 301 AD. "I am the light of the world," Jesus said. Armenians, very literal people, take this to heart.

My father took me to church every Sunday throughout my childhood, while Mom often stayed home or attended only briefly so she could get back to her kitchen and prepare for Sunday company. Dad and church had a natural connection because "Nishan" means mark or sign, understood to be the sign of the cross. So the name Nishan confers both honor and obligation, a lifelong weight that must be borne with dignity. My father held up his end of the deal, and he held up well under the burden. I can attest that he was a good Christian in every way except the one that counts most, the matter of true faith. I can't testify to that because he never discussed it. I do know he was a sensible, skeptical man solidly grounded in common sense. I also know he loved and respected his church but not the charlatans among the clergy and congregation who exploited and misrepresented it. In all my memories, however, I cannot picture my father praying. I see him in his Sunday suit and tie, tending to the business of the church schools in the makeshift office space in the upstairs hall behind the stage. After church, he'd huddle with the other men, sipping coffee and looking very serious.

He was hardly unusual in making little show of piety. The motion of Armenians in church is collective and choreographed. We sit-stand-kneel, sit-stand-kneel while crossing ourselves so quickly and often you'd think we were jabbering in sign language. We do not wail or shout praise or join in communal hymns. The congregation really makes very little noise, joyful or otherwise.

Still, as in any church, there is opportunity to make an impression by jangling-in late and punctuating loud prayers with exaggerated gestures. My father made a point of noting that the most demonstrative were often the most seldom-seen congregants, people who wanted to be sure everyone knew of the great sacrifice they'd made for Christ by coming to church two or three times a year. They were the same ones who complained loudest if the church newsletter was late in noting their occasional donations. My father never hid his disdain for their sort, no matter how big those donations were.

"You see that old lady?" he whispered, gesturing toward a woman with a cane tottering slowly toward the altar to take communion. "The dollar she puts in the plate every week means more than anything a rich man gives. She believes, but nobody will ever name a building after her."

As our church grew and the faithful old parishioners faded away, Dad objected more often and more loudly to people and changes he saw as crass. When the church instituted formal dues for members, he refused to pay, even though the dues were less than he always gave. It was one of the few times I remember my father complaining that Armenians were becoming too much like the Americans. About the time I got to college, Dad got tired of arguing and stopped going to services altogether. He seemed quite content to listen to the Armenian liturgy—the *badarak*—on his Harman Kardon in the comfort of our living room.

This may not be strictly what the church fathers think of as adherence to the faith, but an Armenian can rationalize such long-distance worship better than a Baptist, who craves constant preaching, or a Catholic, who expects constant correction, because the Armenian Apostolic Church instills self-reliance in its followers through the simplicity of its teachings. We are not given detailed driving instructions for our trip down life's winding highway. We are not even called on to confess our sins individually; we get to plead guilty as a class.

There really isn't much more to the fundamental beliefs of the Armenian Church than the Nicene Creed, at least not that a simple man like me can grasp. We haven't adopted any fresh dogma in sixteen centuries, since we decided the Council of Chalcedon wasn't quite kosher, so to speak. I think the simplicity of the Armenian Church is a great strength that suits the Armenian national character. A people trampled throughout the ages would seem to appreciate a little breathing room on Sunday mornings, but not everyone agrees. Some Armenians have always defected to other churches for political convenience. It was good to be a Byzantine Christian when the Greeks were at their zenith, and good to be a Catholic when the Lusignans of France reigned over Cilicia. Today, in America, there are certainly far more profitable networking opportunities at a Protestant prayer breakfast than at an Armenian church coffee hour.

But many Armenian Christians have been converted to other denominations by the promise of moral guidance that they couldn't find in their home parish. I can understand that. I'm at a loss to tell you if the Armenian Church has much to say about issues such as gay marriage or abortion, which is legal and widely practiced in Armenia. I also couldn't tell you if it has anything to say about birth control, capital punishment, or living wills. None of it has come up in the English-language sermons I've heard, although it's just possible I missed something. In my experience, if you ask an Armenian priest about such things he'll tell you to pray for guidance. In other words, "Don't ask me, ask the Boss."

I like that. The idea that God is more likely to reveal His thoughts to a church hierarchy than to the rest of us has never made sense to me. More important, I like the idea of making up my own mind, as I have a very limited interest in being told how to think. But what does the Armenian Church gain by making a guy like me happy? These days, I'm only an occasional visitor. The Armenian liturgy is beautiful, a dazzling visual and aural experience, but the incense makes me cough, and the whole thing goes on too long—two hours if the priest has somewhere to go afterward, and nearly three if the archbishop is in town or if it's a feast day. Except for an English recap of the sermon, it's all in Armenian. Sitting there takes me back to all those childhood hours in old-lady living rooms listening to conversations I couldn't understand.

So I practice the faith of our fathers in a modern adaptation of my own father's way, listening to the badarak on my iPod while drinking decaf on the patio. I am not tempted to stray to anyone else's church, because I am guided by my father's experience: His volatile childhood exposed him to many religious practices. His early life as a Muslim Kurd even gave him a unique insight into the religion that so many Armenians of his generation blamed for their sufferings. "Muslims pray to the same God," he told me. He also admired Catholics for their devotion to a demanding faith, and for their church's refusal to bow to popular whim. He spent a good deal of time with Protestants, too, even singing with the Salvation Army from time to time to break the monotony of Army life. (Until I learned this, I was puzzled about why every once in a while he'd suddenly start singing, "Shall we gather at the river . . .")

Dad's conclusion was that all these religions worked well for the people who were born into them and that if God is listening to any prayer, he is listening to all of them. So he could find no compelling reason to abandon the faith of the Armenian martyrs who died making the sign of the Holy Cross as Muslims' swords fell across their necks. I can't either, but like my father I'm pretty sure we aren't the only ones with God's phone number, and that our religion isn't the key to our identity.

Armenian civilization flourished under the ancient gods. Pagan Armenia reached its cultural and political apogee in the final century before Christ's birth when the brilliant and brave King Dikran II shoved all foreign intruders aside. Unfortunately, the Romans and Persians shoved back. When the Christian era dawned on the world, the Armenians were again caught in a tug-of-war between competing empires. No wonder early Christian evangelists found an eager audience in Armenia. This new monotheistic religion offered the Armenians something no pantheon could: a promise that no matter how bad things got here on Earth, the misery was only temporary. Armenians who embraced the new God could look forward to eternal life in His kingdom.

Who wouldn't at least listen to the proposition?

The apostles Bartholomew and Thaddeus both found their way to Armenia and planted the seeds of Christianity. Adherents of the old religion did not all yield easily—Bartholomew and Thaddeus were both martyred—but a Christian community took root and continued to grow over the next three centuries. No one can say more with any assurance, because Christianity did more than triumph over the old gods. It obliterated them and much of the civilization they watched over.

Among those converted over the next couple of centuries was King Trdat, who decreed Armenia the world's first Christian nation in 301 AD. The king immediately became the world's first fanatic Christian ruler. His soldiers destroyed the pagan temples and all vestiges of Armenia's pagan past, including historical texts. Even the old Armenian alphabet used to create them was erased. As a result, we have little more than a few stone carvings to relate the glories of ancient Urartu. No people could have taken the notion of being born again quite so literally as the Armenians did by destroying our old selves in the process.

Armenia's conversion was soon followed by Rome's. As Christianity spread, so did disagreements and occasional clashes over the new religion's tenets. Among the most most hotly debated over the next century was the nature of Jesus. Even bishops got tripped up, and occasionally excommunicated, while trying to explain of how He could be man as well as God. The Council of Ephesus answered by adopting this Christological formula in 431: "one nature united in the Incarnate Word of God." That seemed to satisfy everyone, including the Armenians, who were more committed to Christianity than ever—and very possibly more than anyone else on Earth.

No one understood this better than the Zoroastrian Persians, who were trying mightily to convert their Armenian subjects. The harder they tried, the more fervent the Armenian Christians became. An army of Armenians led by Vartan Mamigonian met the Persians in battle on the plain of Avarayr in 451 AD, with tragically predictable results: The Armenians were slaughtered to a man, which was the worst possible outcome for the Persians. This may be difficult to understand because Americans venerate victors, but nearly all Armenian heroes are martyrs. It is the cause and the fight that inspire us, not the outcome. The inspiration provided by the Vartanantz martyrs kept the fire of Christianity burning for a generation until the Persians finally acknowledged that their cause was hopeless.

While the Armenians were fighting to defend Christianity, other Christians were fighting among themselves. This led to yet another ecumenical council, at Chalcedon in 451. It's unclear whether the Armenians, who were busy being martyred by the Persians, were invited. In the Armenians' absence, the council adopted a new formula that declared Jesus to be of "two natures, without confusion, without change, without division, without separation." The Armenians were outraged when they found out about the change a half century later. They joined the Copts and a handful of others in refusing to accept the council's decision.

If you ever run into an Armenian priest, you might ask him to explain the critical difference in the pre- and post-Chalcedonian Christological formulas. I've tried but I can't begin to understand well enough to explain it without risking my own excommunication. What's important to the course of events over the following centuries is that Armenia and the vast body of the Christian world had a parting of the ways. As a result, the Armenian Church was pretty much left behind by the modern world, along with Armenia itself.

What I'm certain of is that the Armenians could not have foreseen the consequences of their principled stand. Some two hundred years after Chalcedon, the first nation to accept Christianity became one of the first Christian nations overrun by Muslims when the Arabs launched their earliest attempt at Western conquest. The Christians of the West didn't raise a finger to help. The Armenians survived the Arab occupation only to face successive Muslim onslaughts by Mongols, post-Zoroastrian Persians, and Turks. Each time, the Armenians humbled themselves by asking for help from their Christian brothers. Each time, their Christian brothers reminded them of Chalcedon. The Armenians clung to their faith and accepted their fate.

What if we weren't so faithful, or stubborn? What if we'd embraced Chalcedon and all that followed, including the Roman practice of celebrating Christmas on December 25 instead of January 6? Just maybe, the West would have shown a little more concern when the Arabs came streaming across the desert. Maybe the Turks would have never made it over the Caucuses. Maybe, in other words, the entire course of Western history would be different. Or maybe not. How can anyone even guess at such things? I can't, but I know this: By standing firm, the Armenian Church distinguished itself in a way that also distinguished the Armenian people. Our fidelity to the orthodox faith of the catholic church kept us from being swept up in the internecine battles that eventually divided the Catholic and Orthodox Churches. Our church became the strongest vessel of Armenian identity through waves of foreign occupation. Millions of Armenians may have been spared slaughter over the centuries that followed if we'd signed up with one side or the other, but they would have been spared as Romans or Greeks with little to distinguish their origins.

Unfortunately, the determined defense of the Armenian Church against foreign intrusion would be more inspiring and more meaningful if we'd managed to defend it against ourselves. In church, as in so many aspects of our lives, Armenians eventually managed to become our own enemies.

Here is the dirty secret of Armenians in America: There are two churches in almost every Armenian community, one under the jurisdiction of the Armenian Diocese and one under the Armenian Prelacy. If you could be transported magically back and forth from one to the other in the middle of services, you'd never know which was which. There is no difference in the hymns or prayers or vestments. No difference in architecture. No difference in dogma. And yet, lots of people who attend one church would not set foot in the other. Not one Armenian in ten, maybe not one in one hundred, could begin to explain how the churches split, or why. Even those who know the origin of the Dashnak and Ramgavar parties would be hard-pressed to tell you why any of it is still relevant nearly a century after most of our grandparents came to America.

By now, whoever killed Archbishop Tourian is surely as dead as Communism in Armenia, but that doesn't matter. Armenians are still haunted by the tragedies of ancient times. A century more or less is not nearly enough time to exorcise the ghost of an archbishop.

TRAVELING THE WORLD CLOSE-BY

On the occasional Sunday when no visitor rang our doorbell after church, we rang someone else's.

"Let's go for a ride," my father would say, and I'd run to the door. I knew this meant we'd be visiting someone, some place, but there was no telling who or where until we pulled into the driveway, because my father never drove the same route twice. The guessing game was almost as much fun as the ride.

A good Sunday ride ended at a house with kids, but the best Sunday ride ended at a house with kids that was far away from ours. The main excuse for an afternoon ride in the pre-air-conditioned 1950s and '60s was "to cool off." You'd crank down the windows and imagine that the lung-searing fumes of a New Jersey summer turned magically cool and invigorating at thirty miles an hour.

I loved visiting Andy and Bert Aslanian, but they lived five minutes away in Leonia. Aunt Lillian and Uncle Peter, who was my godfather and also the senior cousin of the extended Nalbandian clan, had no kids, but they lived farther out in Bergenfield so the ride lasted nearly half an hour—and there was always a chance that my cousins Michael, David, and Peter Bakalian would be there.

I also rooted for a long ride because that justified the effort to bring along music. No one had yet dreamed up the compact disc, much less the iPod, but Dad asked a friend in what was then called the hi-fi business to wire up an electrical converter and an extra speaker in the rear compartment of our 1957 Plymouth station wagon so we could bring along a tape recorder. I'd often guess we were going for a ride even before Dad's announcement when I saw him lugging his big, brown V-M (Voice of Music) reel-to-reel tape machine out the door. The distinction of being the rare family with any source of in-car music other than an AM radio was exciting enough to offset the disappointment of listening to Armenian music instead of the top 40 countdown on 77 WABC like other kids.

I remember going to Hudson County Park for a picnic with some of Dad's old-guy Armenian buddies. Dad backed the car up to the picnic area and opened the tailgate so the men could sing along to the music as they cooked the shish kebab. Then it started to rain. Dad shoved the V-M against the back seat to make room in the storage compartment, and one of his pals climbed in with the still-burning grill. We drove in the rain with all the windows open to keep from gagging on the smoke. The kebab sizzled as Shamlian sang all the way home.

Summer vacation was my one chance to travel more than a few miles from home, but only a few. We never drove more than three or four hours, and there was no alternative to driving. I never got on an airplane until I was married and didn't think I was missing much. "There's no place as beautiful as America," my mother assured me. She heard it from her father, who had seen all of the world between Kharpert and California. His conclusion may be open to debate, but at least Mom got more travel advice from her father than I got from mine.

My parents closed their store for two weeks each July, and off we went to one resort or the other—there were only two: Malkas's Place and Varbed's Place. Malkas owned a hotel in Belmar, New Jersey, a shore town just south of Asbury Park. Varbed had a hotel in the Catskill Mountains in Upstate New York. I never heard an Armenian call either place by another name. I liked both but I liked Malkas's Place better because there were more kids, plus there was the beach. The trip Down the Shore, as the beach is known in New Jersey, took a little over an hour if there was no traffic—but how could there be no shore-bound traffic on a steamy Friday night in July?

We'd get the Plymouth rolling just fast enough to draw a stream of warm, sweet refinery fumes through the windows when all of a sudden, an endless, crooked line of flaming-red taillights would ignite just ahead of us and Dad would slam on the brakes. I can feel his sinewy right arm shoving me back against the seat each time he stopped short, the 1950s version of seat belts and airbags rolled into one. The trip could go on like that for hours:

brief breaths of air punctuated by slamming stops and long, hot, suffocating waits. I knew it was nearly over when the oily fumes gave way to a salty ocean breeze.

The main house at Malkas's was one of those big, barely post-Victorian wooden beach houses with an enormous, shaded porch. We usually stayed in one of the bungalows out back, one room with a bath. Everybody who stayed at Malkas's was Armenian and so was just about everyone in the neighborhood. My mother's cousin Rose Shamlian and her husband, Aram, had a house a few blocks away. (Yes, Shamlian as in Shamlian Records. Hovsep Shamlian was Uncle Aram's father.) The Shamlian boys loved to fish. It was in the Shamlians' yard that I first saw brown crabs turn fiery red as they were plunged into boiling water. The Shamlian house overflowed with kids, all of them cousins, but I was never short of playmates anywhere we went in town.

We rarely took a vacation without Andy and Bert, their kids, and all their assorted cousins: Scotty, Randy, Gary, Karen, and the rest. Bert and Andy's daughters, Lynn and Donna, were like sisters to me, except we got along. We'd all walk a block or two to the beach in the morning and set up our blankets and umbrellas. Aunt Bert always brought iced tea, an exotic drink that my mother didn't entirely approve of. I drank it by the gallon. We'd pitch camp in the shade of the green, wooden shack on the boardwalk where a man sold hot dogs and ice cream. I discovered early on that I had a genius for getting sand in anything I ate at the beach. I'd crunch my way through lunch and wash the sand out of my teeth with more iced tea. All around us, Armenians broiled in the sun as far as the eye could see. We'd all carry our beach chairs and sand pails home together at dinnertime. We'd rinse off, change, and resume the party in the yard.

The men would light charcoal fires in portable grills, the smoke curling around the damp bathing suits hanging on the lines stretched between the bungalows. I can still smell the lighter fluid wafting through the sea air. The kids would play Wiffle Ball until the food was ready. For the children, dinner was communal. We'd eat our way from grill to grill. Then after dinner, we'd all walk along the boardwalk to the penny arcade. It was the most exciting place I'd ever seen. Balls thumping, bells clanging, whistles blowing, lights flashing. I could never get that damned claw in the glass cage to pick up the toy car, but I could also never get it through my head that I was a sucker for trying.

It was the kind of vacation that I wished could go on and on, and it did. When it was time to go back to work, my father went home alone and left my mother and me at the shore for another week or more. When that ended, my father would soothe my hurt feelings by promising we'd go to Varbed's Place soon. Sometimes that was even the second week of our vacation, but we'd also go for long weekends. Again, Bert and Andy and the girls often came along.

In the Catskills with Dad and his Plymouth in 1955.

Varbed's Place was a rambling, wooden hotel near Tannersville, New York. The road leading there through the mountains twisted and so did I, craning to see down into the green, misty valley. The view to the inside was all rock wall and forest, sometimes both, with billowing curtains of water splashing down into streams. The twenty-something dimwits who run Hollywood today love to show '50s flashbacks in black and white, as though life before they were born existed only in kinescopes, but the world was never so vivid or vibrant as it was before cars were air-conditioned. We rumbled up to Varbed's place in Dad's Plymouth station wagon with every window cranked down, teased along by a perfume of wildflowers and summer grass.

My view was neither warped by glass nor obscured by grime, but even if it were I could tell when we'd arrived with my eyes closed the moment Varbed's gravel driveway began spitting stones up into the Plymouth's high-arched wheel wells.

The sign out front, obviously a relic, said "The Washington Irving Inn." The Armenians called it Varbed's Place because it was run by Varbed and Mary Chebolian, whom I called Grandma Mary. I cannot picture her with any expression except a smile. Like Malkas, Varbed offered a choice of rooms in the main house or in the bungalows out back. Bungalows were better because they had private baths, but the main house was fun because there was so much going on. So many people, so much noise! The hotel was already old and creaky, and a very scary place for a kid when summer storms rolled across the mountains. My father told me the story of Rip Van Winkle, explaining that the thunder was really the sound of the little mountain men bowling in the caverns. The result was greatly calmed nerves, and a lifelong love of Washington Irving's tales.

We didn't barbecue at Varbed's, because it was a real hotel with a dining room, and Varbed served real food—Armenian food. Kebabs of ground lamb, stews thick with string beans and okra, fat plates of rice pilaf served family style. Mealtime was long and loud, with lots of cross-table hellos and visits.

The shore crowd at Malkas's Place was almost all families, but Varbed got plenty of older folks, which meant endless interruptions at mealtime for us kids to be shown off. "Hello, Honey, do you remember me?" No, never once did I remember any of them, but it didn't matter. There was no answer you could give to avoid the pinch, which was sure to follow. Old Armenians are world-class pinchers, most favoring the cheek but some with techniques that would serve the CIA well for extracting information from enemy combatants. The dreaded Adam's apple pinch was the worst. Somehow, they pulled so hard they could almost pick you up off the floor.

There were no organized activities for kids, so we improvised, hiking through the fields and exploring the woods. Sometimes our parents took us swimming in a nearby stream. I hated it. It was like swimming in the Antarctic. Even at the height of summer, Catskills air never seemed warm, and the water, whether from the tap or fountain or brook, was downright freezing. I preferred to stay dry and keep moving, but the adults spent most of their time sitting. They spread lawn chairs on the grass and fanned out across the rolling, rocky grounds. For all the talking they did inside, they were oddly quiet outside in the presence of the holy mountains. I'm sure even American-born adults like my mother could sense that this was communion with the old country. The men would play backgammon—*tavlou*—the Armenian national pastime, which is usually accompanied by the sounds of wooden pieces slamming against the tiled board and players cursing in Turkish. (Armenians feel free to blaspheme that way because they're sure God listens only to the languages of good Christians.) But when the men played outside at Varbed's, the only sound you'd hear other than crickets and birds was the stutter of dice spilling across the board.

Every one of them took time out now and then to look up into the distance, at the next mountain. On days when white tufts of vapor rose from the valley, I'm sure they could see Ararat through the mist.

The Armenian era in the Catskills began to fade in the 1970s as incomes went up, air fares went down, and the old folks began to die. I hadn't been there in more than forty years when we took a side trip with our daughter, Mandy, during our vacation in New Jersey in summer 2009. To my surprise, the Washington Irving Inn still stood on the outskirts of Tannersville and Hunter along Route 23A—and it looked great. New owners had restored the place to a glory that passed long before I was born. It was very upscale, very charming, the sort of place where you have afternoon tea and scones, not coffee and the braided bread Armenians call *choreg*.

I thought all vestiges of Armenians had vanished, but I was wrong. The manager guided me to a wall near the bar where pictures from the hotel's past were proudly displayed, including the Chebolians' wedding photo and several group shots of now-nameless Armenians. I did a little Googling when we got back home to see what else I could turn up. I found a genealogy site listing everyone buried in Evergreen Cemetery in the town of Hunter. Entry 187 was Marderos (Varbed) Chebolian and his wife, Mary.

Many other Armenian names were on the list. I smiled to think that at least some of them must be the old folks I remember looking silently out across that same valley.

A LESSON FROM LEON

Nothing excited my imagination or provided a more enticing peek into the adult world than riding along with my father on his daily rounds.

Officially, Dad didn't make deliveries, but he made exceptions for friends and his best regular customers. On summer mornings, I'd go along. After he got the boiler fired and the first load of cleaning in the machine, Dad would load the family station wagon, carefully hanging freshly pressed clothes from a bar stretching across the cargo area in back. We'd leave around 8:00 a.m., windows down, just as the heat of morning was beginning to boil up a fume of diesel fuel and grime from deep within the old, cracked asphalt of Kennedy Boulevard. Behind us, suits, pants, and dresses swathed in clear plastic swayed and swished in a static-electric embrace.

I remember the homes and even names of many customers, mostly professionals: doctors, dentists, lawyers. They were the kind of homes where the doorbells played music instead of buzzing like a cat that bit the toaster cord. I got to peek into big estates with brick walls and slate walkways, and I walked down the hushed hallways of high-rise apartment buildings with doormen and elevators. Usually it was the wife who came to the door, but sometimes the maid. The customers were unfailingly friendly, offering us coffee (which Dad always politely turned down) and sending regards to my mother. The truly favored customers often got a plant from Dad's garden along with their clothing, and at holiday times a sample of paklava or cookies from Mom's kitchen. I never got the sense that Dad was treated as a deliveryman. If he'd gotten that sense, the customer would have been instructed to find another cleaner.

Dad turned down the coffee because we almost always stopped for breakfast along the way, sometimes at one of the endless string of diners along Route 46 but more often at George Bloom's lunchroom at Nungesser's, or Rusty's Diner down on Tonnele Avenue. We'd sit at the counter so we could soak up the atmosphere along with our egg yolks. Diners are where true Jerseyites eat because the food is good, it's cheap, and you can have as much or as little to do with everyone else as you care to. You want to argue about the Yankees or the Giants, or gripe about the weather or the traffic or about the governor and his sales tax? The diner is the place to do it. It's better than any call-in radio show because you don't get put on hold and nobody can hang up on you. Plus, you can get the world's best rice pudding. I loved listening to the conversations all around. It was an unparalleled opportunity to find out how adults talked when there were no kids around, because diner talk goes on no matter who's listening and nothing gets bleeped out.

I know my father enjoyed diners, because they brought out the jokester in him, as not many people or places did. If he saw a new counterman or cook, he'd complain loudly about the food in Greek—and sure enough, the guy would look up, startled, then look over the crowd to see where the insult came from, only to see my father laughing. George Bloom wasn't Greek, but he was a genial guy and an easy target. He made the mistake of telling my father that breakfast was his most profitable meal. The next day, Dad arrived with a bag of doughnuts. He greeted every customer at the door: "Free breakfast today."

We made other stops, too. Dad had a network of friends who, like him, worked for themselves. They did business among themselves, through an informal but efficient barter system. Clothes were cleaned, cars washed, chairs upholstered, papers notarized, and arms vaccinated without a cent changing hands. We'd stop to see Charlie the TV man or Oscar the mechanic, maybe to get something done but usually just to say hello and catch up on neighborhood news.

One of my favorite stops was Robinson's Car Wash, an oversized garage on a shoestring-wide side street in Guttenberg across from Uncle Mike's apartment. Mr. Robinson was the only black man in Dad's tight circle of shopkeeper pals. His car wash was always busy, always squealing with the sound of wet tires slamming to a stop and echoing with what they used to call race music that somehow squeaked its way through the tiny, tinny speaker of an old tube radio on the windowsill and drowned out the spray of the hoses and the slap of wet towels. This was pretty close to kid heaven, watching black men Simonize a Pontiac Bonneville—better yet, *listening* to black men Simonize a Pontiac Bonneville—while Dad and Mr. Robinson swapped small talk over a cup of coffee. No talk was too small as far as I was concerned. Just hearing my father's voice made me feel that he was sharing something special with me, even if I was really eavesdropping on his life.

The best stop of all was always at Leon Feldstein's body shop about a mile north of our store on the Boulevard. Leon and my father met before I was born, when Dad needed a fender straightened, and he and Leon developed a genuine friendship. They didn't just visit during business hours. Leon and his family came to our home and we went to theirs, but these two guys clearly enjoyed hanging out together. I probably enjoyed it even more than they did. Leon always had interesting stories to tell, usually about cars, and he told them to me as well as to my father. Leon was the rare adult who didn't talk over or around or in spite of me. He addressed me directly, as though I were an actual participant in the conversation, and he addressed me as an adult, even though I was a kid. He always looked me in the eye, always called me by my name, which in his Polish accent came out *Doh-glus*. I called him Uncle Leon. I enjoyed visiting him so much that, when I got older, I went all by myself.

By then, when I was eleven or twelve, Leon had started selling cars as well as fixing them. He got a franchise to sell MG and Austin-Healey sports cars, later adding Fiats and Rovers. What a stroke of luck for me! No other kid I knew had an uncle who owned a car dealership. I'd wander in after school and hop from car to car, spastically pumping the clutch and yanking the shift lever while making *varoooom* noises. I couldn't drive a car, but I could drive Uncle Leon's salesmen crazy. They'd complain to him, but all he ever said to me, ever so calmly, was, "Dohglus, don't break the car." Apparently I never did, because he always let me come back. Each time I left, my arms were loaded with brochures on exotic vehicles with exotic names like Saloon and Magnette, and bundles of grease-stained technical bulletins on how to repair leaks in the Austin 1800's Hydrolastic suspension or how to synchronize an MGB's twin SU carburetors.

When I was fifteen in 1967, Uncle Leon gave me an entire car, a 1962 Ford Anglia, a strange-looking English sedan that appeared to be going backward and forward at the same time. This Anglia wouldn't go in either direction. Vandals had struck while the car sat on the used-car lot. They slashed the upholstery but didn't damage the body. The car didn't run because one of Leon's mechanics had started taking the engine apart to repair a knock before the vandals attacked. The vandals robbed the Anglia of its meager profit potential, but an ambitious and capable young man could replace the worn rod bearing and bring the odd little sedan back to life. Uncle Leon, sadly, mistook me for such a young man and had the Anglia delivered to our home as a present. I was thrilled. I even persuaded my father to let me get another Anglia, a junkyard wreck, as a parts car. How was I supposed to know the engine parts from a 1958 Anglia wouldn't fit a 1962? The two battered cars sat behind our house for over a year, until it became clear that I was never going to make progress. I was happy just to sit behind the wheel reading *Car & Driver*, making *varoooom* noises in my head. My father finally called a wrecker to tow the cars away. If Uncle Leon was disappointed in me, he never said a word.

Soon after Leon gave me my first car, he gave me my first job. He moved his business to a larger showroom, adding American Motors cars to the lineup, and he hired me as a summer gofer. He led me through the door of the parts department, which was in shambles. I couldn't step more than a few feet into the room. The floor was strewn with empty boxes, taillights, fuel pumps, and spark plugs. Leon said simply, "Dohglus, make a little order in here please." So I did. I swept, shoveled, sorted, and stacked all summer long. I had plenty of other chores, too. I cleaned the showroom, washed and waxed the used cars, and fetched lunch for the mechanics and salesmen. It was all fun to me. I got to play with cars, even if I was still too young to drive them, and I got to hang out with adults, even if some of them were more juvenile than I was. The mechanics especially were grimy and foul-mouthed, fixated on bathroom humor and slobbering over magazine photos of naked women that they taped to their lockers. I was intoxicated by the big-boy atmosphere as well as the smell of gasoline and solvents, particularly the stuff we used to strip the shipping wax off the cars. It was the last job I loved unconditionally, every minute of the working day.

Riding with Leon was even more fun than listening to him. He always drove something sporty, usually with a stick shift, and he drove it quickly and smoothly. His driving style was pure liquid. Every movement blended perfectly with the next—accelerating, turning, shifting, braking—so the car never bucked or jerked or bounced or pitched no matter how fast he drove or how quickly he stopped. Cars obeyed Leon the way lions obeyed Tarzan.

Many years later, long after Leon and my father were both gone, I learned how he came by his seemingly magic command of things automotive.

I'd been living in Florida for about ten years when I got a call at work from Leon's widow, Anna, who was visiting friends nearby. I picked her up and brought her to our house. Our dinner conversation that night was unique in my experience. Anna's speech sounded much like Leon's, but her tone was dark and bitter as she reminisced about coming to America. My parents were among the few non-Jews who welcomed them, she said. She was convinced anti-Semitism was nearly as bad here as in Poland, a word she spoke with clear disgust. She went into painful detail about her own tortures in the camps and the horrific deaths of family and friends. Somehow, she and Leon both survived the Holocaust. After the war, while the world debated the creation of a Jewish state, Leon joined the Zionist underground and helped smuggle Jewish refugees out of Europe and into Palestine. He drove a truck along the back roads, through mountains, often at night and without lights. He had to make time yet avoid notice. He had to be fast and smooth—and never miss a curve. He made countless drives over countless miles without losing a passenger or his truck.

When the mission was complete and Israel was a reality, Leon and Anna wanted to move there, but they decided to wait. Leon had become a first-rate mechanic as well as driver, so he was sure he could make a living in America. They would start a family here, save their money, and then resettle. It took a quarter century longer than they expected, but the Feldsteins finally did move to Israel. My father talked about Leon often after that, always with a smile, until the news came that Leon was dying of cancer. I don't think he was much over fifty years old. My father still talked about Leon after he was gone, but he didn't smile. That's how I know he missed his friend.

Of all the conversations between my father and Leon, the one I remember best is the one my father tried to stop. They were talking about how lucky their kids were to be growing up in the land of plenty when Leon took a logical but unexpected turn that caught my father off balance. Leon started talking about the concentration camp where he'd been imprisoned during the war. He talked about being forced to work without food or water, in the company of men dying of hunger and thirst at the same time. One of the men found a leather belt and they took turns chewing on it, sucking out the moisture. I leaned forward, horrified but fascinated by every word. My father's right hand shot up.

"Leon, stop! You shouldn't talk about these things."

But Leon didn't stop.

"No, Nish, you're wrong. We have to talk about these things."

Wrong? Could my father ever be wrong, especially about something so much a part of his character? This was the most horrifying and fascinating idea of all, one that changed my view of the adult world. I continued paying close attention to my father, hoping always to learn more, but now I understood the importance of watching and listening to other adults because they could teach me something as well.

Like Leon, they might even teach me something about my father.

The brother my father never had

One of my favorite visitors any day was Arpag Mahlebjian, truly my father's best friend.

They met sometime in the early 1950s when Uncle Arpag was freshly back from service in the Korean War and was starting out in the carpet business. He was barely thirty years old, and my father was well into his forties, a couple of hard-working Armenian guys with young families who struck up a friendship at church.

Dad and Uncle Arpag went out together to nightclubs or to play cards or to their secret Dashnak meetings of the Armenian Revolutionary Federation. My father's man-about-town days ended when I was still in single digits—family legend says I ended his morning-after habit of sleeping late on Sundays by hitting him on the head with a hammer while he dozed—but the bond between him and Uncle Arpag never weakened. The Kalajians and Mahlebjians socialized often as families, but the men also had their private time in our living room, sometimes at night but often on a Sunday afternoon.

They did not watch baseball or even play cards or backgammon. They drank scotch, listened to Armenian music, and talked, for hours, in their language. I can still hear them laughing and cursing in Turkish. I loved listening to these two, often sitting on the floor nearby even though I didn't understand what they were saying.

When they did go out, or whenever another visitor stopped by, they always introduced each other as brothers. My father had an answer whenever anyone noted that they had different last names. "We had different mothers," he'd say. He loved that most people readily accepted the non sequitur. It was irrelevant that he and Arpag didn't look much alike, at least not to other Armenians, and they didn't sound alike to anyone. Uncle Arpag was born in Ethiopia, raised in Cyprus, and came to the United States from the United Kingdom. His Armeno-Afro-Greek-Anglo accent and his rich, melodic tone were unmistakable. I always ran down the stairs whenever the door's chime was followed by, "Hah-lo, Seel-vee-ah."

If it was Sunday, I might be in for a very special treat. Uncle Arpag liked to go to New York on Saturday nights to Armenian clubs and restaurants that have disappeared now but that were plentiful in the 1960s and '70s. He'd bring back an aluminum take-out bowl of my one favorite food Mom never made: *midiyeh dolma*, mussels stuffed with rice and currants. I haven't eaten mussels like those in years—plump, black shells full of sweet, pink meat made sweeter by the currants, then sharpened by a squeeze of lemon. My father used to laugh and then look disgusted while I ate them.

What kid eats that sort of thing?

"Oh, Neesh," Uncle Arpag would plead. "Doh-gee has good taste."

Then something very strange happened to Uncle Arpag when I was eleven or twelve. He got divorced. Nobody in our family, nobody I knew, had ever gotten divorced. The event was preceded and followed by a lot of grown-up whispering in Armenian. I wouldn't have understood if they'd shouted, but the whispering let me know not to ask. Uncle Arpag eventually got married again to Carol, who wasn't Armenian but was very nice. The two of them came to our house often for the next few years, and then something even stranger happened. They moved to Texas, and then to Los Angeles. I knew my father was upset because he said almost nothing about it, except he would call Uncle Arpag often and curse at him in Turkish. For almost thirty years after that, he would bring up Uncle Arpag often in conversation, laughing about their good times and then he'd suddenly stop. "Goddamit!" he'd say. "Why the hell is he in California?"

My father often talked about going to Los Angeles to see his brother, but it never happened. Uncle Arpag and Carol finally came to Florida to see Dad in February 1990. My mother had died and my father was living alone near Robyn and me. They stayed at his condo, listened to Armenian music, and talked late into the night. My father drank scotch, but Uncle Arpag had switched to vodka. My father just shook his head and cursed in Turkish. The visit lasted only a week, but my father's spirits were buoyed. "I'll see you in

Los Angeles," he promised his brother. I'm sure he meant it, but it never happened. Dad died the following month.

I used to call Uncle Arpag from time to time in the years after, but I didn't see him again until summer 2002, when Robyn and I went to California on vacation. He was recovering from a stroke, and he and Carol had moved north to a suburb of San Francisco to be near her family. He was barely able to speak, and he was difficult to understand when he did, but the four of us went out to dinner. I ordered a scotch on the rocks. Uncle Arpag smiled and turned to Carol, who could make out the words he formed with his lips. "He wants a scotch, too," Carol said. "It reminds him of your father." Carol, Robyn, and I were talking as we all sipped our drinks when Uncle Arpag leaned across the table. He spoke clearly to me for the first and last time during our visit.

"I still miss him," he said.

A little over a year later, Uncle Arpag and Carol moved to Florida, about two hours north of us. He'd gotten better for a while, then complications set in. Now he sat silent, confined to the house they bought near Carol's sisters. "I think it would help him to hear some Armenian music," Carol said over the phone. When we went to visit, I put on some old time kef music, the sort he and Dad listened to. Uncle Arpag's eyes opened wide and he smiled. Then a muffled sound came from his mouth that made me smile.

He was cursing in Turkish.

A MATTER OF TONE

D ad had more than sentimental reason to safeguard his father's citizenship paperwork: He didn't have his own.

He tried a number of times to obtain documentation of his miraculous metamorphosis from vile giavour to American citizen, but each time he was told that no paperwork was necessary. He was assured that his father's naturalization covered him as well, even though the certificate said nothing of the sort, because the law at the time of his arrival in the United States granted citizenship to children of naturalized Americans as long as they became residents while still minors.

So on the rare occasions when Dad was asked to demonstrate his citizenship, he'd unfold a black-leather case and display the certificate affirming that "Harrotune" Kalajian, 41, became an American on Dec. 12, 1927. This was always met with a puzzled look followed by a barrage of questions. Dad got steamed at having to explain himself. He got steamiest when his application for veterans benefits provoked the same questions from the Department of Veterans Affairs. "You didn't ask any questions when you sent me to get shot at," he said.

You'd think a branch of the US government would know the law, or at least be able to look it up. But while the law was clear in 1928 when Dad arrived in America, it has been amended a number of times since. The rules of derivative citizenship seem to have an asterisk for every immigrant who scuffed the floors of Ellis Island. As a result, the seemingly simple matter of determining just who is an American and how they got that way isn't always so simple.

When I started poking around to understand the situation a little better, I was surprised to learn that the government had tried to simplify the citizenship process for Armenians just a few years before Grandpa Kalajian took the oath. Luckily, the effort didn't succeed or the response to my grandfather and any Armenian seeking to become a citizen would have been "No."

Here's the part that had me scratching my head: The government decided Armenians couldn't be citizens because they weren't white people.

The 1927 citizenship certificate Nishan shared with his father.

The federal government, I learned, made its first attempt to set down the rules of naturalized citizenship in 1790, the year after the Constitution took effect and George Washington became president. The Father of Our Country signed a law restricting naturalized citizenship to "free white persons." It was clearly aimed at black people, as almost everyone else coming to American then was white and European, but the law came in handy when the growing nation's appetite for cheap, disposable labor resulted in a wave of Chinese immigration.

Armɔ
white or
or Asn

More than a century later, being white remained the legal key that un-locked the gates leading to American citizenship, but the vital matter of de-ciding who was white—and who wasn't—was usually left to the whims and squints of courthouse clerks who accepted and processed citizenship applica-tions. An Armenian immigrant in Oregon discovered how arbitrary the pro-cess could be. Tatos Cartozian was granted citizenship in 1923, only to have the government sue him a year later to revoke it. The government argued that Cartozian "is a native of that part of the Turkish Empire known as Turkey in Asia, or Asia Minor . . . and is of Armenian blood and race. It is alleged that he is not a free white person within the meaning of the naturalization laws of Congress."

Cartozian's defense relied on testimony by historians and anthropolo-gists that Armenians had deep European roots. Herodotus, the venerable and long-dead Father of History, even testified by proxy, having classified the Armenians among the Phrygians who migrated from Greece to Asia Minor. His nearly two-thousand-year-old observation was buttressed by tes-timony from Franz Boas, professor of anthropology at Columbia University. The European origin of the Armenian people was so well-documented, Boas testified, that "nobody doubts any more their early migration from Thrace across the Hellespont into Asia Minor."

There was also testimony that Armenians mingled fraternally with un-questionably white Europeans such as Germans and Russians, and even oc-casionally married "native white Americans" without objection from either side. One witness, an Armenian immigrant woman who had married an American from Wisconsin, is described in the court's ruling as "very intel-lectual and highly cultivated."

The court was clearly impressed. Judge C. E. Wolverton of the federal district court in Oregon ruled in July 1925 that Armenians "are of Alpine stock, of European persuasion." Most important, he declared that Armenians were white people "as commonly recognized in speech of common usage, and as popularly understood and interpreted in this country by our forefathers, and by the community at large."

The *New York Times* offered five paragraphs of unsigned commentary on the Cartozian decision soon after it was rendered. The great paper de-clared that the judge rightly distinguished Armenians from other Asiatics, including prior tenants of Asia Minor who had "no talent for business such as the true later Armenians always have shown." Having long reported on

Cartozian ruling

Armenians from up close, the *Times* clearly felt qualified to pronounce that "though many, and indeed all [Armenians] are of dark complexion, they are what we think of as 'white.'" But the *Times* tempered its generosity with a cautionary tone:

"The faults ascribed to Armenians are natural to people long oppressed and forced to live by craft rather than strength. In safer environment they lose those characteristics, and many have done so already in the United States. They are no more 'Asiatic' than many other peoples to whom naturalization is granted here as a matter of course."

The article neglected to list these faults ascribed to Armenians. I guess everyone was supposed to know. It all seems ridiculously arrogant, this idea of America deciding who's in and who's out according to some crazy color code that no two people, not even federal judges or the *New York Times*, could define or describe accurately. The logic of the Cartozian ruling boiled down to this: If my family's origins were in Europe, I must be white and therefore a good fellow—a truly puzzling conclusion in light of Europe's history of fratricidal war and despotism.

The Cartozian ruling was celebrated by Armenians for obvious reasons. How many immigrant communities could boast of being certified white by a federal court? The glow did not dim for years. The Cartozian ruling was reprinted in full in the winter 1953 edition of the Boston-based literary and historical quarterly the *Armenian Review*. The editor's introduction urged readers to "keep this copy not only for future reference but also to have a ready answer whenever the rightful origin of the Armenian people is contested by maligners."

I understand the danger of reading history without recognizing that sensibilities change, but this is not the ancient history of Herodotus or even the dusty textbook history of Toynbee. The obnoxious racial posturing of the courts and the *Times* were very much current events in my father's youth, and the *Armenian Review's* celebration of its namesake people's whiteness occurred a year after I was born. Here were the survivors of the century's first genocide, persecuted and chased from their homeland because of their ethnicity, now praising their new homeland for embracing them on the same grounds. I understand their joy at finally being accepted. After being persecuted as nonpersons by the Ottomans, Armenians in America felt understandably proud—and relieved—to get this government's first-class stamp of approval. But that same history should have taught Armenians the danger of encouraging governments—or anyone—to judge people by their names or religions or skin color or the birth city of their great grandfathers.

I also understand that attitudes and the law were different even well into my own lifetime. In 1953, the US Supreme Court was still a year away from deciding it was wrong to segregate schools. It would be a decade beyond that before the 1964 Civil Rights Act finally put an end to "colored" water fountains and toilets, and then another year before Congress finally guaranteed that black people could vote anywhere in America.

My father, who'd seen the worst of human behavior, thought Americans were particularly decent people despite the occasional chiseler and demagogue. I wonder how much this generally rosy view of America obscured his sense of how America viewed him? He always insisted he'd never been discriminated against, and that Armenians in general suffered from no such problem in this country. "There aren't enough of us to bother anyone," he'd say with a laugh. But clearly, there were, or the mighty federal government would not have concerned itself with the skin tone of Tatos Cartozian.

To my father, the evidence that Armenians were not targets of discrimination was clear: Unlike so many others in America, he'd been able to find work throughout the Depression. To me, that proves only that he was diligent and willing to pick up whatever tool was in demand. The college man sitting next to him on the errand-boy bench surely felt cheated, but did he really know more than the immigrant boy who'd seen so much of the world and read every book in the orphanage library? Did anyone bother to ask this boy if he could quote Shakespeare or summarize the Punic Wars or explain how Caesar wound up in Gaul? At best, I'm sure, all anyone saw was a sinewy young man with a strong back, and all they heard was some sort of foreign accent. That was enough to secure a seat on the bench, but it would never be enough to lift him off that bench.

My father never hinted that he thought about this, much less that it might bother him if he did. He was content with the opportunities that presented themselves or that he created. Dad was confident that greater opportunities would present themselves to me, and he was right. But opportunity in America is not guaranteed, and it still can sometimes be denied unfairly on the basis of skin color or ethnic origin as it was a century ago because we are still wedded to the idea of labeling and categorizing everyone. Take a look at the next census form you receive. There are special categories for people whose ancestors were born in all sorts of places, including islands in the Pacific and even Alaska, but there is no special category for Armenians. The people who come up with these categories are no more grounded in science than the clerks and judges who labeled people like Tatos Cartozian. We justify this silliness by claiming to celebrate diversity, but there's not much for Armenians to celebrate as long as we are denied a niche of our own, or at least a place in one that confers minority status.

Poor Cartozian couldn't possibly have guessed that his victory would be, at best, a mixed blessing for future generations. Three thousand years of invasion, subjugation, and slaughter merit no bonus points. There is no reward anywhere I know of outside Glendale, California, for hiring or promoting Armenians. Or for lending us money to buy a house or start a business, or for admitting us to college.

Yes, I know it is still advantageous in America to be white, but that advantage applies far more to white people who look like Dick Cheney or even Arnold Schwarzenegger than it does to people like me who make blue-eyed blondes nervous when we sit next to them on an airplane.

APSODENT, TAPSODENT

"Compositions," it says on the notebook cover, although there are few real compositions on the lined and yellowed pages inside.

The "C" is highly stylized, a half-moon ribbon staked in place by what was probably meant to be a quill pen but looks more like the Olympic torch. It's hard to tell, really, after so many years. The name below is barely legible, written in the formal, forward-slanted cursive script that betrays the cramped but eager hand of a still-motivated student who had not yet begun to scrawl: "Miss S. Bichakjian. Room 805 Class 8B" earned an "A" on every assignment from cover to cover.

The notebook is small—about six inches wide and eight inches long— but Mom's hard work led to a much more substantial reward, a diploma big enough to fly from a flagpole declaring Sylvia Bichakjian eligible for admission to high school. It is signed by Helen C. Kilroy, teacher, and Amos H. Flake, principal. The date is January 26, 1927.

I found the notebook and the folded, creased diploma in Mom's bureau after she died. I know what they meant to her. She told me many times that she loved school and wished she'd been able to go on. As a kid, I assumed that in those days, people routinely went to work instead of going to high school. It is true and it isn't. Lots of people just as poor kept up their studies, but they did not have either of my grandfathers to answer to.

Mom graduated elementary school just a few months after her mother died. Her father ruled that she would take her mother's place as cook and caretaker for her younger sister and brothers. There was no possibility of appeal, or even discussion. Mom's life might have been very different if her mother had lived a while longer. What I know for certain is that on January 26, 1927, Sylvia Bichakjian's life as an excellent and eager student ended, and on January 27, 1927, her new life in the kitchen and cleaning factories began.

My mother on her last day of childhood in 1927. Earning her eighth-grade diploma meant the end of school and the beginning of her life as a surrogate mother.

I don't know enough about Grandpa Bichakjian to guess whether he ever had second thoughts about that decision. Mom wasn't as secretive about her life as my father was, but her parents were. She gave no hint that they ever shared the stories of their lives before she came along.

She left me just one picture of her father, taken when he was probably in his late fifties or early sixties. He never got much older than that. In this picture, Grandpa is standing next to his younger sister Veron in a field, most likely in Massachusetts. The barrel-chested man in short-sleeve white shirt and dark pants shows what might be a hint of a smile, although it's hard to be certain among the smudged pixels of the creased and faded snapshot.

He looks remarkably like me: same glasses, same mustache, same waist-line. It seems likely the picture was taken just before he moved to New Jersey. I wonder if brother and sister ever saw each other again.

Harry Bichakjian and his sister Veron.

Grandpa was long dead when I was born, but the sister who stayed behind in Chelsea became my window into his side of my mother's family and into their life in Massachusetts. My mother called her Emmeh, and I remember her because my parents made a fifty-mile detour to her house in Somerville each year while taking me to summer camp. It was an old, wooden house, three stories tall and divided into two living areas: the first floor for her and Uncle Abe, and upstairs for their son George and his family. I remember a back porch, a narrow driveway, a busy street, and a cat that seemed to understand Armenian.

The most outstanding feature of Emmeh's house was her immense, wood-burning stove. I saw it the first time we visited and thought it was the most amazing thing in the world. I'd pictured wood stoves as small and pot-bellied, like the one at the shack by the lake in Hudson County Park where the skaters warmed themselves in winter, but this was a cook's stove. It was big and black and flat-sided and had valves and gauges and, for all I knew, maybe a whistle and a caboose. It was a great, roaring, fire-breathing stove, as powerful and imposing as a locomotive. Emmeh swore it was the only stove in the world good enough for baking bread.

George and his wife, Tillie, had surprised Emmeh sometime in the 1950s with a new electric kitchen, which is how her old stove wound up in the basement. Emmeh was delighted with her new stove until she opened the oven door and discovered there was no place to build a fire. From then on, she did her cooking in the cellar. She trudged down with all her ingredients, all year-round, whenever her lavash supply was running low, and she stayed down there until she'd baked a great, heaping pile of it.

My mother took me downstairs to watch Emmeh bake, and I was as fascinated by her as by her magical, other-worldly stove. Emmeh was every bit as sturdy but even more imposing. She did not totter along in old-lady steps, holding on and feeling her way. She charged down the basement stairs and back up again, arms loaded both ways. She ran everywhere. I have never met anyone of any age who moved as fast or as purposefully as Emmeh. She was a blur, always. Watching her, I understood where my mother got her impatience with wasted time and motion, and why she felt such a powerful bond with this aunt she'd seen so rarely since childhood. Even at that age, I was struck by their similarities, but I was also puzzled by their differences.

Emmeh's lavash, for example, was nothing like my mother's. She made it without eggs or butter, but it was wonderful, traditional Armenian flat bread covered with brown bubbles of flaky crust. It snapped when you bit into it, then melted almost instantly. I loved it at first bite, but I wondered why it wasn't anything like Mom's. There was no use asking Emmeh, who spoke as quickly as she moved and always in Armenian. She even talked to her cat in Armenian. She yelled at her cat in Armenian. I understood none of it, not so much as a word here or there, as I did when I listened to my mother's other aunts. The reason, I learned much later, is that unlike nearly all our other relatives on both sides of the family, Emmeh wasn't from Dikranagerd. She was from Kharpert, another ancient city that was the caravan stop before Dikranagerd if you were heading deeper into Asia, or the one after if you were heading in the other direction toward Europe. It is not a long journey between the two cities—less than fingertip to first knuckle on a wall map—but it was far enough in the old days of the old country to nurture and preserve each city's dialect and distinct cultural flavor.

So my mother, it turned out, was the product of a mixed marriage: Half Dikranagerdtsi, half Kharpertsi. I didn't know this at the time of my childhood visits to Emmeh's house, which is just as well because I wouldn't have known what to make of it. But I did know that Emmeh was the living link to my mother's childhood. On one visit, we even took a five-mile-or-so detour to Mom's hometown of Chelsea, a pug dog of a city just north of Boston on the shore of the Mystic and Chelsea Rivers. I don't remember much except old, narrow houses crowded along old, narrow streets. We stopped at one house and visited some Armenians. I don't know if they were relatives or friends, but it was a dark, old-people's house that smelled like onions. The floors were covered in reddish-purple puddles of worn oriental rugs, and the end tables were covered with yellowed doilies. I could tell, even at that age, that Chelsea was not a rich place, and not a place I was eager to visit again.

I've searched my memory for other remnants of our visits to Somerville and Chelsea. Mom told me so little about her parents and her childhood that the tiniest scrap of memory seems like an important discovery, particularly if it seems to shed light on Grandpa Bichakjian. For most of my life, he was as removed from my consciousness as any other long-gone ancestor, but I realize now that he is the lynchpin of family history on both sides. It was Grandpa Harry Bichakjian who enjoined Grandpa Harry Kalajian in the great enterprise that carried them both to New Jersey and that led in turn to my father meeting my mother that day in 1928 after his arrival in America. From the little my mother told me about her father, and the bits I've pieced together since, Harry Bichakjian was a man of admirable courage, vision, ingenuity, and determination, all betrayed by truly rotten luck.

What I know for sure is that he was a hard-working man whose struggle to eke out a living by satisfying other people's hunger left little time for telling his children stories even if he'd been so inclined, which seems doubtful. He acknowledged that his parenting time was meager by lining his children up once a year and slapping each one across the face.

"This is for everything you did that I didn't know about," he'd say. "Don't do it again."

My father was able to vouch for this because he arrived for that first visit to the Bichakjian home just in time for Grandpa's annual slap fest. It didn't matter that Dad wasn't part of the family; he got whacked along with the rest.

My mother's knowledge of her father was mostly limited to what she observed when he was done with the day's cooking, serving, cleaning, and other chores. He would sit quietly in his chair in the family's gas-lit living room and chain-smoke hand-rolled cigarettes until he was ready for bed. He did not take a day off when he was sick, because he couldn't afford to. When he got a toothache, he sat in his smoking chair and slowly worked the rotting tooth loose with his pocket knife. Then he packed the empty socket with cigarette ashes to stanch the bleeding. Grandpa's life was not entirely grim, however. When the family moved to New Jersey, they discovered the wonders of electric power, which included radio. Grandpa used to laugh at *Amos 'n' Andy*. He sang his own words to the Pepsodent toothpaste jingle:

"Apsodent, tapsodent . . . apsodent, tapsodent . . ."

Uncle Mike, the younger of my mother's two brothers, left me one other mental image of Grandpa. He remembered his father going outside in freezing weather without a coat, time after time. Grandpa said the cold didn't bother him. Maybe that was true, or maybe he couldn't afford a coat. He was hauling the trash out to the curb one snowy night when a policeman spotted him and hauled Grandpa down to the station. The policeman could see that any man wearing shirtsleeves on a night like this had to be crazy—and on top of that, this guy was talking gibberish. Clearly, the cop did not speak Armenian, but someone at headquarters must have because Grandpa was soon escorted home, still in shirtsleeves.

Grandpa did pass along a few hard-earned lessons from his years of working in restaurant kitchens: Never order anything covered with gravy, because gravy is mostly fat, plus it can hide the taste of rotten meat. Never order the hamburger, because you don't know what's been ground up into it, including very possibly some else's half-eaten hamburger. Never order bread pudding, because it was probably made from scraps of bread other customers left behind.

My mother did mention one other thing: Grandpa always cooked pork chops for dinner on Friday. I've thought about whether there's some meaning in this. It could have been a symbolic thumb in the eye of the Muslim Turks, who are forbidden to eat pork. It could have been a joke on his Catholic neighbors, who ate no meat at all on Fridays. Or, maybe Grandpa just liked pork chops.

This was very nearly the sum of my knowledge of Harry Bichakjian as of 1988, when my mother died, except for one seemingly small matter that made little impression until much later, when I began researching this book. Mom had shared Grandpa's advice: "See America." Mom said her father had taken a trip out West and was struck by its beauty. The landscape of mountains and deserts dwarfed anything he'd seen between Kharpert and Chelsea. He even saw Buffalo Bill's wild west show. It was the greatest theatrical spectacle in an age of great theatrical spectacles because it featured real Indians and real cowboys and real horse soldiers reenacting the epic struggle for the American West. These almost qualified as current events in Grandpa's day—he was about twenty years old when the Indian Wars reached their bloody climax at Wounded Knee—but it was ancient history to me. When I heard this as a boy, I assumed Grandpa had simply taken a vacation. It didn't occur to me that this would be extraordinary in a family that still didn't go anywhere more than a four-hour car ride from home. I tucked the information deep in the folds of my brain and never thought of it again until I began sorting out the scraps and snapshots I'd culled from all the folders, boxes, and envelopes my mother left behind. Remarkably, the deepest treasure of clues about Grandpa Bichakjian was left not by Mom but by her brother, Uncle Mike, who died two years after she did.

It's remarkable because Uncle Mike did not appear to be a sentimental man. I asked him soon after my mother died to help me identify the cousins and uncles and aunts in her photos. "Why?" he responded. "They're all dead. Just throw it all away." He was serious, as I discovered when I asked him a second time a few months later. "Didn't you hear me? Throw it all away!"

But to my good fortune, Uncle Mike did not throw all of his own mementos away. He left behind a box containing his high school yearbook, a collection of photos from his Army years, a handful of snapshots of his various nieces and nephews, plus a scattering of the family's vital documents, including his father's certificate of citizenship:

To all people to whom these presents shall come, Greeting.

KNOW YE, that at a session of the Lynn Police Court, holden at Lynn, within said County of Essex, on fourteenth day of October A.D., one thousand nine hundred and four, Harootin Bechakjian of Lynn in said County of Essex, born in Harpoot, Turkey, having produced the evidence, and taken and subscribed the oath required by law, and the affidavits of the petitioner and of his witnesses, required by Section 39, of an Act of the Congress of the United States approved March 3, 1903, entitled "An Act to Regulate the Immigration of Aliens into the United States" having been duly made and recorded, was admitted to become a Citizen of the United States of America, according to the Acts of Congress in such case made and provided, and the laws of the Commonwealth of Massachusetts.

The date jumped out at me: 1904, exactly one hundred years before I started trying to puzzle all this out. I wondered just how entrenched Grandpa was in his new American identity when he pledged allegiance at Lynn, Massachusetts. I picked up more than a few hints from scraps that even Uncle Mike was unaware his father had dropped along the way, the sort of scraps we're all dropping around us now without a second thought: census forms, address books, even Grandpa's First World War draft registration. It is amazing what you can dig out when you have thirty years of skill as a journalist. It is even more amazing that anyone with a desktop computer and a credit card can dig out far more—and dig it out in a flash. The only skill I really needed was the ability to type sixteen digits and press "enter."

Without so much as swiveling in my seat, I time traveled back to 1887, when Grandpa Bichakjian landed in America. Did he just up and decide one day to make a new home in a new place in the New World? Was he the adventurer I never was, a young man who heard the call of the road and followed it? I don't know, but I do know there were good reasons for an Armenian in the 1880s to think about a life outside the suffocating confines of the Ottoman Empire. The most obvious is that for the first time in centuries of isolation, there was something very real and tantalizing to think about. Europeans, even Americans, were suddenly everywhere in historic Armenian provinces, opening schools and preaching the Gospel from Protestant pulpits. Preaching Christianity to the world's oldest Christian nation may seem like preaching capitalism to Republicans, but it carried a distinct advantage over trying to convert the Muslim population: It was not punishable by death. Many Armenians turned into enthusiastic converts, while even the less fervent seized the opportunity to learn everything they could from these willing teachers and their books. The missionaries opened a window that allowed Armenians to see the world outside, while the world outside could now see the Armenians.

The Reverend Henry Fanshawe Tozer wrote *Turkish Armenia* in 1881 about his travels across the Armenian highlands, including a visit to Kharpert, then a hotbed of Protestant activism. Tozer described a city that sat on a cliff a thousand feet above a broad plain dotted with hundreds of villages hemmed by the Murad and Euphrates Rivers and stretching about fifteen miles south to the Taurus Mountains. The villagers were overwhelmingly Armenian, while the city was mostly populated by Turks. Atop the cliff face at the entrance to the city stood the ruins of an ancient castle that had been fought over by Crusaders. In spring, Tozer wrote, the view from the heights was a vast carpet of green so rich and vibrant that natives believed it encompassed the Garden of Eden. Tozer's host was an American missionary identified as Dr. Barnum, who lived and preached in Kharpert. Barnum pointed to a spot in the distance and announced that "just where that village stands you may believe that Adam first saw the light."

Why would anyone leave such a place? Tozer's travelogue was published the same year as Raffi's *The Fool*, the stirring, searing account of Armenian impotence under Turkish rule. While the missionaries called Armenians to prayer, Raffi and others were calling them to arms. It was a lot for a young man to think about. I think the one safe guess about Grandpa Bichakjian is that he was no fool. At seventeen, he must have seen that his choices were to cower, tilt at windmills, or make a bold leap.

I know nothing about his family's circumstances, because I know nothing about his family except that a *bichakji* was a knife maker, which hints that they were hardly nobility. But the extent of Western presence in Kharpert suggests that he was at least exposed to the missionaries. He might well have attended a Protestant school, even learned to speak and read a little English. Perhaps it was Dr. Barnum who told him about America, land of opportunity, and pointed the way. There's really no telling which way that was. Did Grandpa simply head south along the Diyarbakir Road, or west toward Istanbul, sharpening knives and saving pennies until he reached a port? Or did he sign on for missionary work, or join someone's army? Somewhere along the way, he learned his new trade as a cook. Did he find work in a kitchen—or, a ship's galley? He never told anyone, at least not anyone who lived long enough to tell me.

I only know the year he arrived in America, as noted by a census taker long afterward: 1887. Grover Cleveland was in the middle of his first presidency; Queen Victoria was in the fiftieth year of her reign. The entire population of this country was only about sixty million, and there were just thirty-eight states. North Dakota, South Dakota, Montana, Washington, Idaho, Wyoming, Utah, Oklahoma, New Mexico, Arizona, Alaska, and Hawaii all followed Grandpa Bichakjian into the United States. My grandfather, it turned out, arrived on the American scene before the airplane, the automobile, the motion picture, the ice cream cone, the Hershey Bar, or the first pizzeria. More than half of America's history has occurred since he stepped ashore. Just reading that paragraph back to myself makes me feel like a son of pioneers.

The first record I could find of Grandpa Bichakjian in America was in the Chelsea, Massachusetts, business directory of 1899, under Boarding Houses, between Bakelmann Anna and Billiard Joseph: "Bichakjian Harry, 233 Walnut." Bravo, Grandpa! Running a boardinghouse is quite an accomplishment for a Kharpertsi who'd been in America for just twelve years. Everything I knew about Grandpa fit perfectly in and around Boston, city of immigrants and center of the largest Armenian population in the United States at the turn of the twentieth century. He established a business there, became a citizen there, eventually got married and had children there.

So, of course, I expected to find him in Chelsea in the 1900 census. Instead, I found him in Visalia, California: "Bichakjian Harry, lodger. Born 1870. Turkey. Occupation Cook." I can't imagine a stranger detour, unless he'd gone back to Kharpert. Maybe, in a sense, he did just that. The fertile San Joaquin Valley, cradled by mountains that seemed close enough to touch, became a magnet for Armenians longing for a place to plant their apricots and figs and walnut trees. Fresno, about forty miles from Visalia, is now an indelible part of Armenian-American lore thanks to the writings of native son William Saroyan. But Saroyan's birth was still eight years away, and the Armenian migration to California had barely begun when the census taker came knocking at 517R Acequia Street on June 13, 1900.

Visalia's origins as a Gold Rush boomtown halfway between San Francisco and Los Angeles were still obvious then. Many of the buildings along the main street were the solid-block sort you'd expect in a prosperous county seat, but the street itself was dirt, and hitching posts outnumbered lamp-posts. Visalia was still very much a mining town where cowboys whooped it up at the end of a long cattle drive. There was money to be made on the railroad, too, legitimate and otherwise. One of the famous train-robbing Dalton Gang was captured nearby in 1891 after a heist and remained locked up in the Visalia jail until someone slipped him a hacksaw blade.

Grandpa must have chugged into town on these same tracks and, somehow—did he actually read a newspaper?—figured out there was a room for rent at the home of Ricardo Mattlee, a saddle maker of great enough renown to be Google-able all these years later. Mattlee, then fifty, had come from Mexico as a young man with a valuable skill. His specialty was carving saddle trees, the forked part of the saddle, from solid oak. He and two partners founded the Visalia Saddle Company in 1869. By the turn of the century, the company had been sold and moved its headquarters to San Francisco, but Mattlee was still living in Visalia with two grown stepchildren and the family's Armenian boarder. Was Grandpa their cook? No telling. There's no telling about any of it. Not about why Grandpa went to California, nor about how he picked Visalia. Not about what he did once he got there, except cook. The only other telling information on the census form is that Grandpa answered "yes" when asked if he could read and write and also claimed he could speak English. He must have spoken enough, at least, to get by in an old cow town in the American West where his neighbors were mostly farmhands and fellow immigrants from places like Mexico and China.

I could not picture Grandpa in such a place, so I called my cousin Ed Murachanian, knowing he could at least picture Grandpa. Ed had the distinction of being the oldest living grandson of Harry Bichakjian until he passed away in 2010. He was twenty-four years older than I am, old enough to remember visiting Grandpa in the Bichakjian family's apartment in Union City. He even remembered Grandpa's storefront restaurant. Their last visit was probably not long before Grandpa died in 1935, when Ed was seven. He remembered that Grandpa, ebullient at seeing his grandson, gave him a dime. But did he remember anything about Grandpa heading west and living in Visalia, California?

"California? You're kidding! I never heard anything like that. Never."

Two weeks later, Ed and I sat down and compared notes on our grandfather. It didn't take long. I gave him copies of the papers Uncle Mike left, including Grandpa's 1904 citizenship certificate. We know Grandpa's stay in Visalia was over by then, and Ed knew a few things that helped fill in what happened after that. Most important: Ed's mother, Mary, was born in 1908 in Chelsea, so we know Grandpa was married by then, probably in 1906 or '07.

Whom did he marry?

Grandpa Harry Bichakjian and his long-nameless
first bride, Rosa Goshdigian, about 1906.

One of Ed's few mementos of Grandpa was his wedding picture. The bride, Ed's grandmother, appears slender and tall for a turn-of-the-century Armenian. She is wearing a white gown with a wispy train. Her hair is pinned up, her eyes focused dead ahead, her lips tight and straight so she gives no hint of emotion. There is no caption, no note, no date on the picture. The bride's name was lost. "I never heard anyone mention it," Ed said. Within a year or two of the wedding, Grandpa's bride was lost along with her name:

Boston, April 12—The greatest fire that has visited any part of the Boston metropolitan district in ten years devastated the manufacturing, tenement, and retail business sections of Chelsea, a suburb of this city, today, burning over more than one square mile of territory and leveling many of the city's best structures and making 10,000 persons homeless.—New York Times, 1908

Gale-force winds transformed an unremarkable Sunday-morning rag-shop blaze into Chelsea's version of the Chicago Fire. Flames were lifted high above the city and hurled down onto rooftops blocks away. Fire departments from Boston and surrounding towns could not outrace the spreading blaze. Chelsea's old wooden tenements dissolved into ash, one after another.

The Bichakjian family home at 107 Walnut Street was directly in the path of the spreading flames. Cousin Ed had been told that Grandpa survived along with his infant daughter, but Ed's grandmother did not. I never heard a word about any of this from my mother, but that raised no suspicion about the story's authenticity. Without ever having met my grandfather, I knew he would see no reason to talk about it. What happened, happened. So move on. Start over. With Armenians, history begins today.

But I was curious about the photo of the nameless bride. So I sent a request to the Massachusetts state archives for the record of Mary Bichakjian's birth, assuming it would include her mother's name. It did: Rosa Goshdigian Bichakjian. The same repository also yielded the record of Rosa Bichakjian's death. I called Ed to tell him I'd solved the century-old mystery of his grandmother's name but had uncovered a family fib in the process.

Rosa did not die in the Chelsea fire. She died two years after that, in a state charity hospital, of tuberculosis. She was twenty-seven and had been ill for more than a year. The trauma is impossible to comprehend. Tuberculosis was the scourge of poor immigrants, a shame and a curse as much as a disease. No wonder it was kept quiet, even long after its victims were gone. Poor Rosa must have died miserably, isolated and separated from her baby and her husband. Then she was nearly forgotten, along with the cause of her death.

At forty years old and half a lifetime from Kharpert, Grandpa started over again in America with no home, no wife, and a baby daughter to care for. But he certainly wasn't left alone. There were other Bichakjians in the area by then, although who they were and how they were related to Grandpa is a mystery. There were plenty of other Armenians, too, so he would have found help with the baby and been welcome to share someone's kebab, at least from time to time. More than likely, he made the kebab—a good cook could always find work, and a hard-working man with an employable skill would have little trouble finding another wife among the many Armenian families in the Boston area.

Grandpa's marriage to Horopsooma Nalbandian—Hormoush or Hormeeg to her Dikranagerdtsi family, Rose to the Americans—was probably arranged over a steaming bowl of lamb and okra. She was in her late twenties, the oldest of three sisters. The register of their wedding revealed a detail that heightened my suspicion that Grandpa spent time in the company of Kharpert's missionaries. The wedding ceremony was performed on February 25, 1911, in Chelsea—not by an Armenian priest, but by Charles N. Thorp, minister of the city's First Congregational Church. I never met my grandmother, but I knew her sisters and they were definitely not Protestants. So I can only assume the minister was either a convenience or he was Grandpa's choice. I'll never know for sure, but it may be that my grandfather brought a new religion with him to the New World.

Rose and Harry's first child, my mother, was born in 1912. Two more children had come along by 1918, when Grandpa left a couple more scraps for me to pick up all these years later. He showed up in the Chelsea business directory once again, this time as proprietor of a lunchroom at 44 Heard Street, which was also the family's address. They must have lived upstairs from the family business. He also showed up at the local draft board to register that September. He was noted as having gray hair and blue eyes. *Blue eyes.* Now I understand why my mother made a point of telling me when I got married not to jump to conclusions if my wife had a blue-eyed baby. There is no birth date listed, but the registrar apparently accepted his age as forty-seven, too old to be much use to the military.

At last, it seems Grandpa was settled. He had a business again, a new wife and a growing family in a growing Armenian community. But this is the story of an Armenian family, so nothing remains settled for long. By 1920, when the census was taken again, just about everyone on both sides of my family except for my father was living in Chelsea. Harry Bichakjian and his family were still at 44 Heard Street, but he listed his occupation as boardinghouse cook. Had he closed the lunch room, or was this a side job? My guess is the lunchroom had closed and he was cooking at the boardinghouse where the man who was eventually to become my other grandfather lived while working in a nearby shoe factory. That must be where Harry Bichakjian and Harry Kalajian cooked up their business scheme, when the factories started shutting down and the Armenians of Chelsea were suddenly lost in the world again. Sometime in the early 1920s, the Bichakjians and Harry Kalajian joined yet another caravan of Armenian refugees, this time to Hudson County, New Jersey.

I don't know exactly how many Bichakjians made the move. I know Mom's sister Mary did because my mother told me so. Mom always spoke with a special and sweet sadness about her older sister—she never said "half-sister." I knew and remembered Mom's brothers, John and Mike, and their younger sister, Ann, but the 1920 census lists another brother, Antranik, little more than a year old then. He did not live long enough to be counted again in 1930. I'd never heard a word about him from anyone. Mary stayed with the family for a while after the move, but she was only fourteen when she married Dick Murachanian, a Dikranagerdtsi nearly twice her age. With Mary gone, the responsibility of keeping house and tending the kids fell to my mom after her mother died of cancer in 1926 at age forty-six.

A widower again, Grandpa was in his late fifties, but he had one more adventure left. He sailed to Cuba to marry for the third and final time. His new wife was one of thousands of Armenian refugees stranded there when the United States tightened immigration quotas in the 1920s. The marriage was a contrivance that allowed the woman to enter the United States as the wife of an American citizen. I don't know what Grandpa received other than a free trip to Cuba. He brought my mother a souvenir: a green, red, and white brooch handmade of painted wood in the exaggeratedly oblong shape of a woman's head, with tufts of string for hair. It looks like a caricature of Carmen Miranda. It is the only memento even remotely related to Grandpa's final, nameless bride, who went straight off to her own family without so much as stopping by for a slice of apricot pie. My mother never told me who the woman was.

Cousin Ed was born in 1928, the third of Mary Bichakjian Murachanian's three children. He told me Mary became pregnant for a fourth time in 1935, but she and the baby both died during labor. She had lived to the same age as her mother, twenty-seven. Grandpa Bichakjian died three months later, on Oct. 16, 1935. His death certificate was among the papers Uncle Mike left behind. It lists Grandpa's age as sixty-three years, eleven months, and six days.

Was he really born Nov. 10, 1871? I figure that's close enough. The transcript from the record of deaths in the County of Hudson, volume 23, page 22, burial number 11093, sums up Grandpa like this: widowed, white, chef. Birthplace: Armenia. Cause of death: congestive cardiac failure and pulmonary emphysema/broncho pneumonia. Grandpa died in Christ Hospital in Jersey City. I was born in the same hospital a little more than sixteen years later. The bill for Grandpa's funeral at William Schlem Inc. in Union City, New Jersey, was made out to my mother. It came to $194.20, including $1.24 tax. Grandpa was buried with Grandma in Grove Church Cemetery in North Bergen, New Jersey. Mom paid $100 for the headstone in April 1936.

Grandpa Bichakjian eventually had eight grandchildren, most born after he was gone. I think he deserves to have them listed in a book, so here they are. Mary Bichakjian Murachanian's children: Anne, John, and Edward. Ann Bichakjian Arcelli's children: Gilbert, Diane, Patricia, and John. Plus me, Sylvia Bichakjian Kalajian's son, Douglas Harry Kalajian. Harry Bichakjian's first grandson, John Murachanian, deserves a special note for his sacrifice to the nation that Grandpa adopted for all of us who followed: He was a boatswain's mate aboard the destroyer USS *Twiggs* when it was blown apart by a Japanese suicide bomber during the Battle of Okinawa in 1945.

I wish I'd thought more about Grandpa when I was younger, when I could have tried harder and pestered more people for answers, even though it's doubtful I'd have had much luck. Cousin Ed tried but he wasn't any more successful. He followed up our initial conversation with a call to his sister, Anne Sargisoff, who was a few years older. She remembered hearing about Grandpa's Western adventure, but she didn't want to talk about it, or about him.

"She said everything about that time is too sad," Cousin Ed told me. "It stirs up too many sad memories. It's the first time I remember her getting angry with me."

That is very Armenian, very much like my father and Uncle Mike and all the rest: Don't ask. Forget it. Move on. It all makes sense, in a sad and frustrating way. You really can't look back unless you are standing still, and Armenians can't afford to stand still. I will have to be content with what I know about Grandpa Bichakjian and with my own musings about him. I picture him at a wood-burning stove in the kitchen of an old house on a dirt street in Visalia, California, working by lamplight on a dark winter morning. It is not quite dawn, dusty and cold outside but warm inside now that the fire is roaring. He slides the first, flat tray of lavash into the oven, then carries a steaming pot of fresh coffee to the wooden table. He pours a cup for himself and a cup for an older, weather-lined Mexican. The coffee scalds him as he pours, and Grandpa lets out a stream of Kharpertsi curses. Ricardo Mattlee laughs, and so does Grandpa. The Armenian cook and the Mexican saddle maker sit and sip and share stories about the Near East and the Wild West.

Neither understands much of what the other says, and that's fine with both of them.

And it's fine with me that there are millions of immigrant stories like Grandpa Bichakjian's: hard life, hard luck, died poor. I have fallen in love with this guy, this barrel-chested old cook in a white, short-sleeve shirt who baked apricot pies and pulled his own teeth and chain-smoked hand-rolled cigarettes as he listened to *Amos 'n' Andy*. I love him because he was born in midair, like all Armenians, but he did not wait to hit bottom. I believe Grandpa stood amid the ruins of that castle on the heights of Kharpert and looked down at the Garden of Eden before God turned his back and let the Turkish devils cast the Armenians out of Paradise. I believe he looked out across the Euphrates River, breathed the blessed air of Armenia, and decided it was his time to leave.

I love my father and my father's father for all they endured, but I love Grandpa Harry Bichakjian for making up his own mind and setting his own course. I love him for coming to America not to seek refuge but to make his way. I love him for never punching a time card, never jumping at a factory whistle, for being his own boss; for being Harry Bichakjian, proprietor, and for being Harry Bichakjian, explorer, who wasn't content to find the other side of the world but who had to keep going and see what was on the other side of the other side.

The template for my image of Grandpa will always be his sister, Veron, my mother's Emmeh. I am nearly as curious about her as I am about her brother. I called her son, my mother's cousin George Parigian, before I started on this book, only to hear terrible news. His wife, Tillie, had died a few months before. I felt sad for him, but sad, too, that I hadn't kept in closer touch. I asked George if he knew much about his mother's early life and her family.

"She came here after your grandfather did," he said. "He already had the restaurant and she worked for him. She told me she used to carry bushels of apples up the stairs from the basement."

I could picture that. But when did she come to America? How did she get here? What did she remember about her parents—my great-grandparents?

"Oh, dear," he said. "I don't know any of that. I wish I did, but she never talked about any of those things. None of them did."

No, none of them did. The old Armenians kept their secrets, and none held them tighter than my grandfather and his sister.

THE UNCLE WHO DIDN'T
LEAVE A TRACE

My mother's younger sister, Ann, was Auntie Annie to me. Mom called her *kooroog*, which means "sister" in their dialect. Auntie Annie called my mother Mom, an inside joke that wasn't entirely humorous.

Auntie Annie was still a teenager when Grandpa Bichakjian died and my mother became her legal guardian. I'm certain they had a few mother-daughter spats after that. Auntie Annie even had to get Mom's signature when she joined the Women's Army Corps during the Second World War, and that couldn't have been easy. Auntie Annie sent her a Mother's Day card every year for the rest of Mom's life.

Although Mom was seven years older, they looked so much alike that it's sometimes hard for me to tell who's who in old photographs. When my cousin Diane was a baby, she cried if our mothers were both in the room because she couldn't tell which was hers. I'm sure there were many similarities beyond the resemblance, but I couldn't see them, possibly because Auntie Annie was so thoroughly Americanized. I never heard Armenian music at her house. Her coffee-table dishes were filled with potato chips and malted milk balls, not pistachios and *basturma*. She cooked ham for Christmas dinner, and she served it with plain white rice instead of bulgur pilaf. She never uttered a peep in Armenian that I heard.

Auntie Annie had even become a Catholic when she married Uncle Artie Arcelli. He was a pinball-machine repairman, which was the greatest thing I could imagine because he brought pinball machines home with him. They were the original video games back before there was video, and Uncle Artie's pinball machines were the best pinball machines in the world because you didn't have to put a quarter in them. He rigged them up to play for free, right in the basement of their house.

Despite being much younger, Auntie Annie beat her sister to motherhood by three years when my cousin Gilbert was born. Unlike Mom, Auntie Annie kept having kids. Diane, Patty, and John came along in several-year intervals. Visiting them was always fun, especially at Christmas, because the house was full of kids and toys and beeping, clanging, buzzing noises from the basement full of games. But it was also a peek at an alternate reality. I was surrounded by other grandchildren of Harry Bichakjian who displayed none of the traits or traditions that I associated with being Armenian. Diane was even harder for me to process because she had the fair hair and blue eyes of my mother's older half-sister sister, Mary, whom I'd never met.

Mom and her sister Ann each pose with the other's son. That's Gil at left in front of my mother.

Gil was just older enough that we never really became close, although he was the closest I came to having a big-brother figure. He not only grew up first, he grew up fast. After high school, Gil joined the Navy and soon got married and had kids. We lost touch years ago. Diane was just younger enough that she and I also weren't close as kids, but we became phone-and-e-mail friends in middle age. She was sweet and smart, a hard-working teacher of deaf children. I was heartbroken when she died unexpectedly at age forty-three, only a couple of years after Auntie Annie.

Looking back, I wonder if my fragile connection to my first cousins had more to do with cultural dissonance than age differential. I'm sure my Armenian father seemed stranger to them than their Italian-American father did to me. None of us ever met our common grandfather, and they certainly heard even less about him than I did.

What would his journey from Kharpert to America more than a century ago mean to them?

My closest connection to Mom's family was Uncle Mike, who shared my room when Mom and Dad brought me home from the hospital. After I literally kicked him out of bed, he found an apartment in the rear of a private home a mile or so from us in Guttenberg, a little city packed tighter than the unfiltered Chesterfields that Uncle Mike smoked. He didn't move out of that apartment until just before he died, when he was too sick to keep house.

Uncle Mike Bichakjian looking confident and happy
sometime between high school and the war.

Uncle Mike was a man of extraordinary fidelity to his circumstances and routine. He never considered moving to a larger place because he needed nothing more than his three, small rooms close to the bus line. He never bought a car because the bus took him where he needed to go. He never got married because—well, he never said, although I did ask. Questions didn't disturb Uncle Mike the way they disturbed my father, but he didn't exactly encourage them any more than he volunteered information. His reply to the marriage question was always the same: "What for?"

He didn't need anyone to cook for him because he could always eat dinner at the Berkshire, an old-style chrome-and-mirrors diner around the corner on Bergenline Avenue. He didn't need a menu because the waitresses all knew what he liked, or at least what he would eat—any meat with a potato, plus a cup of coffee. They also knew his cooking instructions: "Burn it." After dinner he walked home, sat on his couch, and read. He was the only adult I knew who read as much as my father, but you wouldn't know it from looking around his apartment. He had just one, two-shelf bookcase, and it wasn't nearly full. His habit was to read a book once and then give it away, often to me when I got older. "I don't want things," he'd say, and that was clearly so because he owned almost nothing except a few chairs, a green-granite coffee table, his bed, a small black-and-white TV, and an Emerson clock radio. He did have a refrigerator, but there was rarely anything in it. He cooked nothing but coffee.

He didn't need anyone to wash the floor or make the bed because he was scrupulously clean and almost obsessively neat. Whenever I visited him, even unexpectedly, his carpet was always vacuumed, his bed made, the bathroom scrubbed. The only house-cleaning demerit he deserved was for the ever-full ashtray by his side. He smoked so heavily that it never stayed empty for long no matter how often he dumped the ashes. Uncle Mike was so fastidious he even kept to a monthly shoeshine schedule, and he painted the apartment once a year. He let me help him paint once when I was little, and he said I got more paint on me than I got on the brush. It became a lifelong joke. He'd call me and say, "I'm painting the place next week, so stay away."

Uncle Mike lived alone but he was hardly a loner. He went out every weekend with Andy and Anita Avedisian. Andy was his best friend at Emerson High School, and they remained best friends ever after. Sometimes they were a threesome, but more often Andy stopped along the way to pick up whoever Uncle Mike was dating. Uncle Mike always had a girlfriend, but

I rarely caught a glimpse of one and he never, ever brought a woman to our house. His love life was off limits, even to me, but I knew he had one because plenty of people we knew ran into him and his dates at Fred's Restaurant in North Bergen, or up at Leo's in Englewood Cliffs. Uncle Mike wasn't fussy about the restaurant and he cared absolutely nothing about food. Any place was fine as long as it had a bar, and even the drinks were less important than the right crowd. He loved meeting people, finding out what they did and where they'd been. Uncle Mike knew an amazing array of athletes, business-men, and politicians. He met them all in bars, and he used to tell me about them. I grew up thinking that there must be nothing quite so exciting as drinking in bars, and once made the mistake of saying so to my father.

My father looked accusingly at my mother. "That's a nice idea your brother put in his head." He knew instantly he'd made a much bigger mis-take than I had.

"You leave my poor brother alone!"

Any criticism of Uncle Mike, no matter how mild, brought out the moth-er in my mother. After all, Uncle Mike was the boy she helped raise after their mother died. She instilled in me the idea that Uncle Mike could do no wrong, and she was correct in the strictest sense. As an adult, I stayed closer to Uncle Mike than to anyone on either side of my family except my parents. We spent long hours talking, often about books or about world events or human behavior. I remember him as truly literate and insightful, and a man of honor and honesty. Of course, he did nothing wrong. But what did he do right?

I never really got to know Uncle Mike well enough to understand if he was risk-averse or just uninterested in anything beyond his grasp, but he nev-er took a step—much less a leap—outside his comfortable routine. Unlike my father, who came back from the Army to start a business and a family, Uncle Mike went back to his job making jewelry in someone else's shop. He kept at it for the next forty-five years. I saw enough of his work to know he was a talented man, but he was satisfied lending his talent to others. Maybe he recoiled from the example of his father, my bold and enterprising grandpa who worked his way from Kharpert to Massachusetts to California and died broke. I see Grandpa as heroic in the Armenian sense: Losing a battle does not diminish the effort. But I didn't grow up in a cold-water flat or tumble out of the family nest into a world convulsed by Depression and war. I did not grow up in fear of anything, including failure, but Uncle Mike did. He left his clues in a shallow bundle of cards and letters he wrote to his first cousin Lucy Tekijian DeVita. Aunt Lucy, as I called her, was sister-close to Uncle Mike and my mother. I am indebted to her for many things, especially her failure to follow Uncle Mike's instructions to destroy his correspondence. On May 3, 1942, Pfc. Michael Bichakjian, 1st Platoon, Battery C., 14th Battalion, Field Artillery Replacement Center, wrote to relay a conversation he'd had with a fellow recruit:

"I spoke up and said the very thing I have been saying since I got out of high school. At that time I amazed my friends with my utter disconcern for the future. I felt at that time that sooner or later we would have a war and all my dreams and plans would crumble. Well to get back, he said 'we are the lost generation—born in wartime, raised in poverty, finished our schooling in time to enter the business field to find a depression and then just as it began to seem as though we were at last on the road to wealth and happiness we find ourselves in the Army.'"

How sad, really, and how unlike the man I thought I knew when I was growing up. He was an uncle straight out of the movies, a guy who always arrived with a smile, a funny story, and a present: a cap pistol, a fire truck, a race car. He even seemed amused rather than annoyed by my genius for destroying every toy within minutes. He'd bounce me on his knee while singing his own funny words to songs he learned at the Italian club in Union City: "Boomba-doomba, doomba-doom." Uncle Mike was so at ease with all kinds of people that he'd spend hours at that club with his pals, drinking and laughing at the stories told by old men in Italian. They never suspected he didn't understand a word.

My image of Uncle Mike in his forties and fifties—strong, funny, and easy to talk to—fits perfectly with the image that emerges from his high school yearbook. The January 1934 edition of *The Altruist* notes that Michael "Mendo" Bichakjian, business student and varsity football star, was selected Class Physique. His initials were comically interpreted as standing for Mighty Boisterous. His favorite expression: "Don't jerk me around." His chosen career path: "Michael intends to become a certified public accountant. His commercial course, especially bookkeeping, will help."

It was a practical aspiration typical of a class full of working-class Italians, Jews and other assorted ethnic kids. Mike and his friend Andy had plenty of Armenian company, too, judging by the class roster: Deroian, Kochakian, Jamgochian, Kazanjian, Mardirosian—even a Kalajian. The Genocide wasn't history for these kids. They were the children or even the younger brothers and sisters of survivors, so they heard the stories from primary sources. Along with his own yearbook, Uncle Mike kept one from the class that graduated when he was a freshman. In it, amid tales of glory on the football field and high jinks at the prom, Vergen Boyajian—business student, member of the glee club, recipient of both the typing award and a perfect attendance certificate—told the story of her parents' murder in Dikranagerd at the hands of Turks, and of her miraculous survival:

"They tried to frighten us by saying that they would not kill us by just chopping our heads off, but would first take our finger nails, then cut off our fingers, one by one, take off our arms and feet and so on, until we would be almost dead, then they would chop our heads off. This beastly talk did not move one hair on us, and we still preferred death. Then they took a girl and me, laid us on our backs near the stream, and held the swords at our necks. They talked to each other for a while in Turkish and finally decided not to kill us because they thought we would become Turks if we lived long enough. This surely was the Almighty's hand that delivered us from the Turks."

What did the Americans think of this girl who tumbled off the pages of the *Arabian Nights* straight into the halls of Emerson High? I wonder if Uncle Mike and his buddies talked about the tragedy that displaced their families and deposited them in this strange place called Union City, New Jersey. My guess is they tried not to think about such things. They almost certainly never talked to each other in Armenian, at least not in public in a time when being an immigrant was a shame and a burden. I suspect this weighed heavily on Uncle Mike because I can't think of any other reason that he kept the Armenian world at arm's length for as long as I knew him.

I know he spoke Armenian but I never heard a word of it come out of his mouth. He never went to Armenian affairs, not even a church bazaar. I believe he tried very hard to fit in all the time he was growing up, and he succeeded so well that he could hardly have changed after that. Uncle Mike must have been the first person in our family to hold a football, and he won a place as starting right halfback on the Emerson High School team that went 5-3, including a season-finale triumph over archrival Union Hill. As the yearbook recorded: "The record of that game will forever show that Mike Bichakjian starred in some fancy groundwork and that Zuccaro, Bichakjian and Romano played the last and best of their high school games."

That's an inspiring note to graduate on, but what did Uncle Mike graduate to? He was already apprenticed at his brother-in-law Dick Murachanian's jewelry shop. I wonder if his plans to study accounting ever progressed beyond schoolyard chatter. I'd bet he never discussed them with his father, because it's clear what Grandpa would have said: "That's enough school." Grandpa was in the last year of his life by the time Uncle Mike finished high school. His heart was too weak for work, and the Depression was at its depth. So Uncle Mike could hardly turn away from a reliable craft that he was well on the way to mastering. At least he had company. His brother, John, three years older, was already working full time in the same shop. Their work was about the only interest the Bichakjian boys had in common.

Mike was athletic, outgoing, popular. John was a bookworm who grew increasingly distant from everyone he grew up with. The cousins who remember him today remember him from the early 1940s, when he rarely left the family apartment except to go to work but could still be persuaded to chat with visitors if the topic was about anything or anyone except John Bichakjian. He considered even the blandest inquiry about his well-being an intrusion and didn't hesitate to say so. He eventually became so withdrawn that the elder cousin of the clan, Peter Doramajian, paid him a visit to ask what was wrong. Uncle John's reaction bordered on irrational. He not only told his cousin where to go, he wrote a letter to the editor of the local paper urging people to keep their noses out of other people's business. Hardly anyone stopped by to see him after the letter was published.

Uncle Mike had his mysterious aspects, but Uncle John went on to lead an entirely mysterious life. He lived alone, somewhere in New York City. That's all I ever knew until he died. He appeared twice a year throughout my childhood, at our house on Easter and at his other sister's, my Aunt Annie's, on Christmas. Uncle John took the bus no matter the weather, refusing all offers of a ride. He was friendly to me, but not nearly uncle-friendly. More like distant-relative friendly. No bouncing, no funny stories, no Italian songs. He'd just sit in one place, chatting with my father and Uncle Mike. Both understood and respected the ground rules: no personal questions. My father certainly couldn't object to that.

Uncle John always brought me gifts but never the blinking-shooting-buzzing sort that Uncle Mike brought. The only fun thing Uncle John ever gave me was a cannibal-head coin bank made out of a coconut, a souvenir of his trip to Florida when I was four or five years old. Mostly he brought books, except one time when I was seven he gave me the greatest present ever. He gave me his typewriter, a black Remington Portable Model 5 that looked so old even then that Charles Dickens might have used it to type *Great Expectations*. Uncle John didn't explain why he gave it to me, but I was thrilled. I was just starting to take piano lessons, so striking keys with my fingers seemed normal, except that these keys were many times harder to press than any piano's, and my fingers hurt whenever I managed to crash into one hard enough to make an impression. But the great, metallic splash that echoed up from the Remington's belly with each successful stroke sounded so much like applause for a job well-done that I wanted to hear more. My mother helped me carry my new treasure upstairs the next day to show Dad's cousin Anne Sarkisian. Anne, a secretary, showed me how to load the paper, spool the ribbon, set the margins. Most important, she gave me my first typing lesson. I pestered her constantly after that for more. I'm sure I was the only kid at Horace Mann School who could touch-type by the end of third grade.

My antics apparently didn't amuse my serious and mysterious Uncle John.

I wondered, though: Why did Uncle John have a typewriter? "Uncle John was a writer," my mother explained. I got nothing else from her then, but she told me more when I was older. Uncle John spent a good deal of the Second World War in the living room typing while Uncle Mike and all the cousins were in the Army. Uncle John had been rejected by every branch of the service. If my mother knew why, she didn't say, but Uncle John was clearly depressed about it. His withdrawal turned into near total isolation. He just typed and typed. He was apparently no more interested in sharing his writing than in sharing his feelings. Nobody ever saw any of it, Mom said. She was wrong about that. When Uncle Mike died, he left behind a slim folder of Uncle John's papers—his birth certificate, a few insurance receipts, and a single, yellowed clipping from an English-language Armenian newspaper:

> *Ephemeral*
> by John Bichakjian
> *Fading vision of faulty memory*
> *True loveliness must needs pale;*
> *Fearful, when the mind does fail*
> *And no imagery over haze prevail,*
> *Then, cold shadows within unfold,*
> *For fleeting instant what mind would hold,*
> *Vision sweet, with tender grace and gentle mold.*

By the time I came along, Uncle John had apparently written everything he had to write. I like to think that when he gave me the typewriter, he was saying, "OK, it's your turn. See if you can do any better." (I've done this much, Uncle John: I got you published again.) He gave me just one bit of advice about writing, and it's one I still follow: "Use the name Douglas, never Doug. You'll get more respect."

Uncle John had packed away his typewriter and moved out of the Bichakjian household about the time the rest of the clan came back from the war. He was still making jewelry when I was growing up, but he eventually quit and went to work in a factory assembling electronics parts. Uncle Mike said he didn't know why, and there was no point asking. Uncle John's visits became less regular around this time, late in my teens. He started to skip one holiday or the other, and sometimes he skipped entire years, but he made one extraordinary, nonholiday trip to see me in summer 1971. I was nineteen years old and miserable, aching night and day from a duodenal ulcer. The doctor prescribed a bland diet—nothing spicy, nothing fried, lots of cream cheese and milk—but it brought no relief.

Uncle John, to my surprise, insisted he knew better than the doctor. He showed up with an armful of paperback books, including *Let's Eat Right to Keep Fit* by Adelle Davis and *Food Facts & Fallacies* by Carlton Fredericks. He also handed me a paper bag full of bottles containing various vitamins and supplements. Uncle John, I discovered, was a health-food advocate. Some people called them food faddists. My father called them health nuts, although only when my mother was out of the room. Uncle John's theory was that ulcers were not caused by acids and stress, as doctors then believed, but by poor nutrition and vitamin deficiencies. He prescribed a regimen of pills, powders, fruits, and vegetables. "Uncle John knows what he's talking about," Mom insisted. "Just look at him." He looked remarkably the same as ever. He was nearly sixty but looked closer to forty-five, still trim and with a full head of dark, glistening hair.

I decided Mom must be right, as usual, and I adopted Uncle John's vitamin-and-fiber routine. It didn't seem to help, but I didn't think it hurt either. The ulcer eventually faded away, and so did Uncle John. The electronics factory where he worked moved to the suburbs sometime in the 1970s, but Uncle John stayed behind in Manhattan. He didn't visit much at all after that, and I didn't know what he was doing until years later when I found the answer on his death certificate: He became a maintenance man at the Waldorf Astoria hotel. He was still employed there when he died alone in his apartment on West 44th Street in 1986 at age seventy-two. The cause was atherosclerotic cardiovascular disease. In other words, he had clogged arteries. So much for health food, I thought.

Uncle Mike had to go to the morgue in Manhattan to identify the body, even though there was no question who it was. Uncle John had been dead at least a couple of days before someone noticed he was missing and called the police, who found him slumped in a chair. New York Police Department Officer Thomas Mullin inventoried Uncle John's apartment and logged his worldly belongings on property clerk's invoice C297554:

$72 in cash

1 Timex white metal watch

1 white pearl-like necklace in suede pouch

1 room key

1 Two Dollar US Bill Numismatic

1 One Dollar Bill Numismatic
20 Foreign Currency Bills
468 Chase Manhattan Bank checks
1 Life Insurance Policy
1 Chase Manhattan Bank Card
1 St. Claire's Health Card
1 Birth Certificate

I wondered about the necklace. Was it a keepsake from his days as a jeweler, or perhaps something left behind in one of the hotel rooms? It seemed somehow discordant, the only vaguely personal item in Uncle John's store, but there was something much more personal that went unrecorded. Uncle John's sketchbook turned up a few years later in a box Uncle Mike left behind. The drawings appeared to be art-school homework—profiles, anatomies, a few movie-star portraits—nothing brilliant but not bad at all. Uncle John clearly had the eye and hand of an artist. Whether he had the imagination or the soul is another mystery. My guess is that he threw his most telling and personal work in the trash along with his writings.

For as long as Armenians have existed, enemies have tried to erase them from the planet. My Uncle John is the only Armenian I've ever known who erased himself.

THE TURKS WHO CAME
TO DINNER

It didn't strike me as odd that my father never cursed the Turks the way other Armenians did, because there were so many things my father didn't talk about at all.

I asked him why he listened to Turkish music. "I like it," he said, and that was all. Why wouldn't he like it? Turkish music was as familiar to him as rock 'n' roll was to me and my friends, and as relevant. Armenians who lived in Turkey wrote and sang what anyone else would call Turkish music, but it was as Armenian as they were. The deep, mournful resonance of the oud strings spoke to them in a transethnic language.

My father was no musician, but he had a real appreciation of the oud technique called *taksim*—improvisational yet highly disciplined—and a respect for the masters of the form. So it was natural that when two Turkish musicians came to visit Diyeh, my father's step-uncle, Dad went to meet them and listen as they played. I was old enough to stay home, so I did. Their music meant nothing to me.

My surprise came a few days later, when the same Turks came to our house. My father had invited them to dinner.

I don't remember much about them except that one was tall and the other wasn't. They both had mustaches. They wore suits. If I didn't know they were Turks, I'd have noticed nothing at all about them. They looked like anyone else. But to me, fifteen and full of anger, they hardly looked human. I could not believe my mother cooked Armenian food for Turks and served it to them on her best china. I asked to be excused, but my father told me to sit down and be polite to our guests. I tried. They spoke no English, but my father translated their greetings and compliments, which seemed pleasant enough. But I knew better. I knew about Turks and their flattery and their lies. Then one of the Turks turned to me and spoke. I didn't wait for the translation. I felt my throat close in anger. I threw my fork into my plate and ran upstairs. My father followed me.

I don't think I'd ever raised my voice to him before and I never did it again, but I screamed loud enough for everyone in the house to hear. He had no right to bring Turks into our house. No right to make my mother cook for them. No right to tell me to be polite to them.

My father didn't get angry. He tried to explain calmly that these men were guests and deserved to be treated the same as any other guests.

"But they're Turks," I shouted. "We hate Turks."

My father said the most shocking thing I've ever heard:

"I don't hate Turks."

I was so shocked that, without thinking, I blurted out the unmentionable:

"The Turks killed your mother!"

My father looked suddenly sad. "The Turk who killed my mother is dead. The Kurd who saved me killed him."

I felt ashamed, and I still do. I was so ashamed I couldn't speak, but my father finished the conversation for me. "You can hate people who do terrible things, but you can't hate someone who wasn't there and wasn't even born."

I looked at him, now more confused than angry.

"You can't hate an entire people," he said. "You may want to, but it doesn't make sense."

He left me alone to think about what he'd said. I still think about it, often.

THE TURKS WHO CAME
HOME TO STAY

I got over my aversion to the company of Turks after the dinner-table debacle with the musicians, not because of what my father said but what he did: He invited more Turks to our house.

The Turks who came most often were Yahya and Pembe Sengul and their three children. I knew Yahya because he was an upholsterer who worked for Greg Nedurian's father. He was a walking advertisement for unrestricted immigration, a genial hard worker and dedicated family man. I met Yahya's family because my father did something even more surprising than inviting Turks to dinner. He rented this young Turkish family our old home over the cleaning store.

Whenever an Armenian asked how he could do such a thing, Dad shrugged. "They need rooms, I need tenants." I know there was more to it. He liked Yahya, and my mother loved Pembe, who explained that her name meant pink in Turkish.

"It's the same in Armenian!" my mother exclaimed.

"No, that's Turkish," Dad corrected. "You don't speak Armenian. You speak Dikranagerdtsi."

Mom ended the argument with a hand flip.

"Never mind him," she said to Pembe. "We're going to be friends."

We all bonded so swiftly that moments later, I found myself holding Pembe's baby, a boy named Cengiz.

"Like Genghis Khan," my father explained with a grin.

I thought he was joking. Who would name a baby after Genghis Khan?

"To you, he was a monster," Dad said. "To them, he's a hero."

From then on, the Senguls, proud Turks, often served as lessons in differing cultural perspectives. Whenever Yahya stopped by for coffee, he'd relate his children's latest achievements at their mosque or their participation in parades and other cultural programs just as any other American parent might boast about his kids' glories in the Sunday school Christmas pageant or the Boy Scout Jamboree. My father used the opportunity to teach me that everyone has a right to be proud of his heritage. My mother found her own opportunities to teach Pembe a few lessons of her own.

"This is America," Mom would say whenever Pembe started to explain the role of the deferential Turkish wife. My mother urged her to get a driver's license, which she did, and the two of them often went out shopping together. When Pembe brought the kids to the house, Mom put out her usual lunch spread, including ham and cheese. My father was appalled.

"These people are Muslims. They can't eat ham."

"This is America," Mom replied. "They can eat whatever they want."

As it turned out, they wanted ham.

MY ARMENIA

I'd never seen a blue school bus before, and I don't think I've seen one since, but I'm sure about this one. I remember because it looked wrong. School buses were always yellow; at least, they were in 1958. I'm sure this one was yellow, too, when it was new and probably even when it was old, which it already was by the time I was born. Now someone had painted it a pale, chalky blue of the sort you see at the bottom of a dry swimming pool.

I'm sure of the year because I know that I was six years old when my parents decided it was unhealthy for me to spend another summer in their dry-cleaning store. Summer day camp was the obvious solution, but which camp? Mom and Dad did what moms and dads usually do: They asked friends for recommendations. I don't know if their Armenian friends had no suggestions or if the camps they recommended were inconvenient for one reason or another, but I do know my father turned to his pal Leon. Leon enthusiastically recommended the camp his own children attended, which is how I wound up on the Union City Jewish Community Center summer camp bus.

In addition to the Feldstein kids, I knew a few others from school so I had no trepidation about going. I was especially excited to be carrying my very first lunch box. It was plaid-painted metal with a matching Thermos bottle just big enough for one cup of soup. Mom packed a ham-and-Swiss sandwich (the only kind I'd eat) along with a foil-wrapped metal container of frozen liquid. It was supposed to be some sort of super ice that stayed solid longer than frozen water. The idea was to keep the sandwich cold, but it just made one side of the sandwich cold and soggy while the other side got dry and stiff. The outside of the lunch box sweated even more than I did as the

153

old bus chugged its way along Hudson Boulevard toward the highway. That bus ride was the first time I ever heard the song about ninety-nine bottles of beer on a wall. The beer was all spilled and swabbed long before we got to camp. It was a long ride up Route 23 to Wayne until we reached a clearing on a mud hole, one of the man-made lakes that were popular in the days before suburban swimming pools were common. I don't remember much about the look of the campsite, but I remember thinking it was wonderful. There was an arts-and-crafts hall, a wood shop, and even a real swimming pool, in addition to the lake. We played all the usual summer-camp games and climbed back on the bus that afternoon with barely enough energy to restock the musical beer shelf and knock all the bottles down again.

Rainy days meant a shorter ride, just to the JCC building in Union City. I remember nothing about the place except that it was gloriously noisy with all those kids jammed inside. We filled the time we would have spent swimming by listening to Jewish lore and learning Jewish songs. I joined right in. Why wouldn't I? The stories were interesting, and I liked the songs. At six, I knew even less about Jews than I did about Armenians, but I knew that these kids and I shared something in being somehow different from most of the other kids I knew. I fit in so well that first year that I went back the next summer, and the summer after that. I might have kept on going if I hadn't been the victim of reverse anti-Semitism. One day, a kid I barely knew asked me point-blank if I was Jewish. I said no. He said I didn't belong in his camp and told me to go home. A moment later, we were on the ground, flailing at each other. The counselor who broke us up took my side and gave the bully a stern lecture about tolerance, but I decided the other kid was right: I didn't belong there.

When I got home, I told my parents what happened and insisted I wanted-ed to go to an Armenian camp. My father smiled. I'm not sure now what it meant. Was he happy, or amused—or both? Either way, I got my wish. The next summer, when I was nine years old, my parents signed me up for two weeks at Camp Haiastan—Camp Armenia—in Franklin, Massachusetts. It was the official camp of the Armenian Youth Federation, the youth arm of the Armenian Revolutionary Federation. This was just after we formed our AYF Junior chapter at Sts. Vartanantz, so I felt like I belonged even before we got there. Better yet, a bunch of the kids from church were go-ing, too. Our parents caravanned their way from New Jersey to then-rural southern Massachusetts, not far from the Rhode Island border. It was a good four-plus-hours ride on the old thruways, even on a sleepy Sunday morning in July 1961. As soon as we passed through the camp gates, we tilted downhill as the car shuddered over a trail mix of dirt, gravel, and asphalt. We drove past a handful of tumbledown cabins that must have been tacked together before the Second World War. The grass was tall enough that a cow wouldn't have to stoop to eat lunch. I looked out the window of our Plymouth and wondered if it was too late to go back to the Jewish camp. A moment later, I was glad that it was.

Just beyond the old cabins at the top of the hill was a field full of people having a party. A band was playing Armenian music, and the dance line was in full *tamzara*. We had all the car windows open, of course, so the sweet, smoky smell of shish kebab and onions on the grill enveloped and beckoned us. I was instantly both hungry and excited, ready to jump out and grab a plate. I knew immediately that this was my camp, an Armenian camp, where the American kids wouldn't even have wanted to eat the food because it wasn't tuna fish and mayo on white bread. I was ready to hop out, but the caravan kept going past the picnic grounds and around a few more bends until we got to a parking lot at the bottom of the hill.

The music faded and the kebab smell gave way to the deep, lung-expanding scent of pine from the trees all around us. The ground, including the parking lot, was covered with crackling brown needles. We shuffled through them as we got out of the car, so we sounded as if we were doing a soft-shoe dance as we walked toward the whitewashed camp office to sign in. The rest of what I could hear reminded me of the Catskills: birds and buzzing insects and those weird screeching sounds that people who grow up with nature probably find comforting but that sounded to me like a thousand Studebakers with bad fan belts. To a kid who grew up breathing bus fumes and listening to tire chains clanking all night, this was going to be a big adjustment, and it was going to come quickly. Our parents were eager to start the long drive home, so they left as soon as we'd received our bunk assignments. Sunday was always a free day at camp—no organized activities until evening, and no schedule except for meals—so we soon found ourselves in a strange place with nothing to do but look around and wonder what we'd gotten into.

If you've seen *Stalag 17*, or most other prisoner-of-war movies, you have an idea what our accommodations were like. There were a dozen identical cabins arranged in a circle, each just big enough for four steel-frame, double-deck bunk beds high enough off the floor to make room for a couple of suitcases underneath and with protruding bolts that served as handy hangers for duffel bags for our dirty laundry. There was a small window on each side of the cabin, but not much light came through. A single bulb hung in mid-ceiling. We each stood with an armful of bed linen, looking around at unpainted cabin walls braced with two-by-fours. It seemed more like a wooden skeleton than a building. The pillows and mattresses we clutched were thin and limp. The woolen horsehair blankets smelled musty. At least the sheets were clean—but where was Mom to tuck them in?

More important, where in the world was the bathroom? Camp Haiastan did have indoor plumbing, but it was not inside our door. The johns, as they were called, were in a concrete bunker in the woods behind the cabins, a short and easy walk—except at night, when even following the lighted path seemed like a perilous hike through the wilderness. Getting to the outdoor-but-covered wash basins and the shower building meant an even longer hike. Our quick peek at this strange little world left us disoriented but hardly discouraged, because we were energized by the thrill of setting out on a great adventure. Best of all, my friend Aram Aslanian was assigned to the same cabin and took the bunk directly across from me. He and I quickly stowed our gear and headed out to explore.

We hiked up to the picnic grounds, then down to lily-covered Uncas Pond, the camp lake. We peered through the impossibly dense screens into the mess hall and ran back and forth across the grassy athletic field that was really just a clearing in the woods. All the while, we watched other cars full of kids and their families arrive and unpack. The license plates traced the migration of Armenians across America: New York, Pennsylvania, Ohio, Michigan. That evening, when the parking lot was empty and the cabins were full, the counselors led us all down to the pool for a get-acquainted cookout. I remember being disappointed when I saw the hamburgers on the grill. No kebab? Then I took a bite. My teeth sensed the crisp, moist profusion of chopped onions even before my tongue did. The taste was instantly comforting, although it was obliterated a moment later by my first swig of bug juice, a syrupy sweet form of ersatz Kool-Aid that was to become our standard meal-time drink. Its color was as unnatural as its flavor, a glowing, pulsing red that seemed to have been drained from a neon sign. The stuff must have been 90 percent sugar with just enough water to reach pourable viscosity. I thought it was great, and I drank about a gallon.

We were exhausted when we slid into our bunks that night, but we sensed instantly how to peel away just enough linen so we wouldn't have to remake the bed from scratch in the morning. I fell asleep, dizzy from the excitement. Then I woke up in the middle of the night, still dizzy. I slid out from under the covers and stood up, but I only felt dizzier.

"Aram, wake up. I don't feel good."

"You're just homesick," he said.

"I'm really sick."

"No you're not."

I started to tell him he was wrong, but all that came out of my mouth was bug juice. The entire gallon—and the hamburger, too! Aram managed to escape the flood and get out the door to find the counselor, Unger Mesrob. Unger was his title, not his name. It's pronounced more like "inn-gehr," with a rolled "r." It means friend, but it's really more like comrade. Unger Mesrob was probably a college kid, but to us he was a man. He could have been forty, or sixty-five. He was, at least, a pleasant man who smiled and kidded us. As he was calling the cabin roll that first day, he'd teased Aram and me by exaggerating the Anglicized pronunciations of our last names. "As-lay-nee-inn?" "Kuh-lay-jee-inn?" I indignantly corrected him, and then we all laughed. I think it was the first time I'd ever shared an Armenian joke with anyone. Now, mere hours later, nothing seemed funny about this Camp Armenia.

Unger Mesrob was unflustered by my illness. "It's OK, just clean it up and go back to sleep," he said. That wasn't the advice I wanted. I didn't want advice at all. I wanted my mother, and I said so. "No phone calls," Unger Mesrob said. "Just clean it up." What happened to the funny guy? What happened to my life? A day before, I was a coddled kid in New Jersey who got all the sympathy he could ask for. Now that I was away from home for the first time, I was sick, I was crying, and I was being held incommunicado. I wanted comfort but all I got from my counselor were rags and a bucket. All I got from Aram was a lecture.

"You're just being a baby. You're not sick. You've got to be tough."

At least Aram helped me clean up. Eventually, I got back to sleep, just in time for reveille. I sleepwalked through morning calisthenics and trudged to the mess hall for our first camp breakfast: pancakes and little link sausages, which I'd never seen before. No bug juice—thank God!—just chocolate milk. I barely finished a few bites, then took off running. At least I cleared the mess hall door before the next torrent poured out. I called for Aram, but he was busy finishing my breakfast. I spent the rest of the day lying in the cabin while Aram and the others were introduced to the daily routine that included instructional swim, arts and crafts, and a rousing game of softball, basketball, or some other athletic contest. By evening I was feeling better, but Aram was still feeling superior.

"You should have come with us. You're not really sick."

What I was sick of was being lectured by another nine-year-old. My revenge came that night, when I was awakened by familiar words.

"I'm sick."

This time, it was Aram. He woke up spewing bug juice into his laundry bag.

"You're just homesick," I said. "Go back to sleep."

That morning at flag-raising, it was clear that Aram had a lot of company in his misery. Kids all around us were holding their stomachs and covering their mouths. It turned out that the bug juice really was buggy after all. The well that supplied the camp's drinking water was contaminated, so everyone got sick. A new well the next year solved the problem permanently, but we were over the trauma within a few days as our stomachs worked out their differences with the microbial intruders.

I never went to a non-Armenian overnight camp but I think it's a safe guess that 95 percent of Camp Haiastan life would be familiar to anyone who did. We sang songs and told stories around the campfire. We swam, we rowed, we ran. The difference is that we sang the songs of the Armenian Revolution and told stories about the brave fedayees. And whether we were swimming, rowing, or running, we imagined we were heading into battle or returning victorious. You played cowboys and Indians? We played Armenians and Turks, and the Armenians always won. We started each day by raising the American flag and pledging allegiance to the United States. Then we raised the Armenian flag and sang "Mer Hairenik" ("Our Fatherland").

Our mess-hall menu was standard high-school cafeteria fare, prepared most years by odar cooks: meat loaf, fish filets, stuffed cabbage. But we prayed in Armenian before every meal, and we ate under the stern gaze of fedayees in old, faded, black-and-white photos. We felt the presence of these men and their cause every waking moment. We were not allowed to forget. Even our calisthenics were more like military training exercises than like high-school gym class, at least for the older boys. When we were twelve or thirteen, we were introduced to the camp tradition of running uphill while carrying a telephone pole. I'm serious. We'd line up along the main road at the bottom of the hill, shoulder to shoulder, and pick up an old telephone pole with our bare hands. We'd lift it waist-high, then turn in unison and charge uphill. Do you know how heavy a telephone pole is? I have no idea in pounds, but it felt like we were carrying an Oldsmobile. When we got to the top, we'd put down the pole and begin our exercises—push-ups, sit-ups, leg lifts, running in place—while the warm and understanding Unger Jim would scream, "Are you tired yet, ladies?" When he was satisfied, and we were exhausted, we'd pick up the pole again and run back downhill.

None of us would even think about complaining. If anything, we tried to prove each day that we could take just a bit more of whatever Unger Jim dished out. I've never served in the military, but I've heard many people describe it as a uniquely and powerfully binding experience. Veterans talk about their comrades as more than friends, sometimes more than brothers. Camp Haiastan wasn't exactly combat, but our shared exertion, enthusiasm, and emotion laced us more closely together than even the experiences I shared at church. I don't remember any jealousy, meanness, cliques, or bullying beyond the usual older-kid hazing of newcomers. Even that didn't amount to much. Maybe I just don't want to remember anything ugly, but I think I'm right. We really did like each other. Sundays were fun not only because we were free to eat shish kebab at the picnics but because new waves of campers would arrive. Meeting all these different people from different backgrounds was a hoot.

They were all Armenian, of course, but some were rich and some poor, most from the United States but some from Lebanon or Syria or Iran. We'd sit up nights in the dark cabin taking turns just talking about where we were from and what it was like. I thought it was all interesting. In a cabin of eight kids, you'd almost always have one who rode limos, one who rode subways, and one who rode camels. Even the counselors were interesting. There was an aspiring actor who'd had a bit part off-Broadway, and another who was trying out for the Canadian Olympic team. And a woman who'd been a go-go dancer on a TV rock 'n' roll show.

I went to Camp Haiastan for at least part of each summer until I was fifteen, then went back later for one summer as a counselor. That was over forty years ago, but the memories are indelible. I am now a retiree who buys suits from the "executive-size" rack. I get tired holding up my cell phone, never mind a telephone pole. I still remember the words to "Mer Hairenik," but it does me no good because somebody changed them when Armenia finally became independent again. The song is more politically correct now—among other changes, they seem to have dropped a line about destroying the land of the Turks—but I still get misty when I hear it. I do not picture Armenia, which I've never seen, but rather a hundred kids in rumpled shorts and T-shirts huddled in a little circle of grass on a cool New England morning, all looking up at the fluttering red, blue, and orange flag.

My father never took me to his Armenia, but I finally took Robyn and Mandy to my Armenia in summer 2005. It was an impromptu visit in the midst of an impromptu vacation. We were supposed to be in the mountains of North Carolina, but an ear infection scuttled Mandy's flight plan. We met in New York, where she lives, and then we drove north for a short stay in Rhode Island. One day we got in the rental car and started toward the mansions of Newport, but the word "FRANKLIN" leaped off the road map. The women agreed it would be fun to see the place I'd been talking about all those years. At least, they put on a good show of pretending.

It was June, and the place wasn't open for the season yet. The picnic grounds were still there, but empty and silent. No music, no kebab. We drove down the hill, which seemed shorter than I remembered and not so steep at all, unless you were carrying a telephone pole. They'd built an Olympic-size pool to replace the one I learned to swim in. Uncas Pond was still covered in lily pads, but there was a golf course and new homes on the other side where we used to pitch camp on our overnight expeditions. Most of the cabins and other camp buildings looked new, at least since my day, including a director's office at the top of the hill where the old overnight cabins used to be. I didn't see anyone I knew, but Robyn did. The executive director, Roy Callan, turned out to be someone she went to college with in Chico, California, probably about the time I'd last visited Camp Haiastan. He invited us into his office for a chat.

He gave us an update that satisfied my curiosity about the camp's future. The place is jammed, summer after summer. Many are second- and even third-generation campers. There's constant interest from odars, too—not to attend, but to buy the place. Franklin is now a booming suburb attractive to commuters because it's reasonably close to Boston and Providence. But to generations of former campers who are now the camp's main support, selling Camp Haiastan would be like selling Armenia. There is holy soil under all those pine needles.

As we were talking, my daughter noticed a plastic bag on a table next to her.

"Oh my God! Are those bullets?"

I explained that they were empty shells, probably policed from the grounds after a winter's season of hunting.

"Can we leave now?" she asked.

Some things just don't translate from generation to generation. Mandy grew up in Florida with plenty of Armenian contact but nothing like the immersion I experienced. She went to an Armenian church camp for parts of several summers, but they sang hymns, not revolutionary songs, and they shot photographs, not imaginary Turks. My youth was mine, as my father's was his, and my daughter's was, in turn, her own. As we left Camp Haiastan, she said she wished she'd had a chance to experience Armenian companionship on that scale but not necessarily in that setting.

At least, not unless they moved the bathrooms inside.

THE TIGHT CIRCLE OF YOUTH

L iving so close meant church was almost impossible to avoid, which was mostly fine with me.

I knew nearly everyone in Sunday school because we'd all started class together in a borrowed Episcopal church a few years before our church was built nearby. My attendance was never in question because my father was Sunday school superintendent, but the whole gang had a powerful incentive to be there every week once we moved to the new church: The entire ground floor was an auditorium-gymnasium that included a full-size basketball court.

After class we'd scramble downstairs and play. We didn't necessarily play basketball, or any ball. We ran, we jumped, we hopped up onto the stage and banged at the piano or danced, or just goofed around. Our parents built us the world's greatest romper room. We were warned, over and over at high volume, to take off our street shoes and tread softly on that very expensive wood floor. We paid no mind. Somehow, despite the scuffs and streaks and water marks, those long, slim strips of spruce held firm through the coming years as the church gym became the main arena of our battle with adolescence.

We learned to play real sports there, and to both win and lose. We learned to dance and romance, at least to the extent that such a thing was possible under the gaze of Armenian parents. We learned to sing and recite and even speak off the cuff on that impossibly high and formal stage, shriveling under the heat of those red, blue, and orange overhead lights. I got the willies just standing on that stage, looking down and out across the gym. It made my hands sweat. Some of the older boys discovered one day that they could jump off the stage and grab hold of the support bar across the basketball back-board. They'd swing like jungle apes, give a shout, and then jump down to the floor. When Aram did it, I decided to try. I was so short I had to stand on a chair before I jumped in order to have any chance of reaching the bar. Aram yelled, "Douglas don't!" but I did anyway. My slippery hands barely skimmed the surface of the bar, and down I went—down and out. I woke up lying on a wooden tabletop in the church kitchen with the priest standing over me. Aram was crying. He thought I died. I don't know how long I was out, but someone called the police. In those days, a mere fifty or so years ago, there was no such thing as 911. No paramedics, no emergency services van. A police officer gave me a ride to a doctor's office, then took me home. My head hurt for days.

Our years at church were full of little dramas, though most weren't quite so painful. We experienced all the aches and angst of youth there because we spent so much time there. There was no pass from Sunday school unless you were serving on the altar, which I rarely did. The incense and heat from the candles made me woozy—a weak excuse that proved its worth when I passed out during a christening. That didn't mean I escaped church. Class was al-most never dismissed until we'd marched quietly upstairs to attend the end of services. Only after that were we cut loose to play, but the fun could last well into the afternoon. Our families almost always lingered in the church hall to chat, to have coffee, to catch up on news of the community. Often, church was followed by a *hantess*, a program of some sort. The worst ones for us kids were conducted in Armenian. Instead of playing ball, we had to sit quietly in the same hard-metal folding chairs we'd been sitting in all morning and listen to an hour or more of speeches or poems or God-knows-what in a language we didn't understand. Actually, there was one thing worse—when we had to participate, memorizing our parts phonetically. I can only imagine what really came out of our mouths.

Even cheat sheets didn't help much, because we couldn't read Armenian letters well enough. We had to use English transliterations, which don't really capture Armenian sounds very well. So all you got from the print was a hint, like an off-stage cue. You had to keep the rest in your head, unfathomable as it was. Filling my head with Armenian words was as uncomfortable as it was difficult, like having a stranger share my toothbrush. Holy Week was the toughest. I couldn't escape altar duty because all the boys were pressed into service to chant solos. Adding a foreign musical scale to a foreign tongue multiplied the stress level.

Being on the altar in front of the entire congregation meant we couldn't deal with our discomfort the usual way, by goofing around. Except for Aram, that is. We were standing on the altar in our long, white *shabik* robes, holding candles and taking turns with the prayers. I had barely started chanting the story of Jonah and the whale when Aram tilted his candle my way and set my scripture on fire. I don't remember my exact words, but they were not in Armenian and definitely not in the Bible. If you think this got us banned from further participation, you don't know Armenian priests.

Ours was Father Kourken Yaralian, who was young, towering (at least over us), and dynamic. He was a *der hayr*, a married parish priest who can never be elevated to bishop, much less Catholicos, because the Armenian Church hierarchy is reserved for celibates. A der hayr's congregation is his highest calling, and the children in particular were Father Yaralian's. He got down to our level by shooting hoops or playing ping-pong, but he also brought us up to his level with the dreaded Adam's apple pinch. He could lift me clear off the ground, and often did. This wasn't punishment—not always, anyway—but a very effective way of getting and holding our attention. His message was simple but clear: This is your church. That meant we were not only invited to attend, we were obligated—and that obligation included Saturday as well as Sunday.

Saturday was Armenian school, an all-day series of classes in Armenian culture, history, and language. I loved the first two subjects but proved remarkably nonabsorbent in the last. Adding to my frustration was the knowledge that my American school friends were out having fun. I couldn't join them, or go to parties or ball games or whatever else regular kids did on Saturdays. One day I told my parents I'd had enough of Armenian school. "It's OK with me," my father said. "Go tell Der Hayr." Dad's sense of humor was never keener. Like a little dope, I walked right into the trap. I was soon dangling high in the air, the skin under my neck stretched like a rooster's. I could barely gasp my regrets at having had such a crazy idea.

By age nine or ten, the last window of weekend freedom slammed shut when we all began attending Friday night meetings of the AYF in the Sunday school hall. We mostly did what other church youth groups did: We held socials, went bowling, helped out at the church bazaar. We also listened to lectures, read pamphlets, and wrote reports that helped indoctrinate us in the beliefs of our parents. These were not necessarily the beliefs of our church, or of any church. The AYF is the youth arm of the Armenian Revolutionary Federation, the Dashnaktsutyun. We were being indoctrinated in the ideology of Armenian nationalism and liberation—and I loved it. Our meetings were giddy, chaotic affairs punctuated by kid pranks and accelerated by the urge to get back on the basketball court, but they were precious to me because they were closed to anyone who didn't belong, even other Armenians. I loved the idea that I was now a very junior member of my father's secret society, the one that filled our living room with cigar-smoking killers.

Now our Armeno-immersion was as near total as it could be while still allowing time for American school. You might guess that some of us would rebel when we reached our teen years, and some did. Even those who didn't rebel sometimes thought about it. Who didn't feel left out when our American friends started going to Friday night dances at the school gym or playing football on Saturdays or taking the bus to New York and then hopping the subway out to Shea Stadium for a Sunday afternoon Mets game? As we got older, more and more of us skipped out from time to time to do such things, American things, and some just kept on skipping. Girls became cheerleaders. Boys dated blondes. In the world of second- and third-generation Armenian kids, this was crazy stuff, like joining a hippie commune or getting a tattoo on your forearm. Parents talked in whispers about the kids who did these things and then silently shook their heads.

I don't think I ever gave my parents such cause for concern, at least not until 1 was much older. My American friends were great companions at school and sometimes after, but my Armenian friends were family. It seemed natural to be with them as much as possible, and I was far more comfortable in their company. If you had a party, you didn't think of excluding any of the kids from church or AYF anymore than you'd think of excluding a relative from Sunday dinner, even the ones who chew with their mouths open. Family is family, after all.

I don't know quite how to explain this, but I felt almost like two different people until I was in my late teens. The Armenian Douglas was confident, funny, focused. The American Douglas was awkward, shy, geeky. I'd swear there was a real, physical difference, too. The American Douglas was a fumbler, uncoordinated and weak, the last guy picked by either team in gym class no matter what the sport. The Armenian Douglas was tough and confident, and a handsome kid, too. Neither Douglas could make a layup on the basketball court, but the Armenian Douglas was at least fast enough to anchor the church relay team.

We may have sometimes chafed against our enforced participation in Armenian activities, including endless hours of praying, singing, and even being lectured in a language none of us understood, but most of us were having too much fun to resist very hard. This is what strikes me as both odd and wondrous now, after so many years: a heritage of misery and persecution that made my father so sad was somehow transformed into something almost joyous one generation later.

The only person I knew who crossed back and forth with me to the world of the Americans was Sarkis Shirinian, who moved to Ridgefield from California about the time we started high school when his father became our new priest. Sarkis adapted to his new surroundings better than I would have, despite the burdens of being the new guy and also of having a foreign-sounding name at a time when that was hardly common. You'd think I'd have gone out of my way to help him try to fit in, but you'd be wrong. I spread the word that he'd just come from Armenia and didn't speak English. It was months before some people caught on that I was kidding. Sarkis still doesn't appreciate the humor in my little joke, but we became friends anyway and he joined the AYF-Camp Haiastan-Sts. Vartanantz boys just as our adventures turned away from mindless, preadolescent high jinks to mindless, midadolescent high jinks. We got away with way more fun than our parents suspected as long as we were all together.

The same parents who reacted in horror if any of us proposed going into New York City with our school pals to see a Knicks game were overjoyed if we were going there with our Armenian friends to an AYF dance. When the oldest of the gang started driving, we all experienced a euphoric surge of freedom that must have been something like the East Germans felt when the Berlin Wall fell. Suddenly, we could go almost anywhere, anytime—Boston, Philadelphia, Providence, Washington, DC—as long, of course, as we were going together to do something Armenian.

It was understood that we were all responsible, sober, and mature. Hah! We'd tumble into Greg Nedurian's Cougar or my Oldsmobile 442 or Aram's red Camaro and drive way too fast down the Jersey Turnpike or up the New England Thruway, more likely singing *Honkey Tonk Woman* than the Armenian national anthem. We stayed up too late, drank too much beer (how much is too much at, say, seventeen?), and, more often than not, slept

166

a dozen to a motel room. Once, when a group at church rented the insanely funny Marx Brothers movie *Monkey Business*, we commandeered the projector and watched it about a dozen times in a row. On our next road trip, we each checked into the motel as Maurice Chevalier. If you've seen the movie, you'll get the joke. If you haven't, I'm sorry for you.

The point is, we were pretty typically immature and occasionally reckless teenagers, but we did always do something Armenian, whether playing in an AYF basketball tournament or dancing the *haleh* or eating kebab at a church picnic. We bonded with other Armenian kids our age and compared notes on our remarkably similar childhood experiences. They weren't just any Armenian kids. They were nearly all Dashnak kids, like us, who'd heard the same stories and learned the same revolutionary songs and entertained at least passing fantasies of liberating Armenia.

The first exceptions I remember were a handful of guys from somewhere in Massachusetts who showed up at the annual AYF Olympics in Providence, Rhode Island. Those Olympics are an Armenian-American phenomenon that draws thousands of people of all ages from all over North America each Labor Day weekend. The sports events are much the same as you'll find in any other track-and-field tournament, with backgammon thrown in for good measure. The real draw for many is the all-night kef that always starts in a big hotel ballroom and then sets its own course as the Armenian dance line, linked pinky to pinky, snakes its way down the hall and out the door. Heaven help any odar who accidentally books a room at the headquarters hotel, or anywhere near. Nonparticipants should treat the Olympics with the same respect as, say, a Hiroshima-scale nuclear device. Of course, the Olympics are much louder.

The guys we met in Providence were experiencing all this for the first time, and they threw themselves into the party with the zeal of converts, which, in a sense, they were. I remember them because they came up to us and asked, "You guys *ay*-uhn?" We thought they were asking about laundry—like, do we do our own ironing? "No, your names. Do they end in *ay*-uhn?" Ah! So that's how you pronounce "ian" with a New England accent. That seemed to be all they knew about Armenians. Somehow, their parents had told them nothing except that Armenian names end in "ian." To them, the Olympics were a glorious eye-opener. They skipped all the pain and guilt and sadness of being Armenian and started right at the good part. All they knew was that being Armenian, especially at Olympics, is a hell of a lot of fun. Who else gets to be instant pals with complete strangers just by walking up and saying "*ay*-uhn?"

A year later, we were introduced to a different side of being Armenian, and a different sort of Armenian, when we went to Olympics in Montreal. The ride took about ten hours by bus. It could have taken ten days for all we cared, because we were all together. Once we arrived, the games and the kef were both familiar, but we met some people who struck us as pretty strange. It was the first time I'd met a large group of Armenians my age who weren't born in America, and I'm not talking about Canadians. Many of the guys from Montreal were originally from Beirut and other parts of the Middle East, and they had a decidedly challenging attitude not only toward us but toward America. We couldn't be entirely sure, because they were speaking Armenian, but they seemed to be making fun of us for speaking English. OK, in fairness, we were making fun of them for speaking Armenian—or, sometimes, speaking English with Armenian accents—but we were still angered. If we really had been mature, we'd have shrugged it off and acknowledged that, after all, we were the foreigners. What a strange idea. It was the first time I'd ever left the United States, the first time I had a chance to experience even a shadow of what my father did so many times as he moved from place to place. None of that sank in. I just thought, "What a bunch of jerks," and we tried to steer clear. We were successful until our bus was about to leave one of the tracks where the events were being held. Before the door closed, some of the Montreal guys got on. One of them started speaking loudly, in Armenian. When no one answered, he switched to English.

"You don't speak Armenian? You know why? Because you're not Armenian. You're Americans. So what are you doing here? This is Armenian Olympics, not American Olympics."

We were so startled by this that I think we were all more amused than annoyed, until the soliloquy turned nasty. "Why do you kill people? Why do you kill all the people in Vietnam? Who asked you for your war? Take your war and your President Nixon and go home." I was sitting behind Mike Azarian, who responded: "Hey, Nixon may be a shitty president, but he's our shitty president."

We were out of our seats in an instant, fists balled, but no punches were thrown. The Montrealers retreated. Looking back at the events on the bus, I felt heartsick at the idea of being spurned by other Armenians for somehow not being Armenian enough. Even worse, for all the times I'd heard my mother castigate me for acting like an American, I never imagined anyone could actually dislike me for being one.

Of all our encounters with Armenians outside our own little circle, the most eye-opening resulted from the formation of a church basketball league when we were in our midteens. All the Armenian churches in the New York-New Jersey area formed teams, including the "other" churches. We all knew there was a parallel universe of Armenian kids, but who imagined both could converge on a basketball court? I was too short, too slow, and too near-sighted to play, but I hung around to cheer the other guys on. Looking back, I shouldn't have hesitated to join in. There have been some outstanding Armenian athletes—Steve Bedrosian was an ace pitcher for the Atlanta Braves, Garo Yepremian kicked field goals for the unbeatable Miami Dolphins, Andre Agassi won a tennis tournament or two—but not in basketball. The federal judge who was trying to decide if Armenians were white should have come to our games. The case would have been open and shut.

Pete Jelalian from New York was a notable exception, as intense and purposeful on the court as he was laid-back and jovial off it. The other exception was Aram. He had the aim and range of a teenage Bill Bradley, and his deadly but off-kilter jump shot was a right-handed mimicry of Dick Barnett's. He could run, gun, and pick and roll with the speed of Walt Frazier, and he could jump like—well, unfortunately, he jumped like Fat Albert. Poor Aram. If he could have jumped, he would have played in the NBA. Of course, if he could have breathed underwater, he would have been a fish. We are what we are, and Aram was the reason the Sts. Vartanantz boys were the Armenian church league's basketball powerhouse.

The better we got to know our on-court competitors, the more we learned about the curious similarities between our communities. We had AYF, they had ACYOA, the Armenian Church Youth Organization of America. We had Camp Haiastan in Massachusetts, they had Camp Nubar in Upstate New York. We compared notes on our churches, our dances, our picnics, and even our parents, and we discovered nothing very different except that we Dashnaks saluted the flag and sang the national anthem of a country that was erased from the world map before any of us were born. That certainly didn't explain why our parents were so insistent about keeping to themselves and keeping separate churches. By the time we were in our late teens, we were routinely attending each other's social functions, formal and informal. Some of us became good friends. Richie Doudoukjian was the best example.

He came from their side, but he clearly didn't care about sides. He just cared about having fun with other Armenians, and the Sts. Vartanantz gang was always fun. We liked Richie so much we elected him president of our AYF chapter. It didn't matter to any of us that he wasn't actually a member. It was a deliciously subversive gesture, but it did nothing to break down the political divisions.

The walls that separated us from other Armenians turned out to be porous, but there were no walls at all to keep us inside any Armenian community. We were the first generation where that mattered, because we were the first generation headed for college. For most, that meant leaving home and leaving our church. I don't think any of us thought about it in those terms. Being Armenian, being with our Armenian friends, was so much a part of our lives that it just seemed obvious it would go on and on. We didn't need any institution, any building or social club or political organization, to hold us together. Even in our late teens, as we drifted away from the rigid, weekend-long regimen of Armenian activities, we drifted as a group. We took our road trips, we double-dated, we organized our own parentless expeditions to the Jersey Shore. Long after we were freed from our Saturday Armenian school obligations, you'd find most of the same group crowded into the garage at the Nedurian house.

Greg decided to turn his Cougar into a hot rod—an idea firmly rejected by his hard-working father, who, after all, had paid for it. We all thought the plan was brilliant, and we joined in. My natural mechanical talent equaled my basketball talent, but that didn't matter. None of us had any real idea what we were doing, but we figured out how to loosen bolts and operate a hand winch. We got the engine out of the Cougar just before Uncle Harry pulled into the driveway. His words echoed for blocks: "Goddam Gregory!" He kept saying it, over and over, in disbelief. That was over forty years ago, but I haven't called Greg anything else since.

Of course, we couldn't figure out what to do next, so Greg "borrowed" Uncle Harry's upholstery van and we towed the Cougar to the Sunoco gas station across from church. The guy who owned the place apparently found us amusing. We made a mess, but it was an entertaining mess. We eventually got the engine souped up and running. We even got it back into the Cougar, although we had to jump up and down on top of it to get the new, giant-size exhaust pipes to fit into the engine compartment. It took weeks, maybe months, to get the Cougar back on the road, complete with rumbling exhaust and giant tires. What a roaring hot rod it was, too. And fast! Most of the guys lost interest long before we finished, but Greg and I drove the Cougar all across New Jersey and New York, tires squealing. Today, especially with so many Armenians in California, there are actually Armenian car clubs. But back then, the Cougar was the first Armenian-built hot rod any of us had ever seen. We talked about painting it red, blue, and orange but never got around to it, which is probably for the best. I even wrote a song that Greg and I sang at Armenian parties:

Uncle Harry bought Greg a Cougar,
With bucket seats and carpets on the floor.
It's a real nice car, but you can't get very far
'Cause the Cougar doesn't run any more.

Who knew that if just one tiny screw dropped down into the carburetor, the whole engine could blow up? You live and learn. But all that meant was we got to start on a new project, turning the hot rod back into a regular Cougar. We did it, somehow, using an engine we dragged out of a junkyard. When we were done, the Cougar looked normal again and seemed to drive OK, but I was troubled by the pile of leftover parts in the driveway.

"Greg, don't you think we should figure out where these were supposed to go?"

Greg just shrugged.

"Don't worry about it."

Today, Greg is a surgeon. It's probably best that his patients don't know about the Cougar.

Soon after we got the car back in one piece, more or less, Greg sold it. Our road-trip days were just about over by then anyway. Greg didn't go far, just across the Hudson River to Wagner College, but his premed coursework was demanding. Aram went away the following year on a basketball scholarship to the University of Connecticut. Sarkis headed to Villanova outside Philadelphia. Most of the other AYF boys and girls took off, too, but not me. I stayed home and commuted to a nearby school. I stayed connected to church and what was left of our circle, but not for long. The fun of growing up Armenian lasted only so long as I was growing up. That left very little to offset the serious part of being Armenian, the gloomy and guilty and angry part. The times made it all seem that much angrier.

Once we left our Armenian-kid cocoons, we were no longer insulated from the ugliness of burning cities and burning campuses, or from the acrid enmity between hippies and the people who hated them and everything they seemed to stand for. In the early 1970s, everyone in America had some reason to be angry, and the Armenians, as always, had more reasons than most. People my age, people who went to Camp Haiastan and shot at the same tin cans, were now talking about a real revolution. Some of them wanted to fight it right here in America.

I remember talking to a very scary guy from New York. He'd never seemed scary until this night, when he told me he wanted to blow up a movie theater that was showing a Woody Allen comedy because a character told a joke about Armenians. It would be a statement, he said. I agreed. "It would be a statement that you're an idiot." I argued with him, and with others, that it would be not only wrong and illegal but immoral for Armenians to hurt America or other Americans in any way.

I was always more political than most of my Armenian pals. I spoke up loudly and publicly at every opportunity. I may not have been our AYF chapter's best athlete, but I was the most enthusiastic speaker. I breathed fire into the microphone at holiday assemblies, paying tribute to the fedayees and urging loyalty to the cause. I was so sincere, so dedicated, that I was one of the few speakers, young or old, who wasn't censored beforehand. My father, Dashnak to the core, always seemed proud and sprung to my defense whenever anyone suggested that perhaps I should tone things down a bit. So I was surprised at his lack of enthusiasm when word came that I was being considered for a special honor: Would I be interested in a scholarship to an Armenian university in Beirut? I could become fluent in Armenian, a scholar in historical and political affairs, and I would be guaranteed a job with the party when I graduated. While my friends were choosing among mundane pursuits like medicine and law, my future seemed assured as a revolutionary propagandist.

"I'd love it," I said. "I believe in everything the party stands for."

My father knew better.

"How do you know what you'll believe a few years from now?"

Then he sharpened the point.

"Political parties change. Just like people. How do you know what the party will stand for when you're ready to graduate?"

I conceded the point, reluctantly. I became an English major at Fairleigh Dickinson University in Teaneck, New Jersey, which wasn't nearly as exciting as Beirut had become. I barely finished two years of college when I quit to become a newspaper reporter. By then I was arguing with more and more people like the guy who wanted to blow up the movie theater. Armenian revolutionaries were firing guns, setting off explosives, and killing Turkish officials all over the world. The party I'd once believed in didn't publicly condemn these actions, much less do anything stop them. I thought this was foolish and wrong—and I told this to anyone who would listen, but there weren't many left to tell.

With my friends gone, I felt no connection to Armenians other than my family for the first time in my life. I had no time to mourn the loss. I was working long, long hours learning the ropes of the newspaper business, covering fires and car crashes and city council meetings. That first job, at a twice-weekly paper, paid $2 an hour, which worked out to $80 for a laughably hypothetical forty-hour week. Minus taxes, of course.

That didn't leave me enough to support myself, so I was still living at home with my folks in Ridgefield. The church I'd grown up with was still just a block away, but it might as well have been a million miles.

Lessons I will never learn

If you could peek into the living room of my childhood home when my father and his friends were making kef or playing backgammon or just having a drink and talking about the old days, you'd see a clearly happy man at ease in his surroundings. You could not mistake the broad smile on his face or the bright tone of his voice even if you didn't understand a word he was saying in Armenian.

As a child, this puzzled me. I couldn't reconcile this picture with the father I saw so often in less comfortable surroundings. Day to day, my father was impatient, irritable, and occasionally angry for reasons I couldn't understand. He had no interest in small talk with strangers, even when it was good for business, which is why my always genial mother waited on the customers whenever possible. I once heard my father tell a man that his clothes were too dirty. "Go find another cleaner," he said, shoving the guy's pants back across the counter.

Dad would not wait for anything, anytime. If there was a wait to get into a restaurant, we left. If there was a wait at the barber shop, we left. If there was a line at the movies—well, he never went to the movies. My mother and I went alone because my father had no interest in sitting in a dark room full of strange people. Besides, what movie would he want to see? John Ford was just about done making the world's best westerns by the time I came along, and Dad didn't care for much else. The only movie I remember going to see with my father was *America, America,* Elia Kazan's semiautobiographical saga about a Greek from Anatolia. Dad pulled me out of my seat during a scene where Turks set fire to a church full of Armenians. It was the second time

I saw my father cry. I've still never seen the end of the movie because I can't get past that part.

My father was never rude or even unkind to me, at least not in words. His impatience, though, became a real barrier to sharing normal father-son experiences. I think he really wasn't sure what to do with me after I got too old to pick up and bounce on his knee. My father, after all, had grown up with no father of his own to emulate.

In most ways, he ad-libbed remarkably well. I know this isn't revisionist thinking because I was quoted at length by the local paper in a 1972 story on Father's Day. "American fathers tend to want to be liked so much, they ignore the role of father," I said. "In an Old World upbringing, there's an almost physical distance between father and son; the bond of mutual respect is greater." At twenty, I recognized there was more to his fractured stories about Armenia than idle interest in history. "There was always a strong sense of ethnic identity and heritage in our house; everything tied back to a long and impressive history. It gave me a sense of my place in the world that elevated the sense of my own goals, a personal pride that held me up until I could begin to take pride in my own accomplishments. I wasn't just a nameless face in the crowd."

Looking back, I certainly wouldn't have traded that for a father who played catch. Of course, it's no mystery why we never played catch—he probably never saw a baseball until he was well past Little League age—but we never really played anything. No sports, no board games. I asked him to teach me backgammon, at which he excelled, but he put me off. I was probably in single digits then. The subject didn't come up again until I was in my twenties and had learned to play the game on my own. When I pestered him, he agreed to play a single game, which he won in a flash. He closed the board before I could ask for a rematch. We never played backgammon again.

I knew that other fathers took their sons to ball games or went camping or fishing. I didn't necessarily want to sleep on the ground or even see Mickey Mantle up close, but I was jealous that other boys got to spend time with their fathers. The most time Dad and I ever spent alone together was in the car, when he let me ride along as he delivered clothes. They were wonderful times because we were together, not because we shared our thoughts. Instead of my father's voice I listened to an endless loop of traffic jams and subway shootings set to the clacking teletype soundtrack of News Radio 1010 WINS ("You give us 22 minutes, we'll give you the world.").

My father didn't want me to become a dry cleaner so it made sense that he never showed me how to do his job, although I watched as closely as I could from a distance without bothering him and pestered my mother to provide explanations when she could. He really only offered three hands-on lessons in any life skills, and I was foolish enough to ignore one of them. He was oddly pleased to have me tag along as he tended his plants and even demonstrated grafting and potting and other skills. I'd hang around for a while, then go back to watching television with Mom. The second lesson was how to land with a parachute. This was much more interesting, although not very useful, as I didn't have a parachute. But Dad watched me jump off the three-foot stone wall in the backyard, insisting I always remember to tuck my knees and tumble with the momentum, just in case. In case of what? When I was eight years old, I fell while trying to swing like a monkey from a basketball backboard. I landed on my head and got knocked out. "Did you forget what I taught you?" he asked when I woke up. No, I just didn't have time to remember before the ground hit me.

The third lesson would have meant the most if he'd carried it through. One day when I was fifteen, Dad told me to get into his Fiat station wagon on the driver's side. "I'm going to teach you how to drive a stick shift," he said. I slid the gear lever into first, applied the gas, and slowly let the clutch out—and, of course, the car stalled. Everyone stalls the first time. Before I could step on the clutch to try again, my father said, "Get out." And that was the end of our father-son driving lesson. I couldn't ask for a second chance because he got out before I did. I blamed myself for failing and for disappointing my father. Worse, I could tell from the flip of his hand as he walked away that I'd upset him, which I'd tried so hard never to do since my mother's warning years before. Looking back, I realize I did nothing wrong. I'm sure he knew that, too. I wonder now if he was disappointed in himself for not sticking with it and giving me the lesson I deserved—for not even saying, "Good try, son" before he left. No matter, as the moment passed and it wasn't coming back. When it was time for me to get my license, Dad hired a driving instructor.

None of this means I didn't learn from my father. I learned a great deal from his example and his occasional observations, just not from his instruction. His example served me well throughout my childhood, except when it didn't apply to my life, or when he had no example to offer. I never thought about this. I just took my mother's word as gospel: My father was the smartest man in the world. So how could I not do well to emulate him? He listened to Chopin, so I listened to Chopin. He read books, so I read books. He read the newspaper, so I read the newspaper. (My classmates at recess had so little to say about Senate debates and Supreme Court decisions that I began to suspect none of them started the day by reading Andrew Tully's National Whirligig column.)

It's probably normal and healthy for most boys to take after their fathers, as long as their fathers aren't con men or gangsters—or survivors of war and genocide who had no experience on the schoolyards and ball fields or in the classrooms of America. My father's advice regarding school was simply to respect my teachers and never disobey. He also told me to do well, but he didn't tell me how. He rarely asked anything at all about what I was learning, and never asked to see my homework. The first time I asked him a question about schoolwork, he looked pained. I don't remember my question, but his answer left a deep impression. "I can't help you," he said. "I didn't go to school."

If my father were an ignorant man, I might have been embarrassed for him or embarrassed by him. Instead, I felt strangely proud to think that my father never went to school but he became the smartest man in the world! I see now that he was self-conscious about his lack of formal education and that the gaps in his learning showed up in ways that weren't obvious to me because he didn't want them to be. I asked why he almost never wrote anything in English, even a grocery list, and he explained that he'd never learned proper punctuation. I'm sure that was true, but it didn't satisfy me, and I'm certain his imperfect sense of English usage didn't satisfy him even though he'd read enough to absorb the common level of punctuation, spelling, and grammar. I can't know the embarrassments he experienced over the years or the setbacks that stuck in his craw, because he kept that all to himself, and he wrote his notes in Armenian. I was left to my own interpretation, which didn't always serve me well.

I took my father's advice to heart through the first several grades of school, applying myself to learning the alphabet and then to reading and writing. I got excellent grades and lots of praise, which propelled me to work even harder. My idea of hard work at that point involved more reading, which I enjoyed. I read every word that passed in front of my eyes: newspapers, comic books, cereal boxes, soup cans. The more words I read, the bigger my vocabulary got, which resulted in more praise. I remained fixated on words through the third grade, putting up with arithmetic only because my mother told me it was important. By the fourth grade, however, other subjects began to intrude on my reading time, and school became less fun. My love of words betrayed me one day when I corrected my teacher's grammar. Someone asked her a question, and she responded, "I forget." I eagerly raised my hand. "You should have said, 'I have forgotten.' That's the present perfect." I still think she should have thanked me. Instead she told me in a rather snippy voice to be quiet. Right then, I decided I obviously didn't need school any more than my father did, as I was already smarter than the teacher.

I stuck it out for another ten years or so, but I never felt comfortable in a classroom and never learned well from teachers. I followed my father's example and absorbed what I needed in the library and figured the rest out by trial and error. I didn't set any academic records, but I managed to stay afloat except in the one subject that only my father could have helped with: I never learned to speak Armenian.

The closest Dad came to offering help was to give me a few well-worn paperback books of Armenian grammar lessons. He pointed out the alphabet but never so much as recited it for me. My instruction was supposed to come from attending Armenian school on Saturdays at church. What kid wants an extra day of school? This was worse than drudgery, however. This was painful because all the teachers spoke in Armenian and expected us to understand and repeat after them. I never absorbed much of it. I'd look at the foreign letters on the blackboard and listen to the foreign sounds coming from the teachers' mouths and imagine that I'd been taken hostage in some strange place. This went on for years—it seems like about a hundred, but I may be mistaken. Regardless, I never learned to say or understand more than, "Hello. How are you? I'm fine." That's still my nearly complete store of Armenian language ammunition, and the battle is long over.

When I was young, I excused my ignorance of the Armenian language the same way I excused my ignorance of many things—it was someone else's fault. I blamed my father, my Armenian-school teachers, the authors of the many Armenian-language textbooks I stared at so stupidly as if I expected them to talk for me. I'm only a bit more willing to accept responsibility now. To the charge of linguistic ignorance, I plead guilty with an explanation: Everyone I know who speaks and understands Armenian learned it at home or by immersion in an Armenian-language setting here or abroad. I've heard of others who learned Armenian in college, and I'm sure there are autodidacts who managed to absorb more than I ever will from books and tapes and computer programs. I have them all, and then some. They are no substitute for the sounds of the grandparents I never knew, or the father who wouldn't speak to me in the language he knew best.

Like my father, I thought there was time for me to fix all this somewhere down the road. My father recognized that the time for me to learn had passed when he sent his books to Armenia. I wonder now if he had something in mind by letting me know he planned to give them away. Was he trying to jar me into applying myself at last? Did he think I'd start spontaneously speaking in the mother tongue, perhaps by begging him to change his mind? I can't blame my father for my failure, but I wish he'd been more direct. If he had said, "Speaking Armenian is important for you, and it's important to me," I would have tried much, much harder. Instead, he left matters to me. I think deep down he must have known how that would turn out.

Regardless of his intent, when my father decided not to speak to me in Armenian he abandoned me at a cultural dead end, and I'm still stuck there. I've come to the painful realization that I'm guilty of false advertising for so casually claiming my Armenian identity when I should have known better. I've often heard myself saying to non-Armenian friends, "In our culture . . ." This could be followed by a lofty observation about how strongly Armenians feel about their nation or a casual observation about how Armenians like to eat salty cheese with fruit. But none of it ever sounded authentic even when it was accurate. I'd hear the words coming from my lips, and I'd feel a twinge of surprise, or maybe even guilt. I knew that my knowledge of Armenian culture had come mostly from observation at arms' length, and my arms aren't very long.

I hated to consider the obvious, that I was culturally American. For one thing, it wasn't nearly as interesting, which meant I wasn't nearly as interesting. More important, it seemed somehow a betrayal of generations past. Throughout my life, so many people had lectured me about my responsibility to carry on Armenian traditions that the imperative seemed beyond question, even though the question was obvious: How could I carry on with something I didn't know?

For years, I've considered the question of whether language is an essential part of the Armenian identity—simply put, can I be Armenian if I don't speak Armenian?—as a philosophical question. I'm no philosopher, so it was easy to put out of my mind. The more practical matter of what I was missing was also easily set aside as long as I thought in terms of jokes told around the table at coffee hour after church. How funny could they really be? What I can't dismiss, and can't get past, is that not being able to understand Armenian means I can't read Armenian even if I memorize the alphabet. This is a great shame, and I choose the word carefully. How could I not feel shame at remaining illiterate at this advanced age? The loss is mine but so is the insult to the many Armenian writers who dedicated their lives—and in many cases, sacrificed their lives—to tell their stories.

The irony of my illiteracy is that it would have been normal just a few generations back in the old country. Even educated Armenians under Ottoman rule couldn't read their own literature or history because it was all written in an archaic, formal language that no one understood except priests and scholars. Not only was the Armenian vernacular splintered into many local dialects, it had no grammatical form suited to writing. There was no need for such structure while Armenians were busy serving their Turkish masters. Armenian writers wrote in Turkish, just as Armenian musicians played in the Turkish style. The Ottoman culture was seamlessly enriched by the work of Armenian artists just as the Ottoman treasury was enriched by the work of Armenian laborers and businessmen.

The Armenian awakening of the nineteenth century, cultural as well as political, ushered in a wave of Armenian writers who accepted the extraordinary obligation of creating a modern language that was rich in evocative, literary tools but still accessible to the masses. They used this language to encourage a renewed sense of pride in speaking Armenian, in reading Armenian, in simply being Armenian without disguise or apology. It was a message their rulers could not abide. The most stirring of these writers were among the first victims of the Genocide, rounded up and slaughtered in 1915.

I know their names: Daniel Varoujan, Krikor Zohrab, Siamanto. God rest their souls. I am awed by them, but I cannot truly honor them because I don't know them. I cannot learn the lessons they still teach. I cannot take part in the great conversation about the meaning of Armenian life that they continue to moderate. I've failed to recognize their works on bookshelves and felt pained when I later found out what I'd missed even though I couldn't have read the books if I'd known. It was as though I'd walked past the authors' graves without pausing to pay respects because I was unable to read their tombstones. I know their works only by imperfect English titles that even the authors wouldn't recognize. Some of their poems and novels have been translated, but I've read only a few. I'm always self-conscious when I do, mindful that even the best translation is a representation and not the real thing. Reading a translated book and claiming to understand the author is like hearing someone describe the *Mona Lisa* and claiming you've been to the Louvre.

While I can't learn from their work, I continue to learn from their deaths. I know who kills writers: people who are afraid that others will pay attention to them. It is foolish behavior, whether carried out by Turks or Nazis or Communists. The message of the Armenian Renaissance is still being received, repeated, and embellished by successive generations of writers who defied purges, goons, and gulags. Unfortunately, fools who visit misery on others sometimes stumble into good fortune. In eradicating so many people, the perpetrators of the Armenian Genocide simultaneously erased much of the culture those people nurtured.

For me, this cultural genocide may be the greater crime because the tracings of that culture are beyond my comprehension. It is largely lost to me and most of my generation of survivors' children in America. My conscience is eased at least somewhat by the knowledge that others with more intelligence and enterprise are working hard to recapture and preserve the culture of Western Armenia, including the folk music and other art forms. The same thing is happening at ground level in the reborn Republic of Armenia, and I find this even more remarkable and wondrous.

Hagop Goudsouzian, a filmmaker who lives in Canada, has made several excellent documentaries exploring the talent and tenacity of Armenian musicians—artists so dedicated to their craft that they fashion their own duduks out of apricot wood. They don't have the option of ordering instruments from catalogs because there's not enough money to be made from playing music in Armenia. What I found so remarkable about these artists is their fidelity to tradition. It is striking to see so many young, talented people in Armenia singing hymns written in the Middle Ages, and others who have migrated from the diaspora so they can perform and create in an unadulterated Armenian sphere. The most important lesson for me in watching and hearing the people Goudsouzian interviewed is that many insist they've made no sacrifice. "Our wealth is our culture," one explains.

Hearing this, I understood the reason for my own anger a little better: Long before I was born, I was robbed of a fortune.

Closing time

If you saw a photo of Mom from the 1930s or '40s, you might guess she worked in a Manhattan office or an upscale dress shop. She wore high-strap heels and stylishly tilted hats, and suits that looked custom-tailored, because they most likely were.

Dad was every bit her sartorial match, even in his Army uniform. No matter where he was stationed, he'd find a tailor to take the slack out of his slacks. His shirts were not only fitted but pressed to a razor-sharp crease.

Sylvia and Nish looking typically sharp in the late 1940s.

The workday clothes I remember most clearly were more pedestrian, of course: a simple pullover dress for Mom, pants and a T-shirt for Dad. Even then, Dad always insisted his T-shirts have breast pockets because he didn't want anyone to think he was cleaning clothes in his undershirt, although no one other than a deliveryman or my mother was likely to see him.

My parents impressed on me the importance of dressing with dignity, particularly when leaving the house. We all "got dressed," whether we were going visiting or to church or to the grocery store. That meant I had to put on dress slacks and a clean shirt. On me, however, nothing stayed clean for long. Worse, every sidewalk seemed to have a magnetic attraction to my knees. I never wore a pair of pants more than a couple of times before ripping a hole in one leg or the other—sometimes both. My father never scolded me, but he scolded my mother on my behalf. "Why can't this kid stand up?"

I quit dressing up when I reached my teen years but I never quite dressed down the way much of my generation did. There were no tie-dyed shirts or faded jeans with the back pockets torn off in my closet. My father never understood why people lucky enough to afford decent clothes wanted to look like beggars. I didn't either, but there was no denying the sea change in attitude toward dress. If you watch teen movies from the 1950s, even the juvenile delinquents wore jackets and ties to the school dance. By the '70s, many grown men had stopped wearing jackets and ties to the office.

Regardless of fashion, the new wash-and-wear fabrics didn't need dry cleaning. My parents never talked business in front of me, but I could see they weren't as busy as they were in my youth, even though they were working harder than ever. They'd let their part-time presser go, and Mom took on much of the added work, as my father was sidelined by a series of ailments. I found out years later that he'd had a heart attack at one point but just kept working. In 1971, during my freshman year in college, I skipped more than a month of classes to pitch in at the store while Dad was hospitalized with yet another malady he didn't bother to explain. Even then, Mom tried to keep me in the front of the store and away from the heat and fumes. Tending the register, I finally saw how little money was coming in.

Dad was slow to gain strength when he came home, and I could hear him breathing hard just from walking across the room. I helped out by making deliveries, but there was less and less to deliver. I knew Dad was really starting to tire when he finally asked me to help scrub the cleaning-fluid filters, a stinking job that left me dizzy every time. He'd never have allowed that if he'd had a choice. He still insisted everything would be fine when I asked if they could really afford my college tuition. I didn't believe him. It wasn't the only reason, but it was a big factor when I decided it was time to go to work instead of sitting in a classroom.

In winter 1974, as my parents were about to turn sixty-two, Mom slipped on an icy sidewalk and broke a leg. It was one obstacle she couldn't simply ignore. They sold the store soon after that to another Armenian dry cleaner, who offered my father a part-time job at his other store closer to our house. Dad gave it a try for a few weeks, but that was all. After forty-five years of work, he was just worn out.

GETTING MARRIED

M ark Hogan called to change my life about 7:30 pm Saturday, January 31, 1976.

I don't have to double-check the date.

Mark and I had met a few years earlier when I finally moved out of my parents' house and went to work at *Patent Trader* newspaper in Mount Kisco, New York, about an hour north of Manhattan. Mark and I were a reporting team, the Yorktown bureau, covering small towns, cops, and schools in quaint and woodsy Westchester County. The Yorktown bureau was actually a pair of side-by-side metal desks in the downtown Mount Kisco newsroom, but Mark and I were insistent in our fiction that we were invisible to everyone around us, including editors who kept shouting at us to quit goofing off and write something.

We actually wrote a lot, although most of it wasn't suitable for publication. Mostly we wrote humorous headlines:

Editors Tell Hogan, Kalajian:
'Quit Goofing Off and Write!'

They seemed humorous to us, anyway. We soon discovered that newspaper editors have a chronic humor deficiency. I decided the problem was probably limited to small-town newspapers. I'd seen *The Front Page* and was convinced life at a big-city tabloid would be one zany, madcap romp. Within a few years, I was testing that theory at the *New York Daily News*. Unfortunately, reality was not scripted by Ben Hecht. The biggest difference between the *Daily News* and *Patent Trader* turned out to be that at a big-city paper, everybody goofed off; it was a union rule. It just wasn't as

185

much fun goofing off without Mark, who'd become a high school drama teacher. Luckily, he didn't go far. Mark found a job in Red Bank, New Jersey, while I'd moved back to my parents' house in Ridgefield. We managed to get together for occasional weekends of goofing off at beachside bars along the Jersey Shore.

My other constant companion of the time was another odar, Roy Evans, a college pal who was possibly the world's most enthusiastic and knowledgeable collector of obscure 1920s and '30s jazz records. Evenings with Roy and his oversize, broadcast-quality turntable in the unfinished attic of his parents' postwar Cape Cod house in Bergenfield were true theater, like being in the audience for an underground radio show:

"Most people think Bing Crosby only recorded this on Victor, but here's an alternate take of *Wrap Your Troubles in Dreams* on Decca. This is great. Crosby forgets the words to the second verse and starts cursing . . ."

Few of my Armenian pals who'd gone off to colleges around the country showed signs of coming back. Our old routine of weekends at church and summers at camp was long past. I felt the void but didn't think much about it. My focus was on my budding career and my hope to further it. I may have been the least important character on the staff, but I was working at the biggest paper in the country, and I was certain my talent would be recognized and rewarded. I also continued to spend a lot of time in my room typing. I wouldn't call it writing, because I still had no idea what to say, much less how to say it, but I was sure something original and fascinating would emerge if I just kept trying.

Dating was problematic. I had no trouble getting women to go out with me, but I had a world of trouble staying awake and interested during the age of disco and fern bars. I couldn't pretend to be excited about any woman who wanted to know my sign. I was more interested in discussing Kerouac than the zodiac. As for dancing, the very mention of *Saturday Night Fever* gave me the cold sweats. This narrowed the field of dating possibilities considerably, even among Armenian women. I dated a number of them, but nothing clicked. I considered myself lucky. At twenty-three, I had no interest in a long-term relationship, much less marriage. If anything, I shied away from Armenian girls because odars seemed to be safer in that regard. I wanted to be free to accomplish big things, although I wasn't sure what they were.

My father had succeeded in discouraging me from seeing the world, but I hadn't abandoned the idea. I was just waiting for the right time, and the nerve. Aram wanted me to go on the road with him across America, but I said no and he went anyway. He sent me postcards from Denver and San Francisco and everyplace else Jack Kerouac had stopped:

June 1975, Olympic Nat. Park—Jack's Mt. Baker was truly an orange sash in heaven. Everything in California is Primo! Primo, Primo.

Greg Nedurian thought we should buy an old beater of a car and drive the Pan-American Highway to the tip of South America. I said no to that, too. He wound up going off to medical school in Mexico and came back with stories of hightailing through *bandito* territory in a beat-up Camaro. Meanwhile, I cruised through Hoboken with Roy, listening to tapes of a 1930s English music hall comedian named George Formby singing about window washing.

I'm not sure I had any plans at all for January 31, 1976, until Roy called to solicit my sympathy over a bout of girl trouble. He figured an evening of old records and beer would cheer him up and asked me to join him. I was about to leave for Roy's when Mark Hogan called with his own urgent request. He'd been trying to get a date with the school librarian and had nearly worn her down, except she claimed she couldn't go out because she was having dinner with a female friend, a home economics teacher at their school. "No problem," Mark said. "I'll find a date for her, too." This is where I figured in: The friend was Armenian. Mark persuaded the librarian to put her on the phone and said, "*Inch bes es?*"—Armenian for "How are you?" He told her about his Armenian pal and how he was sure they'd hit it off. She told him she'd never heard of this guy Kalajian but was sure he was a loser if he had nothing to do on a Saturday night but wait for his friend to go fishing for a blind date.

Mark, a charming Irishman if there ever was one, got her to suspend judgment while he called me. I wasn't interested in his proposal. Besides, I'd promised to entertain Roy. Mark told me to stand by, dialed the librarian's house again, and suggested she find a third girl for Roy to even things up. His suggestion fell flat, but he wouldn't quit. He managed to get Roy and me to make the hour-and-a-half drive to Red Bank while the girls hurried through dinner and got ready for—what? A three-man, two-woman date? Or perhaps a mere gathering of good friends, most of whom had never met? Mark is one determined and persuasive guy. The people who keep trying to broker Middle East peace agreements should enlist his services.

Gloria the librarian answered the door, while her friend Robyn Dabbakian was a few steps behind, just coming in from another room. Robyn was wearing blue slacks, a pink pullover sweater, and a silky blue scarf. Best of all, she was wearing desert boots, which were a peculiar sort of flat, lace-up shoe made of blue suede and about as stylish as a Rambler Ambassador—except that on this girl, this night, they looked ultracool, just like the rest of her. She had brilliantly black hair, short and wavy, and bright, brown eyes with just a hint of almond taper at the corners. She looked as though she'd stepped out of an Armenian painting, an idealized portrait of a beautiful Armenian girl. I looked at her and thought: "Too bad! She is not going to be interested in me."

Much later I learned she looked at me and thought: "I hope he's the Armenian guy. I'm going to marry him." I still can't figure it. I looked like what I was: a way-too-serious young man trying to look older and smarter than anyone could possibly believe. I was wearing my pseudointellectual's uniform: brown sport coat, white turtleneck, shaggy hair, and beard. I was smoking a pipe filled with tobacco that smelled like a toaster full of burning Pop Tarts.

We got into Roy's car with no real idea where we were headed and wound up at a very casual, very '70s bar—enough wood to build a fleet of arks, more hanging plants than the Gardens of Babylon. Mark's plan quickly unraveled as Roy and Gloria spent the evening comparing tales of unhappy relationships. Mark seemed quite happy drinking beer by the pitcher. Robyn and I talked for hours. We discovered we'd led eerily parallel Armenian-American lives: Weekends at church, summers at the shore. Pistachio nuts and shish kebab. Shamlian Records. She was even Dikranagerdtsi on her father's side.

What made this eerie wasn't coincidence upon coincidence. It was that we'd never met until then. How could that be? We'd grown up twelve miles apart. We had not one or two but dozens of mutual friends and acquaintances. Comparing notes on Armenian events, we were sure we'd been in the same place at the same time more than once, and yet we'd somehow never seen each other. Believe me, I'd have remembered. The only reasonable explanation is only partly satisfying: Robyn went to the "other" church. But so did most of my mother's relatives, and we discovered we even shared some of them: The Nalbandians, my mother's cousins, were Robyn's father's cousins.

My mother said time and again, "Everything happens for a reason." I think she was right. Maybe Robyn and I weren't meant to meet until that night, but we were certainly meant to meet. We were married on August 7, 1977, at St. Leon Armenian Church in Fair Lawn, New Jersey.

We still thank Mark Hogan every time we see him.

FRIENDLY RELATIONS

Our wedding reception was large, loud, and lively. It was a fitting reflection of our shared, dual identities.

We had two bands, one to play Armenian music and one to play American. Of course, even the guys in the American band were Armenians, but the Armenian music was a real sensation: Onnik sang, accompanied by the phenomenal oud player, John Berberian. I'd grown up listening to these guys in my parents' living room, live as well as on record, but this was special. It was like having Louie Prima or Frank Sinatra sing at an Italian wedding. Everybody was up and dancing all night.

The kef continued through our first year of marriage. We rented an apartment in Pompton Lakes, which was at least twenty miles from the closer of our families, but we managed to visit one or the other most every weekend. We reconnected with Armenian friends and even made new ones. We went to church—her church—as well as to Armenian dances, picnics, and cultural events. We even spent lots of time with Armenians at the shore, and we didn't have to rent a bungalow: Robyn's family owned a summer house in, of all places, Belmar, scene of so many of my childhood memories.

Buying the house was her father's idea. Andy Dabbakian was a true Dikranagerdtsi who loved company. He was also a man of vision. Just a few years before I met Robyn, he'd spotted this ramshackle house on the Shark River Inlet: three stories and six bedrooms laced together by a long, wide, and shady porch. Others saw rotted windowsills and a buckled seawall; he saw a front porch overflowing with Armenians. He pictured himself as master of a summer-long kef, beckoning an endless parade of friends and relatives to pull up beach chairs and grab fistfuls of pistachios.

The Dabbakian family relaxing on their seawall in Belmar, N.J. in the mid 1970s. From left are Dawn and husband Ara Hourdajian; my bride-to-be, Robyn; Robyn's mother Mary and her father Andy.

Andy put both shoulders as well his savings into an all-out effort to make his vision a reality. He persevered even when it became obvious the rot reached deep into the walls, even when most of the backyard washed out to sea. His enthusiasm spread to the entire family. Not that anyone had a choice. Weekends were devoted to fix-up, patch-up, paint-up projects. I joined the team late and with little to offer except goodwill. It was a perfect opportunity to learn essential home-repair survival skills. The Dabbakian family restoration project hardly resembled TV's *This Old House*, where a half century of neglect can be remedied in a half-hour episode by a team of experts with a massive infusion of hired labor and cash. The only paid help in Belmar was the neighborhood handyman, who didn't seem much handier than the rest of us.

In fairness, hardly anyone could out-handy Andy, who had a genius for salvaging everything from switches that wouldn't switch to toilets that wouldn't flush. He got long-stuck windows to open and even got them to close again. He silenced creaky doors and unleashed a gush from dry, rusty pipes. His progress was hardly slowed by the intrusion of a new son-in-law who moved a ladder without taking a full-and-open can of paint off the top step. He actually seemed to find the sight of me bathed in green paint mildly amusing.

Andy had been a hardworking man all his life. He escaped the dry-cleaning business by becoming a machinist after he got out of the Army and kept grinding away at the Bendix Aviation plant until he was past fifty, when he decided to go to college. He and Robyn became classmates of a sort at Montclair State College, although she went to school during the day and he took night classes. He graduated a year after Robyn and became a metal-shop teacher. Robyn's older sister, Dawn, had already gotten her start as a high school guidance counselor. That meant they all had summers off, a common thread that bound them even more closely to the Belmar house. They named the place Hye Dune, a bit of whimsy playing on the Armenian words for "Armenian House."   *Asbury Park*

The name was apt, as kef was in full swing right along with rescue-and-renovation work. A steady stream of friends and relatives found their way to Hye Dune's porch, especially on summer weekends. There were still plenty of Armenians around Belmar, although not nearly as many as I'd remembered from our visits two decades earlier. Malkas's Place was long gone, as were the other Armenian gathering spots like the Hye Hotel and the Van just to the north in Asbury Park. Second- and third-generation Armenian-Americans didn't feel bound to the tradition of vacations with their own kind, and they were prosperous enough to really travel. One of the many reasons Robyn struck me as worldly and sophisticated—beyond the obvious, that she really was worldly and sophisticated—was that she'd been to Europe, more than once. She'd even been to Hawaii with her family, when the farthest my family had traveled to was Boston. But like comfortable old shoes, the easy and simple pleasure of a summer Sunday spent toasting on hot sand at the Jersey

Shore could not be discarded. The Armenians who came to Belmar now were as likely to drive Cadillacs as Chevrolets, but regardless, the ones who drove along the Shark River Inlet were waved up onto a gray-planked porch on First Avenue.

Even on a blustery weekend when potential visitors stayed home, Robyn and I had plenty of company at the Belmar house. In addition to Robyn's father and her mother, Mary, regular weekend sleepovers included Mary's brother, Walter Vartanesian, and his wife, Arpie; Robyn's younger brother, Drew; and Dawn and her husband, Ara. Plus the real head of the house, Robyn's maternal grandmother, Yeranuhe Vartanesian, affectionately known as Nanny. She was not a tall woman, but she towered over the rest of us, hawk-like in her attention to the most minute detail of everyone's habits, particularly spending habits. Nanny was not merely a force to be reckoned with, she was to be obeyed.

Or lied to, whichever worked.

It's no insult to anyone else to acknowledge that Nanny was my favorite among Robyn's relatives. I told Robyn more than once that I married her for her grandmother. I was only partly kidding. Robyn was lucky as well as unusual among Armenians of our generation in having three grandparents who lived long enough to leave her with clear impressions. Nanny, the last one left, became the only grandparent I ever had. I'm glad I didn't miss her.

When I met Nanny, she was in her late seventies but looked truly ancient, like someone you'd see in *National Geographic*. "Ageless Woman of the Caucuses: Can She Really Be 200 Years Old?" Nanny had the shrunken, shapeless form of an old woman weighted down by a long, hard life. Her face, bunched tight by the kerchief wrapped over her hair and knotted under her chin, showed the wrinkles of a shar-pei. She wore modern clothes in a way that caricatured an old-country costume: cotton-print house dresses over purple or Day-Glo green polyester slacks. She moved slowly but deliberately, and with deceptive strength. Nanny was old and tired, but she was hardly run-down. She lived alone on the upper floor of the two-story house she'd bought in the 1940s, on a steep hill in a working-class neighborhood in Clifton, New Jersey. Nanny walked a half-mile downhill almost every day to buy groceries, and she carried them back up the hill, rain or snow be damned. Then she carried them up a narrow staircase steeper than the hill. She had no more interest in moving to the ground floor than she had in asking for a ride or accepting help carrying her bags. Like my father, she was born of another time but in a place even more remote and removed from the modern world: Musa Dagh. In a real sense, she remained there all her life.

A famous book published in the 1930s, Franz Werfel's *The 40 Days of Musa Dagh,* told the story Nanny had lived as a child. The book, an international best seller, was a romance with a core of historical truth about the battle of Musa Dagh, which is Turkish for "Moses' Mountain." It is a peak in southeastern Turkey along the curve of the Mediterranean near what is now the Syrian border. In 1899, when Nanny was born in the village of Haji Habibli in the mountain's shadow, there was no border because the Turks still ruled Syria. But they did not rule the Armenians of Musa Dagh, who lived in a handful of tiny villages around the base of the highest mountain. The Armenians sought refuge from invaders there six centuries before Nanny was born, burrowing deeply into the harsh, hostile landscape. They'd come so far from their landlocked homeland that they could finally look out to the sea if they climbed to the top of Musa Dagh. They might as well have been looking at a painting, for all the practical good of their proximity to the water. The almost sheer western face of Musa Dagh dropped straight to the water, so this seaside was useless as either beach or harbor.

The Armenians, hemmed in by Kurds and Arabs as well as mountains, had little land flat enough to farm, but the slopes and valleys were brimming with trees, including mulberries. Many of the villagers became master woodcarvers. Others became silk weavers. At least once each year, they would wind their way through the tortuous mountain passes to the Silk Road to make their trades. It was the only contact the villagers had with the outside world. The Armenians living around Musa Dagh were so isolated that their language evolved into a dialect even more puzzling to other Armenians than Dikranagerdtsi.

The mountains were the villagers' secret and near-impenetrable shield. Outsiders could hardly find the few, narrow passageways, and those who did stood little chance of mastering them. The five thousand Armenians who lived in a half-dozen villages around Musa Dagh felt safe until 1915, when no Armenians were safe anywhere in the Ottoman Empire. The villagers of Musa Dagh were among the last to receive deportation orders, but they'd been among the first to shelter survivors who followed the path of their ancestors into the mountains. They knew deportation meant death, and they'd had time to prepare. The Armenian defenders loaded their rifles and sharpened their bayonets, but it seemed unlikely these mountain

Musa Dagh

villagers could defeat the Turkish army that finally reached Musa Dagh in mid-July. The Turks surrounded the Armenian villages, then continued up the great mountain, commanding the heights and cutting off the remote chance of retreat by sea. But the Turks got only so far and stopped, stymied by the jagged slope. They had too much trouble just holding on to climb higher. The Armenians seized the moment. While the Turks slept, the Armenians slipped out of their villages and climbed silently past them, sure-footed even in the dead of night. The Armenians, now with the height advantage, attacked the off-balance and panicked Turkish forces and drove them off the mountain.

The Turks regrouped and charged up the mountainside, but the Armenians chased them down again with a torrent of bullets and boulders. The battle continued this way for weeks, but the terrain that aided the Armenians also appeared to doom them. The Turks couldn't climb up, but the Armenians couldn't climb down, and nothing edible grew on the mountaintop. When the last sheep were slaughtered and eaten, the Turks wouldn't have to fight at all. The Armenians would simply die—unless, somehow, help came from the sea. Before the First World War, passing ships were a common sight, but even warships steered clear now. The Armenians had scanned the sea-lanes throughout the siege without spotting a single vessel. Still, it was their only hope. An Armenian Protestant minister who'd been schooled in English helped make a banner that read, "CHRISTIANS IN DISTRESS: RESCUE."

The miracle they prayed for appeared through the mist on the fifty-third day of the siege: a French ship, leading a convoy. The Armenian defenders emptied the last of their ammunition into the Turks as the women and children were carried down the cliff face. The survivors—4,058 in all—arrived at Port Said, Egypt, on Sept. 14, 1915. Musa Dagh remains a singular triumph in the Armenians' summer of despair.

Nanny was sixteen years old when she climbed down that mountain, just about the age for marriage. She would have to wait through five more years of turmoil. She was twenty-one when her family finally arranged a match with a much older man from Haji Habibli who had made his way to America. Nanny sailed alone from Beirut to Marseille to Ellis Island, where she married a stranger named Oskan Vartanesian. Robyn says she can still picture him clearly. As a child, she thought he was Uncle Ben, the black man on the rice box. The Vartanesians settled in Connecticut but later moved to

Paterson, New Jersey, the Silk City. Oskan worked as a weaver until some-time during the Depression, when his eyes weakened along with the boss's tolerance for his already slow and painstaking pace. Nanny, now a mother of three, managed to find work at a coat factory. Her husband went back to work only briefly, then retired in his fifties.

For Nanny, life in America proved nearly as stark and challenging as life in Haji Habibli. Only two of her three children survived to adulthood. My mother-in-law remembered her little brother Eddie getting sick at age eight, but she wasn't sure the doctor even tried to explain to their parents what was wrong. It's for sure the doctor didn't explain it in the language of Haji Habibli. Nanny accepted Eddie's death stoically, as she accepted all other hardships, including her role as sole support of the family. Nor did she complain about her subservient obligations as an old-country wife. Instead of going to work, her husband went to a coffeehouse every day to play cards or backgammon with his countrymen. He expected dinner on the table when he came home, then allowed only a short break before the games resumed. He invited company every night, including his brother and wife, for more cards and coffee. Nanny could not rest until she was done serving and cleaning up.

Nanny's only real dominion was over the family finances, and she ruled tyrannically because she had no other choice. Not a penny—truly, a penny—was ever spent without her consent. The Vartanesians not only ate day-old bread, they ate day-old fish, when they ate fish at all. Meat was a luxury. Dinner was more likely bulgur or lentils with vegetables. They had no car, no telephone. Like children in so many other Depression-era fami-lies, Mary and Walter learned to make their own fun instead of squander-ing money on movies and store-bought toys. Unlike other parents, Nanny did not yield her draconian frugality when the Depression ended, or even when the kids grew up.

Nanny worked so hard and saved so much that she was able to buy her family a house with a side yard big enough for a second house. Mary and her new husband, Andy, moved in with Nanny and Oskan. Then Walt and Arpie had a house built for themselves in the yard alongside. By the time Dawn, Robyn, and Drew came along, Nanny had managed to transform her slanting stretch of West Second Street into a miniature Haji Habibli, with grapes fattening on the arbor out back, red peppers drying in the sun, and children running up and down the slope. Oskan even quit going to the coffeehouse, content to weave at his loom and ferment raisins in the bathtub to make arak. (Robyn remembers the pungent vapor that escaped from his still—and the police who came to the door looking for a bootlegger.)

By the 1950s, Andy and Walt were both union men at Bendix, bringing home what used to be called good money, which got even better with overtime. Mary and Arpie worked, too. These were the sort of Armenians I knew growing up, hard-working people devoted to their families, especially the children. Mary and Andy worked so hard that eventually they were able to buy a new, split-level house with a brick front, a shady yard, and two-and-a-half bathrooms. For a first-generation Armenian-American family in North Jersey in 1957, this was a palace. For Nanny, this was treason. Never mind that they were spending money without her approval; Mary and Andy were moving with their kids an entire mile away from her. Who does such a thing? No one in Haji Habibli had ever done it, for sure. No one in any place the Armenians had landed had done such a thing, except in America. Nanny had worried and warned for years about the corrupting influence of the Americans—and now this! My poor father-in-law, the outsider Nanny had welcomed into her home, bore the brunt of her anger. I can only imagine what it was like, considering she was still steamed when I met her nearly twenty years later.

I can not only imagine her wrath, I can feel it. About six months after Robyn and I were married, I was driving through Nanny's neighborhood and decided to stop in for a visit. I climbed the steep, indoor stairway and knocked on her kitchen door. She opened it, smiled with delight, and then slapped me across the face. I staggered back and grabbed the railing to keep from falling down the steps. I'd barely pulled myself upright when she slapped me again. I held on with one hand and grabbed her wrist with the other before she could swing again.

"Nanny, why are you hitting me?" I asked.

"Because I mad at you."

"Why are you mad at me?"

"Because you wait so long to come see me."

I made a point of never visiting her again unless Robyn came along—and I made sure she went in first.

ARMENIA COMES WITH US

I'm sentimental about objects, but only about objects I know were important to someone I cared about.

My father's rocking chair, for instance. I would never give away my father's books either, not just because they were his possessions but because they are books, which means the knowledge in them became a part of him and by reading them I am having a conversation with him again.

I'm not sentimental about places, however. I don't know if this is an Armenian trait or a personal peculiarity. I could argue for either one. Armenians have been chased away from home so many times that they should be immune to homesickness, but that's hardly the case. My father said that his father talked about going back all his life, even though there was nothing and no one to go back to. My father, who had no memory of happy times where he was born, never considered it.

So when the possibility of a job in Florida turned up in the fall of 1978, I knew I could leave New Jersey without regret. I'd miss my parents and friends, but I was excited by the prospect of a new vista and fresh challenges. To my relief, Robyn felt the same way, although her reasoning was different.

"Oh, we can move there. I know there are Armenians in Florida."

She immediately began fishing through her night-table drawer for the Armenian church directory. This is before she knew anything else about Florida. About the cost of living. About crime. About schools (which is really amusing, considering she's a teacher). Even about hurricanes. No, once she confirmed the existence of an Armenian church, her only question about moving to Florida was where to buy bulgur and other Armenian groceries.

"I'll have Mom ask Grace," she said.

The course of our lives might have been very different if Grace and Jack Karagosian, friends of Robyn's family, hadn't already retired to Florida and reported back that there were indeed other "ians" in the Sunshine State. I certainly would have faced significant domestic resistance when the *Miami Herald* offered me a job. This is no joke. Like most journalists, I had friends at lots of papers around the country and got word occasionally about openings here and there. I learned that there was no point in even mentioning any possibility to Robyn unless I knew there was a substantial Armenian community with a church and a grocery store. As it turned out, she should have asked one more question before we moved to Florida. She should have asked if there were any Armenians under seventy.

Soon after we moved, we went to an Armenian dance at a revolving penthouse lounge with a spectacular view of the Intracoastal Waterway and downtown Fort Lauderdale. The setting was romantic as long as we sat looking out through the glass at the moonlight glistening across the water and the rooftops, but it was depressing when we turned toward the dance floor: We were the youngest couple in the room by far. Our prospects of making friends with other young Armenians were about even with our prospects of snow for Christmas.

The community not only turned out to be older than we'd imagined but far smaller than we were used to, and it got even smaller after Easter when many winter residents went back north for the summer. Sunday services were held in a borrowed church, with none of the familiar trappings and with little extraliturgical social activity. The adjustment was difficult for Robyn. Unlike me, she'd never veered from church and community life even after she moved out on her own. Our marriage had actually drawn me back in, although this time it was to her church, the other church, which seemed instantly familiar and yet somehow not quite exact. I was disappointed by our new circumstances in Florida but hardly devastated. My new job kept me busy enough, and I had plenty of new faces to learn without any additional Armenians. But Robyn had come to Florida for me, with no job and no company all day except five fuzzy channels of precable television and a pile of laundry.

She insisted we get out of the house on weekends and look for signs of Armenian life, or any reasonable facsimile. We drove south to Miami and north to Palm Beach week after week but found nothing even vaguely Near Eastern except a Greek grocery store with nearly barren shelves—not even a jar of grape leaves. Our consolation was the certainty that this move was temporary. We'd only be here a year or two, and then we'd move back to the cradle of Armenian-American civilization, New Jersey. In the meanwhile, we would try something radical: making friends with odars. We didn't really think it over. It just happened.

Robyn found Louise in the laundry room. Louise and Ralph lived next door to us in a nearly identical two-bedroom, shag-carpeted apartment over-looking the parking lot. They were an instantly familiar and likable pair of Italian-Americans from New York, older than we were then but younger than we are now. Robyn and Louise became fast friends, making the rounds of discount outlets and fabric shops. Ralph was a gem of a guy, but he worked night and day driving a truck or a backhoe or whatever paid the rent, so our couple-bonding time was limited. I found my own odars, however, right where I spent my own days and nights. How can anyone explain why certain people become friends, real friends? I certainly can't explain Kevin Hall and David Blasco.

Even the people who hired Kevin warned me he was dangerous, a bra-zen advocate of rational thought. He was the only person in the office who recognized my habit of reading our newspaper aloud each morning as sub-versive. We quickly developed the sort of friendship rooted in intellectu-al respect that in an earlier time, in Paris, say, would have involved many long nights of drinking absinthe while discussing Proust but that in Fort Lauderdale in 1979 involved long Saturday afternoons drinking beer and watching *Boxeo* from Mexico. As for Blasco ("Everyone calls me Blasco"), I recognized him as a kindred car spirit with distinctly eccentric tastes. His considerable knowledge of automobiles hadn't stopped him from buying one of the worst cars ever made, a Chevrolet Vega. What set Blasco apart is that once he knew for sure he'd bought a world-class stinker, he went out and bought another. Why settle for owning one of the worst cars ever made when you can own two? He shared my observation that the great age of American cars had passed recently enough that the best cars were now owned by poor people who couldn't afford anything as new and awful as a Vega. We devoted our meal breaks to wandering neighborhoods known for random violence, admiring the rusty but still-rolling remnants of boat-tail Buick Rivieras and four-door Thunderbirds. We were poking through a used-car lot off Broward Boulevard one day when a prophet disguised as a car salesman suddenly ap-peared from behind a white 1967 Pontiac Tempest and announced, "Cars are getting scarce." Blasco immediately recognized the wisdom and bought the car.

Luckily, each of these guys came with a normal, sensible spouse, which encouraged the Armenian instinct for family synthesis. Thanksgiving with Kevin and his wife, Barbara, was followed by Christmas with David and his wife, Bonnie Gross, year after year. The real surprise is that we were all still around year after year. South Florida's population churned furiously in the 1980s, as hundreds of thousands who had been drawn by the promise of cheap living in paradise headed back north within a few years, repelled by the reality of corruption, crime, drug wars, crowded roads, and shoddy construction. Some people are picky, I guess. I saw no reason to flee because to me, all of that made Florida seem a lot like New Jersey, except that Armenians were as rare as oil refineries and frost heaves.

The misery experienced by so many in South Florida made for great newspaper stories, and I had a bird's-eye view of the drama from my seat as assignment editor in the *Herald's* Fort Lauderdale office. Day after day, crazy people did crazy things, like firing machine guns in shopping malls and shooting up courthouses to spring their pals from custody, and gunning speedboats loaded with marijuana through the canals where kids were water skiing. For me, it all made the day go faster—and it made the years go almost as fast.

More than thirty-five years have now passed since we left New Jersey, and the change in both Florida and America is remarkable. The Armenian community in South Florida today is much more like New Jersey's than I suspected it would ever be. There are hundreds of Armenian families here now, many of them young and eager to jump in. We have a real, brick-and-mortar church in Boca Raton and another south of Fort Lauderdale. There are plenty of Armenian social and cultural events to attend and organizations to join, but you won't find my name on any membership list. Robyn, by far the better Armenian, better Christian, and better all-around human being, often goes to church on Sunday mornings while I'm locked in the den, writing. When she comes home, we always have the same conversation over lunch. "You won't believe what's going on," she says, but I believe every word because I've heard it all before many times: So-and-so is angry with so-and-so and there's a new clique that wants to throw out the old clique and someone else complained to the diocese and now the archbishop is supposed to fly down to knock some heads together. I just nod and chew my sandwich. I find that not going to church reduces stomach acid much better than Maalox and Zantac combined. When I want to socialize with Armenians, I do it in my home or in theirs, and always in small groups.

We no longer have to hunt for grape leaves because we can buy them at the supermarket. That is true these days almost anywhere in the country. I know because Robyn and I have a habit of wandering store aisles and thumbing through phone books whenever we're out of town. We look for anything Armenian: names, food, music. You'd be surprised who and what turn up. We even buy things we don't really need just because it's fun. If we see an Armenian CD in a thrift shop, I buy it to play in the rental car, even if it's something I'll give away when I get home.

If we're on the road and find Armenian string cheese in a supermarket, we take it back to eat in our hotel room with strong coffee—regardless of whether we're hungry or thirsty—because it makes us feel good, as though we're not just home but home with all the friends and family who have come and gone.

THE PICTURE THAT OPENED A DOOR

Mom's photo album fell apart years ago.

The front and back covers are rough-cut wood, which will last a million years, and the black, construction-paper pages are also still mostly intact. But whatever bound the pages is long gone, and the punch holes are all torn. The pages have been shuffled a thousand times, and there's no way to guess their original order. That doesn't much matter because there's also no way to guess who half the people were. Only a handful had names written below in white ink, and now those names mark nothing but smudgy spaces where snapshots glued in place before I was born have broken free.

Luckily, the best picture of all was tucked in back but never glued in place.

It is a formal portrait mounted on cardboard and shot by an Armenian photographer in Boston sometime around 1909. The date isn't marked but I can make a good guess because Mom did something unusual, at least for her: She wrote all the names on the back. The reason for her devotion to detail is obvious. It is the only picture of her mother along with Grandma's brothers and sisters, the founders of the Nalbandian clan in America. If I'm right about the year, this photo was shot before Grandma met Grandpa Bichakjian and not long after she came to the United States. Seeing these people in this place at this time is like seeing characters from a familiar story that hadn't yet been written.

My guess about the year is based on the ages of the two remarkably beautiful little girls in the foreground, my mother's cousins Rose and Mary. The older of the two, Mary, was born in 1905 and appears to be about four in the picture. Rose was a year younger, but the girls are dolled up like twins, with white dresses and stockings, black high-strap shoes, and flowers in their long, dark hair. My other guess about this picture is the reason the family got all trussed up in formal collars and starched shirtwaists to make the lurching streetcar trip from Chelsea to the Diran photo studio in Boston. I believe they wanted proof to send back to Dikranagerd that they were all together and safe. Rose and Mary, the first progeny born in America, were the best proof of all that the sacrifices of the previous years were worthwhile.

The extended Nalbandian clan united in America circa 1909. My maternal grandmother, Hormoush (Rose), is at center flanked by her sisters Baidzar, at left, and Touma. The men, from left, are Hagop the gouvedge-making grocer; Baidzar's husband, Megerdich Doramajian; Uncle Charlie, the kef maker; and Uncle Aram (Ray), before he sold Packards. The girls are Baidzar's daughters Rose, at left, and Mary.

The clarity of the image is remarkable after all these years, despite the greenish-gray tinge that must have been Diran's version of sepia. The details of the pose—women standing stiffly at the rear, men seated with cigarettes in their hands—are less revealing than the details that bypassed the photographer's eye. The workman's hands of Megerdich Doramajian, for example. He was Aunt Baidzar's husband, father of Rose and Mary. His fingers appear stained in a way that made me wonder if he was a mechanic or if he worked in a tool shop, but now I know he was one of the first of the Chelsea Armenians to find work in a shoe factory. His hands must have been stained by dye. Uncle Charlie's shoes are another telling detail. They are not just scuffed, they are battered and pocked. He had not been in America long enough to wear out a pair of new shoes here. Could they be the shoes he wore when he left Dikranagerd, or were they his first pair of hand-me-downs from his older brother, Hagop, who came to America first?

I've spent hours looking at this picture over the years, wondering about these people who look as though they cannot possibly allow themselves to feel safe, much less happy. I finally called Charlotte Ermoian, daughter of little Mary, to ask what she knew about the lives and times of the Nalbandians. Charlotte gave me advice that should have been obvious: Ask Alice. Alice Bakalian is among the last survivors of the original Union City Armenians, youngest child of Megerdich Doramajian and Baidzar Nalbandian Doramajian. I have great memories of Aunt Alice and her husband, Uncle Azie, and of their sons, Michael, David, and Peter, especially from the warm and sunny Belmar summers of childhood. I was delighted and surprised to discover that Alice could be reached by e-mail. She responded in a flash, not only with tales of the Nalbands but of the extended family and of that era:

Our Family Tree, as I remember it.

The Nalbandian family

Mother's side

Grandparents Bedros, Susan

Their children Hagop, Garabed, Aram, Hormoush, Baidzar, Touma

What a strange moment, to suddenly read for the first time the names of my mother's maternal grandparents: Bedros and Susan (or Shooshan, or some variation). I had no idea anyone remembered their names, but I will remember them from now on because they are more than links in the biological chain that attaches me to the old country. They were selfless people who sent their children away because there was no way to protect them. If they hadn't done that, I wouldn't be here.

Not having the money to send them all at once, they decided to send two children at a time. Hagop and Baidzar came first, stopping in Marseille, France so Hagop could find work to pay for the rest of the trip to the States. After a short stay, they continued their journey to America. They landed at Ellis Island, then contin-ued to Chelsea, Mass., where Baidzar married Megerdich Doramajian, who was waiting for her. He had left Dikranagerd, where they had known each other. Soon after, they sent for Baidzar's siblings. Two by two they came over and stayed at my parents' house until they also married. Hormoush came with Garabed, and Touma came with Aram. This is the reason they escaped the Genocide . . .

Unfortunately, their parents never reached America.

Alice said Bedros, who was her grandfather and my great-grandfather, died soon after the first of his children arrived in America. How much longer his wife survived is a mystery. How any of them survived on either side of the Atlantic is a mystery. When factory work dried up in Chelsea, Alice's father joined the exodus to Union City, New Jersey, where he became a tinsmith, the work he was trained for in Dikranagerd. He died within a few years, at age forty-eight. Mary and Rose were married by then. Their younger broth-er, Peter, in his late teens, had to support Alice and their mother.

Can't remember how many houses we were put out of because we couldn't come up with the rent. I do remember always wearing shoes with holes in the soles and looking for cardboard to line them with. Quish-Quish were the sounds I'd hear from my shoes when it rained, especially when I went to school and had to sit there all day with soaked feet and then they quished when I got up to walk around. These things didn't bother me because nobody had anything in those days.

Alice continued with reminiscences of the kef nights at Uncle Garabed's house, when the men played music and sang, and of days of communal cooking:

At the end of summer, the women in the family would get together, usually at Aunt Satenig's house, and have a kavourma cooking day. There were large vats of cut-up lamb cooking with apples and quince bobbing on top. This lamb was later deboned and put into large garasses, which are made of pottery with covers. This meat was stored in a cold place. My mother kept it on the fire escape all winter and dug into it whenever she made bulgur or anything that needed lamb.

They all made chormees—dried lamb, another staple—ground-up, spiced, put in bags, which were the bags salt came in and dried on the fire escape on hooks in a wooden grocery box so the rain wouldn't get at it.

Another e-mail contained two bonus memories. Alice remembered Grandpa Bichakjian, the cook and Western traveler, because he was her uncle by marriage. She could picture his storefront restaurant in Union City, where her mother used to pitch in from time to time:

As I walked in, I would face an ice box and on top of the ice box were these wonderful pies. Always apple and apricot, which he baked once a week for the restaurant and he always gave me one to take home. I loved that man. Actually, I was in awe of him. He'd come to our house and sit on the sadr (sofa) and talk to my mother for hours with worry beads in his hand. He was never without them. They were yellow amber.

More pieces of the puzzle fell into place: The apple pies explained the bushels of apples that George Parigian mentioned, the ones Emmeh used to carry up from the basement of Grandpa's restaurant in Chelsea. The apricot pies were Grandpa's legacy to my mother. Robyn bakes one every holiday in memory of Mom, but now it will also be homage to Grandpa. But it was Alice's reference to the amber beads that made me dizzy. Armenian men click away at a string of worry beads while they sit and talk the way American men whittle or chew tobacco or drum their fingers against a table leg. My father left his string of amber beads behind. He always had them, and I never asked where they came from. They were within arm's reach on the bookshelf to my left as I read Alice's e-mail. Could these have been Grandpa Bichakjian's, a gift from my mother to her husband? There's no way to know, but I've decided they were because I want it to be true.

The other bonus was Alice's surprising memory of my other grandfather, Haroutyun Kalajian, the singer who became as well-known to the Armenians of Union City as he had been to the Armenians of Dikranagerd:

He had a great voice. I remember on a Sunday morning hearing a man singing either a saaba or a maya. These are Turkish songs of lament and sadness and longing. Such a soulful sound it was. My mother told me it was your father's father singing in the kagva, the coffee house. This was after a night of drinking or whatever they did there.

This is the most important piece of all. I'd wondered about the story of Grandpa Kalajian returning to Dikranagerd too late to save his family and how his song of lament was so powerful it could be heard—and his voice recognized—across the city. Now I have testimony that years after, his voice was still so strong that all the Armenians in the tenement canyon of Union City could hear him, and that his sadness was still so deep it stirred the soul of a little girl who would keep the memory for more than seventy years.

THE GOOD TURKS

Lots of Armenian families have a Good Turk story. Good Turks hid Armenian neighbors in their root cellars, disguised Armenian children as little Turks, and passed food and water to starving refugees. Here are two Good Turk stories.

Story One: A Good Turk helped my wife's paternal grandfather escape from Dikranagerd as the Turkish army prepared to round up young Armenian men. Without the help of this Turk, Hovsep Dabbakian would most likely have been slaughtered with the rest, and my wife and daughter would never have been born. Here is what I know, as recorded by Hovsep's daughter Zabelle Dabbakian Keil, affectionately known to us as Aunt Zippi:

Hovsep had a devoted boyhood schoolmate who was Turkish and very much aware of the plan to kill Armenian young men. Plans were made to help his escape. One very dark night, my father bade his family farewell and he and his friend went to the river at a designated point where they felt an escape could be possible. The friend watched as my father began to swim quietly across the river. The river was heavily patrolled so it wasn't surprising that soon the soldiers heard noises at the water's edge and began shooting their rifles. By this time, Hovsep was only partially across the river so it was almost inevitable that one of the bullets would find its mark. My father was hit, and although wounded managed to swim to the other side of the river where another friend was waiting for him. The bullet that hit my father lodged in one of his ribs and stayed there. Many years later when doctors examined him for various reasons, the bullet was quite evident in his X-rays. As God would have it, the bullet remained in his rib until one day he passed away some 50 years after the incident. My father was one of the lucky ones that escaped. Had it not been for his boyhood friends this incident could have ended differently. Hovsep survived the river escape and went on across Europe with the help of friends and finally made it to America.

Story Two: A Good Turk helped Azie Bakalian's family escape the wrath of the Turkish authorities.

I've known Uncle Azie all my life, but I never knew he was born in Dikranagerd until Robyn and I stopped by to visit him and Aunt Alice on a trip back to New Jersey in spring 2006. Azie is short for Azad, which means "free." He got the name because his birth coincided with the end of the First World War, and his parents believed—as all Armenians wanted to believe— that the Western powers would honor their promises. For a while, it seemed to be true. Azie's father prospered in business with a Turkish partner, and the family lived as well as they had before the war, until the local pasha came to visit. The pasha wanted to take Azie's aunt, his mother's younger sister. It was impossible for an Armenian to refuse such a demand, but Azie's father pleaded and even offered the pasha gold in place of the girl. The pasha cursed the insolent infidel and spit on him. Azie's father responded by plunging a dagger into the pasha's fat belly.

No Armenian could help the Bakalian family, but a Good Turk did. Azie's father went to his partner and told him what happened. "I can buy you twenty-four hours, no more," the Turk said. It was enough time to get the women and children out of town and for Azie's father to retrieve as much gold as he could carry and take refuge in the local well. He stayed deep in the well for weeks, until the Turks stopped looking for him, then slipped out to join his family. His father's partner could easily have turned in these murderous and troublesome Armenians. He could also have taken the money they used to make their way across Turkey to Europe.

Good Turk stories are remarkable because the punishment for helping Armenians was death. Armenians should tell these stories more often not only because Good Turks deserve to be honored but because the instinct needs to be encouraged, everywhere.

Home is no longer home

My father left a message for me in the form of a pencil mark shaped like a small, white bean on page 849 of *A Treasury of Great Poems* in the margin next to this passage from *The Rubaiyat of Omar Khayyam*:

The Moving Finger writes; and, having writ,
Moves on: nor all your Piety nor Wit
Shall lure it back to cancel half a Line,
Nor all your Tears wash out a Word of it.

Armenians must know this truth better than anyone, even if we pretend we don't. We live with our history. It crowds us, cheers us, smothers us, inspires us, taunts us—regardless, we cannot change it.

We move on.

The Old Dutch settlers of Bergen County, New Jersey, had moved on long before we arrived in Ridgefield. Our neighbors were Italian, German, Irish, Jewish—an old-neighborhood mix of people who had moved there when it was more country than suburb in the 1940s and '50s. By the time my parents retired, the mix was changing again.

Ridgefield, Fairview, Cliffside Park, and others in a long string of small towns in eastern Bergen County had been the first step up the suburban ladder for a couple of generations of frayed-collar families. The population swelled in the 1960s as the middle-class flight from New York City accelerated, but the flight path widened to the west and north in the 1970s as these same families fanned out in search of bigger yards, less traffic, and two-car garages.

My old elementary school was closed because there weren't enough kids around anymore, but it soon reopened as a private school serving a new, booming population of Japanese immigrants. Small homes, narrow streets, and traffic jams made eastern Bergen County seem like home not only to Japanese but to Koreans and others. By the mid-1980s, the area's ubiquitous storefront Italian restaurants were being displaced by Asian markets.

There were new families from Western Asia, too, mostly Turks, plus more from Eastern Europe and the Middle East, including Armenians. Going home for a visit was not like being home at all, at least not when we were outdoors. It was like visiting a familiar-looking but surprisingly foreign place. Accompanying my father on his daily shopping rounds was like taking a world tour. The deli-newsstand where he bought the *Daily News* every morning was now owned by Koreans. At Kocher's, our German butcher shop across from my old school, Japanese parents who'd just dropped off their kids crowded around glass cases filled with prime meats. The real fun came as we stopped at little corner-store specialty shops to get olives or bread or whatever sweets caught my father's eye. He'd check out any new shop that had a sign written in Armenian, Greek, or Turkish and greet the owner in his language. Then off they'd race, in whichever language—laughing, arguing, discussing the weather. How would I know? I had no idea, but I loved it. I loved listening to echoes of my father's early life there along the same streets where I'd grown up. It was as though the Hudson River had become the Bosphorus, and my father had finally taken me back to retrace his path.

Inside our home, everything looked the same except older and tired, like my parents. Mom still cooked every day, but her frantic get-ready-for-the-weekend routine was over. The friends who used to pop in had mostly moved, or died. Diyeh was gone. Uncle Arpag had moved to California. Time and again I asked my parents to at least think about moving to Florida to be near us, but my mother would cut me off. "I'm not going anywhere," she said. "We have everything right here." She wouldn't say so, but I know she worried about my father, about taking him away from the doctors who knew and treated him for various ailments.

Dad was walking slow, breathing hard. He'd quit smoking at fifty-six, but years of inhaling dry-cleaning chemicals compounded the damage. He'd had at least one heart attack, his arteries were clogged, his circulation poor. He wore heavy, white socks even in summer, and he still shivered. None of us said what all of us knew: My father would die first, and only then would Mom think about moving to Florida.

Mom was right about so many things, but she was wrong about this even though she was late in accepting its truth. By summer 1988, I knew she was dying and there was nothing I could do about it—nothing anyone could do about it. Each day I woke up the same way I went to bed, with a vision of my mother drowning. I could see her, but there was no way to reach her because I was a thousand miles away, watching her through a telescope.

I really was a thousand miles away, although I could reach her in a little over two hours by plane—but what good would that do? I talked to her doctor again and again, and he never wavered in his judgment that her condition was hopeless. I knew this was not a tragedy, not like some child getting run over by a car or a young father being shot to death by a stickup man on his way to the grocery store. I knew that this was the way of the world, as explained to me by my mother when I was a boy. "The old people have to die to make way for the babies." She said that every time one of our older friends or relatives died. It was supposed to make me feel better, but it did not help now. Why did some baby have to shove my mother off the edge of the world? Mothers are supposed to live a lot longer than seventy-six years. My mother was supposed to live forever.

I felt certain no one could sense my panic because no one would expect it. I never panic. As a newsman, I was conditioned to expect the unexpected, even the horrific, and to deal with it calmly and logically. Planes crashed, criminals shot cops, parents beat their children to death, families were burned alive in their sleep. For years, I dealt with all of it, every day. I'd send a photographer, send a reporter, commission a graphic of the death scene and order more space to make room for all the gory details while asking: How many dead? Do we have the names? Can we get the children's pictures? Can we interview the widow?

I did this very well, and then I'd go home to eat dinner. I never talked about any of it. I'd swallow it, and then I'd swallow my chicken and rice. This is the way I learned to deal with the ugliness of the world, the Armenian way. I learned it from my father. Don't talk about sad things, and don't let anyone ask. Don't think about it, if at all possible. Just keep moving. But now, for the first time in my life, I could barely swallow anything. My throat felt as though someone were choking me, and my chest felt tighter than my throat. I'd never been a good sleeper, but now I became an insomniac who stayed up

wife
daughter

until all hours watching terrible movies on television. I couldn't bear to read a book because books made me think and I couldn't stand to think because I'd only think about my mother dying.

I felt just plain sick, and so did Robyn. She sat up late, too, but not for the same reason. She had pains in the abdomen every time she ate, and they were so bad some nights that she doubled over. The doctor referred her to a specialist who thought she might have an ulcer or something wrong with her small intestine, or maybe her large intestine. He ordered tests and more tests, and meanwhile the pain got worse. The specialist finally decided the problem was stress. "You have to learn to deal with it," he said. Then one night after we'd been out late, Robyn doubled over in pain again—and this time, the pain wouldn't stop, so I took her to the hospital. The problem, it turned out, wasn't stress at all. The problem was her gall bladder, which had stopped working a long time before. The doctor called in a surgeon who said not to worry. He'd operate in a few days, after the infection cleared up. I got a phone call the next morning at my office: The infection had become worse. Robyn needed surgery immediately. When the doctor cut her open, he discovered gangrene. Her gall bladder wasn't sick—it was dead, and Robyn had nearly followed.

The doctor operated just in time, and I was both relieved and terrified. Even with Robyn safely home from the hospital, I couldn't get over the feeling that something else would go wrong. I sat up watching TV night after night until I was ready to pass out, and then I stumbled off to bed, often barely in time to shut off the alarm clock. Then one night, a little over a week after Robyn's surgery, I was jarred from my sleep by Robyn's voice, shrill and quavering and distant. She was calling our daughter's name, over and over: "Mandy! Mandy! Mandy!" I reached out, but Robyn's side of the bed was empty. Her voice was coming from down the hall, from our daughter's room. I ran there to find Robyn crying. Mandy lay in bed, motionless but not asleep. "She isn't breathing," Robyn screamed. "I heard noises, like she was choking, but I couldn't wake you up."

So Robyn, still bandaged and hobbled from major surgery, made her way down the hall alone to find our daughter inert. I snapped alert, calm and focused as always in a crisis. I put one ear to Mandy's mouth. She was breathing, but shallow. Her body was limp. Her head flopped backward when I try to pick her up. I told Robyn to call 9-1-1 while I gently tried to shake Mandy awake. "Mandy, talk to Daddy. Tell me what's wrong. Mandy, Mandy. Can you hear me?"

We spent the rest of the night at the hospital, then a good deal of the next day at a neurologist's office, where we learned that our perfectly healthy six-year-old daughter had suffered a seizure for no apparent reason. She seemed fine now, but she seemed fine when we put her to bed the night before. She had no cold, no fever, no aches or pains. She was smiling then and she was smiling again as she played in a corner while this strange doctor told us it may never happen again—or this may have been the first sign of a serious disease and we'd just have to keep an eye on her. I wanted to do more than keep an eye on her. I wanted the doctor to tell us how to fix what was wrong, but he said there was nothing we could do. Just like there was nothing anyone could do for my mother. I have never before or since felt so worthless.

A day or so later, I was sitting in my private office at work, looking through the glass wall into the newsroom, trying very hard to think about nothing but the news. My head hurt, my back hurt, and my stomach hurt. Everything hurt, except my hands. I had no feeling in either of them. Pain pulsed down my arms, into my wrists, but it never reached my fingers, as though some neuro-impulse work crew had set up a roadblock somewhere south of each elbow. They must have put up a detour sign, too, because suddenly the pain came pulsing back up my arms and into my chest. I was breathing hard, but I didn't feel any air reaching my lungs. I was gasping, my head was floating, and I couldn't see a thing through the glass. I saw nothing but fog.

Now I was having my own crisis, and I was just as determined as ever to stay calm, think it through, deal with it. I simply refused to pass out or shout for help. I stared at my desk until the telephone came into focus. I slowly, deliberately flipped through my Rolodex for my doctor's number. "I'm not feeling well," I said. "No, it isn't serious, but I need to see the doctor now."

How did I know it wasn't serious? I was clear-headed enough to know I needed a doctor, but nothing else I did made sense, least of all driving myself to his office ten miles away. All the way there I wondered: "What if this is a heart attack? What if I never get there?" And still, when I did get there, I smiled at the receptionist and assured her there was no rush. She saw my pallor and the sweat on my brow and got me through the door swiftly. In a minute, I was lying on an examining table with wires taped to my ankles and chest sending impulses to an EKG monitor. I felt like a human pinball machine. It is a very odd sensation, lying there, knowing a machine is sensing every pulse beat, half waiting for the thing to go "BLEEEEEEEEEP" in some horribly flat and fatal tone signaling that I'm gone. I wondered if I'd hear it? Luckily, there was no "bleep," and there was nothing wrong. The doctor said I was ticking away just fine except for a quickened pulse, and everything else looked tip-top, too.

"Are you under any stress?"

I told him the question annoyed me. I related Robyn's experience with the doctor who couldn't tell the difference between stress and a gangrenous gall bladder.

"Your wife nearly died," the doctor said. "That had to be stressful. Is there anything else you're worried about?"

I told him about Mandy, and then I told him about my mother. He stared at me and shook his head.

"And you had to think about whether you're under stress? You felt like you were losing every woman in your life at once. You wouldn't be normal if that didn't stress you out. No wonder you're in here on your back."

He advised me to get some exercise, give my body an outlet for all this nervous energy so it wouldn't just clamp my muscles tight and send my heart racing for no reason. He also prescribed an anti-anxiety drug. I shrugged off both suggestions. "If it's only stress, I just won't worry about it." Then I added with a grin, "I can always have a scotch to relax."

The doctor was insistent, but I knew my father would agree with me. Dad sometimes took sleeping pills, but an anti-anxiety medication sounded too much like something a psychiatrist would prescribe, and my father definitely didn't approve of that sort of thing. The Armenians of his generation didn't have psychiatrists to help them deal with their troubles, he said many times. I accepted the premise without thinking about it because my father said it, even though it made no sense. The Armenians of his generation had no heart surgeons either, but that doesn't mean they didn't die of heart disease. My father and most other survivors of the Genocide had to deal with the demons their own way. That doesn't mean it was the best way.

I missed the midnight movie that night for the first time in weeks, but my blissful rest lasted only a few hours. I woke up in a flash a little after one. I was suddenly awake, alert, and scared out of my wits, although I didn't know why. Did I hear Robyn calling me? Did I hear Mandy? My heart was pounding harder and faster than I imagined it could without bursting. I quit trying to sleep after that and went back to my TV-movie routine for the next week until I came down with the flu, or a convincing imposter. I knew that wasn't stress because I had a fever and chills and all the classic intestinal symptoms. The doctor agreed with my diagnosis. He told me I'd feel better in a few days, but he was wrong. The fever went away but the chills and the intestinal misery remained. I couldn't keep any food in my stomach, not even soup, for more than a few minutes. This time I was happy to lie down on the doctor's table, but afterward I couldn't stand up. The doctor said I was dehydrated and sent me straight to the hospital.

"You'll feel better when we get some fluids in you."

This was an even stranger experience than the EKG. At thirty-six, I was hospitalized for the first time since I'd had my tonsils taken out when I was five. I had no broken leg, no incision, no communicable disease, and yet I was lying in a hospital bed with an IV needle in my right hand. It hurt, and my hand swelled up. The fluid made me feel stronger but hardly better. If anything, I felt worse. I wanted to sleep but I couldn't because of all the noise from blinking readouts and interruptions of people coming in to check my temperature or my IV bag or my bedpan. I was distracted, and yet I was not distracted enough.

Without my work, I could not help thinking about all the things I'd been trying to avoid. When I closed my eyes, I could see my mother through the telescope's lens, drowning. I was surrounded by doctors and nurses and medical equipment, but I felt nothing but dread. When I told the doctor this, he reminded me of the pills he'd prescribed. "You're over the flu," he said. "There's nothing wrong with you except anxiety."

He said I could go home the next day provided I could eat a meal without immediately expelling it. Breakfast stayed put long enough to justify my release. When lunchtime arrived at home, I decided to eat light, but even helium-on-rye wouldn't have been light enough. Lunch made a lightning-quick exit, and I got back on the phone with the doctor. He told me to be patient—the colon has a mind of its own, and it returns to old habits when it's good and ready—but I was in no mood to be patient. Something was clearly wrong and I wanted it fixed. Over the coming weeks, I willingly submitted to the manipulations of a medieval torturer who called himself a gastroenterologist. Every venue of digestion or excretion was probed, scoped, scraped, and photographed. I got a very small measure of satisfaction along with a fresh infusion of anxiety when he announced that my complaints didn't seem to be stress related at all. He couldn't be certain what the problem was, however. He was certain only that I needed more tests.

This became my routine for the next month: One day I felt a lot better, the next a lot worse. I digested one meal perfectly, then the next one sent me sprinting toward the porcelain before I'd swallowed two bites. I couldn't work or sleep or eat until the doctor finished his tests. When that day finally came, he shrugged and said he'd found nothing wrong. "It's probably just stress after all." The strange thing is, this actually made me feel much better. If stress was the problem, I knew the cure: I would simply ignore it. When I got home from my doctor's visit, I ate a hearty meal and it stayed put. I congratulated myself on my complete recovery. I not only felt better, I looked better. In a little over a month, I'd lost more than thirty pounds. I went out and bought new pants to celebrate. We all celebrated. Robyn had made a robust recovery from her surgery, and Mandy hadn't shown any signs of repeated trouble. The neurologist seemed pretty confident the seizure was a fluke. Not long after school got out for the summer, we all bundled into the car and headed north to see Mom.

How strange it was to ring the doorbell at 529 Bergen Boulevard instead of just opening the door with a key and shouting, "I'm home." Stranger still, the woman who opened the door didn't look like my mother. This was a very old, small, frail woman with white hair who moved very slowly. Where was my silver-haired, mile-a-minute Mom? She should have been in the kitchen, sliding a tray of hot lavash out of the oven, but the oven was cold and so was Mom. It was July, but she was bundled up in fluffy white socks and the blue booties she knitted herself and a blue cotton robe as thick as an Arctic parka. Maybe I'd come to the wrong place, to the igloo of an old Aleut woman perhaps? But I knew this was Mom because of her smile. She was dying and smiling at once, as I should have expected, but I didn't know what to do. I hugged her as though I were hugging a paper mache doll because I was afraid she might break.

I was afraid every minute of every day of our visit, but my mother and father weren't afraid, because they refused to believe anything so awful as death was about to intrude on the life they had shared since they were teenagers. My father was clearly worried, however. He sat on the couch, shrunken and silent, staring at Mom. She sat a few feet away in a tan, vinyl recliner, her lap and legs covered by a blue-and-white blanket she knitted to match her booties. Her arms were pulled in tight to trap what little heat her body still generated. Both hands were cupped to her right side, just below her ribs, where the cancer was eating away at her liver. I couldn't help staring. For two months, since the day I got sick at the office, I had been holding my right side in the same spot. I went to the kitchen to put on a pot of coffee and my father followed. "She could be like this for a long time," he whispered. "I'm going to see about having a shower built downstairs because she can't walk upstairs anymore." I started to tell him it was too late for that, but I didn't have the energy, or the heart. I was worried now about both of them, and they were worried about me. They wanted to know what my tests showed, but we all knew my real problem: I was reliving the worst time of my father's life.

I had grown up in the shadow of the Turk who killed my father's mother. My mother and I both had to bite our tongues and swallow our anger, our frustration, and sometimes even our love because my father lost his mother when he was three years old. Now I was losing my mother, and I was as helpless as a three-year-old to do anything about it. This cancer was a Turk. I knew this was foolish, but it didn't matter because it is what I felt, not only in my gut but in my right side just below the rib cage. I felt angry beyond reason and beyond words, but at least I knew how to deal with it because I had watched my father for so many years.

I dealt with it by saying nothing.

I drove back to Florida with one hand on the wheel and the other cupped against my right side.

A SLOW BOAT FROM CHINA REACHES FLORIDA

When Mom was sick, I'd call her oncologist from Florida for updates and he'd ask me—plead with me—to explain to my parents that she was going to die.

"Neither of them seems to understand," he'd say.

"They understand," I told him. "They're just not interested."

The poor guy would try to explain that the outlook was hopeless, and my mother would tell him to stop being so hard on himself. "You'll think of something." Toward the end, my father and Uncle Mike and I spent long days by her side at the hospital. My father would hold her hand for hours in silence. Then she'd wave him away and whisper to me, "What are you making for dinner?" I'd go through the menu, ingredient by ingredient. "Don't forget the bouillon cube," she'd say. "But don't tell your father. He thinks I never use them." And we'd both laugh.

Eventually, Mom was too weak to speak, and it was impossible to tell whether she knew we were there. The doctor told us the end was near but there was no telling how long. I took my father home and made him dinner, but neither of us ate. I washed the dishes and then sat next to him on the living room sofa as the sun was setting. The room was nearly dark, but I didn't want to leave his side, even to get up and turn on the lights. He was telling me not to worry, that he would manage to take care of Mom when she came home.

I told him, again, that she wasn't coming home, but he wouldn't listen. "What do the doctors know?"

We sat there, saying nothing, until the hospital called to say it was over. Dad answered the phone, calm and measured.

"Thank you," he said. Then he sat down again, and we both cried for a long time.

My father, survivor of war and genocide, lost his way completely after Mom died. He hardly spoke and barely moved. The old paratrooper and businessman suddenly couldn't sign his name to a check to pay the light bill.

"You do it," he'd say, no matter how simple the task. I was happy to, but I had to go back to work in Florida. I didn't ask him if he wanted to go with me. I told him he had no choice. Robyn helped me pack up the house before she flew back. Dad and I followed by train a day or two later. I didn't like to fly, and Dad wouldn't even consider it. He hadn't been on a plane since the Second World War. "He's not afraid to fly," my mother once told me. "He's afraid to land." I still don't know if that was a joke.

No plane ride could have been as bumpy as our lives over the next year and a half. Dad was gracious to Robyn, but he was hard on her, too. She would cook, he wouldn't eat. He'd want to get out of the house, then complain about wherever she took him. He didn't like our grocery stores, our neighborhood, or very much at all about our lives. Florida was too hot, too crowded with too many stupid people. Dad was even tougher on me: Why had I insisted on bringing him to this place? I was tough on him, too. I had his car shipped down, but I wouldn't let him drive. I was afraid of what might happen in his distracted state. So it was my fault that he was trapped in the house all day, pacing as he waited for Robyn to get home from teaching school. Then he'd pounce the moment she opened the door, insisting she take him to this store or that. The only one who escaped his anger was Mandy, now the light of his life. She was seven, and she loved Grandpa. He talked to her, he sang to her, he tried to teach her Armenian. The man who had so little patience all his life and even less now was the most patient man in the world with his one and only granddaughter. But Mandy had to go to school, and after school she wanted to play with her friends, and then she went to bed—and Grandpa was left to sit and think and complain and get angry all over again.

"Listen," he said one day when I came home. "I'm going back."

He would not listen when I told him there was no one and no place to go back to. We'd given away most of the furniture and packed everything else for the movers. The Ridgefield house was for sale. The electricity and water were turned off. He wouldn't hear any of it. In the blustery fall of 1988, Dad took a train back to New Jersey. He tore open box after box, but he didn't find what he was looking for because he wasn't really looking for anything except my mother, and she was gone. He sat in that cold, empty, lonely house in the middle of an ungodly mess for two months before it finally dawned on him.

"OK, I'm coming back," he said, and that was that.

When he got back to Florida, we all went to look for some place where Dad could feel independent but still be close by. We found the perfect place right away, a condominium that was a short drive from our house and a short walk to the grocery store. He rented the place for a while, decided he liked it, and then bought it—and almost immediately after that, decided he hated it. The neighbors upstairs made too much noise. "I can't live like this," he said again. He insisted on buying another place, without waiting to sell the first one. We found a two-story townhouse around the corner. This time he couldn't complain about noise upstairs because there was no one upstairs. It even had a little courtyard where he could plant a garden.

A year passed before Dad was finally settling in, if not exactly settling down. He enjoyed being on his own, but we all had dinner together almost every night. Often, he cooked—and he cooked well. He never quit the habit of buying meat for the weekend, sometimes even when Robyn had already cooked or we planned to go out. Then in mid-week we'd stop by and find the refrigerator packed with meat that should have been eaten days before. We finally had to visit the local butcher and tell him to call us before filling Dad's order.

No matter where we ate or who cooked, Dad and I would have a drink together before dinner and we'd sit and talk. Our conversations weren't always deep, but they were important to me because I was talking to my father, now more than ever, and he told me more than he ever had. It was during this time that he told me about eating crabs on Corfu and about playing with the children at a New Jersey park and about nearly starving in the refugee camp when he arrived in Greece. He still wouldn't tolerate questions, still turned away when the memories became too painful, but I was learning more about him, filling in the gaps and feeling good and proud that he now trusted me enough to tell me more.

One night when we were planning to eat out, Robyn asked Dad what he wanted. To her shock, he said, "Chinese food." Robyn had tried to get him to eat Chinese several times and failed. She figured he knew he'd disappointed her and had decided to be chivalrous. Regardless, she was thrilled. We headed for the nearest Chinese restaurant. When it came time to order, my father just shrugged and pointed to me. "I'll have what he has," he said, so I ordered for both of us. My father did have one request.

He asked the waiter for chopsticks.

Robyn and I both stared at him and then at each other. We figured this was his idea of humor. But when the meal came, he picked up the chopsticks and started using them, flawlessly. I understood immediately that this was a clue.

"Dad, where did you learn to use chopsticks?"

"China," he said, and we both laughed.

"Finally," I said, "I'm going to hear the story."

"There is no story," my father said. "Pass the tea."

On Wednesday, March 14, 1990, we all went out to eat at a French restaurant near home to celebrate my thirty-eighth birthday. It wasn't a ritzy place, but the food was good and Dad was as happy as I'd seen him since Mom died. He'd been ebullient all week, calling friends and relatives around the country and promising to visit. He even called his cousins in France, the grandchildren of the aunt who had sheltered and saved him in the old country. He wanted me to help get a passport so he could visit them. I told him that was a long trip to take alone. He laughed. "I found my way here all the way from Dikranagerd by myself, didn't I?"

When I called the next day, he sounded awful. "Goddam Frogs," he said. "I should have known better than to eat at a French restaurant." I drove over to see him. He was bundled up on the couch in a blue-and-white blanket my mother had crocheted.

"I'll be OK," he said. "It's just a little stomach trouble. Remember: I'm a survivor." He handed me the latest copy of the *Armenian Weekly*. The headlines were all about the rapidly changing situation in the Caucuses. The Soviets were collapsing, the Azeris were rioting, the Armenians were ready to fight. "You must be happy," I said. "Armenia will be free soon." He didn't smile. "At least the Communists kept people from killing each other," he said. When I called the next day, he felt better. We agreed he should rest up, then we'd all have dinner together the next night. "We have to celebrate St. Patrick's Day," he insisted. "I want corned beef and cabbage." I'd never seen my father eat corned beef, and he certainly didn't celebrate St. Patrick's Day.

Maybe this was like his Chinese surprise and he'd suddenly tell us he'd taken a trip to Ireland?

There was no answer when I called him that morning, Saturday, March 17. That wasn't unusual. Dad often walked to the minimall a few blocks away. He'd make the rounds, ordering meat at the butcher's, stopping to chat with the guy at the juice bar (a former dry cleaner), checking out the plants, and then having lunch at the Italian restaurant. I wasn't worried, until later. It was late morning when I went to check up on him. I found Dad lying on the kitchen floor. I knew instantly that he was dead.

He was in his bathrobe, the *Miami Herald* was still in its plastic wrapper on the kitchen table, the coffeepot was on the stove. There wasn't a drop in it. The burner was still on. Dad had simply dropped dead in the middle of his morning routine, a little less than two weeks before his seventy-eighth birthday. It was just how he'd wanted to go. He told me once that the Turks had a term for heart attack that meant "the gift from God." They believed that swift death was a righteous man's reward. Dad deserved this reward, but I didn't. I was crying before I reached him and knelt down. I missed him immensely, immediately—but I was angry, too. I was thinking about everything he knew, everything I wanted him to tell me, all of the stories he never finished.

Everything I would never know.

Now it was my turn, again, to hold up and carry on with the business of living. I made the necessary calls and then sat at Dad's table with a police officer who filled out a report on an elderly man who had died alone of natural causes. He needed a list of illnesses, medications, doctor's name. Name of mother and father. Occupation. Marital status.

Place of birth.

I didn't hesitate.

"Armenia," I said.

I didn't mention that he was born in midair, that all Armenians are born in midair.

THE TRIP MY FATHER DIDN'T
LIVE TO TAKE

The breeze in my cousin Arsene Dirkelessian's backyard during our visit in summer 2001 was always perfect and perfectly mysterious.

He does not live near the sea nor in the mountains. His home is about ten miles northeast of Paris, France, in an ordinary, working-class suburb of small houses surrounded by fences and flanked by wash lines and detached garages. If you tacked on aluminum siding and storm windows, you might be in Clifton, New Jersey, or Cleveland, Ohio. But ignore a few minor details and this was as close as I'd come to Dikranagerd since Diyeh died.

Robyn and I sat at a wooden table on a flat-stone patio between a grape arbor and a hedge of shoulder-high rose bushes in full bloom. Across from us were Arsene, his wife, Odile, and their then-seven-year-old daughter, Marie-Luz. There was enough food for a wedding feast: Spanish soup, French cheeses and breads, Armenian meats and salads, baked and syrup-soaked sweets from throughout the Middle East. My stomach was full but my plate was not getting empty.

"This is special, from Allepo," said Arsene, piling on slabs of something that resembled bologna studded with bits of carrot and pistachio nuts. There was no point in arguing with him. It became clear early in our eight-day visit that Arsene never hears the words "no thanks."

Arsene took special delight in serving food from his native Syria, but he was happy to serve anything at all, usually with his fingers. He used his own utensils to pass along whatever had to be pierced, sliced, or scooped. I wouldn't have it any other way. The intimacy of our meals was far more important than the food. Getting to know Arsene and his sister, Haygo, was the reason I'd come to France. I'd known about them all my life but never met them until a year earlier, when I rushed through Paris on assignment.

In a sense, I came back to continue a conversation that was interrupted long before any of us were born. Our fathers were first cousins, born a few years apart in Dikranagerd. Arsene's paternal grandmother was the aunt who took my father in after he was turned out by the Kurds. My father considered her his mother, and her sons, Yervant and Hagop, his brothers. They were the second family he lost before his eleventh birthday. He never saw any of them again after the Armenians were evicted from Dikranagerd forever in 1922. He landed in the orphanage in Greece. His cousins settled in Syria. Dad made his way to America, while his cousins eventually migrated to France.

Over the next six decades, they exchanged letters, photos of their families, and promises to meet again. Yervant become a chauffeur, Hagop a barber, and my father a dry cleaner. Each was too busy making a living to keep the promise. Even after Yervant and Hagop had passed on, Dad stayed in touch with their children. He was talking enthusiastically about a trip to France the week he died.

A few years later, I came across some of the photos and letters and decided to make contact. I found an address for Arsene and sent a friendly but brief letter expressing my best wishes and curiosity about his family. His response was in French, but a friend who translated it for me was struck by its warmth and by Arsene's delight in my having written. Instead of writing again, I called. We spoke in a halting combination of English and Armenian, but we had no trouble understanding what really mattered.

"I love you," Arsene said. "I kees you."

This man I'd never met, twelve years older than I and born on the other side of the world, suggested Robyn and I fly to France and stay in his home. He was more than sincere, he was insistent—more so after our first encounter.

In the years since my father's death, I'd taken care of some unfinished business: I got my college degree, wrote my first book and eventually made a transition from editing to feature writing at The Palm Beach Post. I flew to England with a photographer in September 2000 to accompany a Second World War Army veteran on an emotional trip back to Normandy, where he'd landed on D-Day in 1944. We took a ferry across the English Channel, then followed the route of the Allied forces inland across the Cotentin Peninsula. Our last stop was Paris, where we had a bit more than twenty-four hours to rest before boarding a plane back to Florida. I called Haygo and Arsene from my hotel, hoping to steal a few minutes of their time. Instead, they stole me for the night.

Brother and sister showed up in the hotel lobby within minutes of my call. I didn't have to rely on their photos to identify them. Their elegant clothes and speech were French, but their body language and manner were all Armenian. We hugged and a moment later I was being propelled out the door, one cousin at each arm. I tried to explain that I couldn't leave the hotel because I was traveling with a party and had to be up early to continue work. They understood, but they weren't interested. We had to talk and, like all Armenians, we could not talk without food. It did not matter to them that I'd already had dinner. We went to a restaurant down the street where, for the first time since I arrived in France, I didn't have to puzzle over the menu. Haygo and Arsene ordered without consulting me. Minutes later, the waiter brought a single plate of steak and placed it in front of me. My cousins knew that all Americans like steak. They ordered nothing for themselves because, like me, they had already eaten. But they were quite certain that Americans are always hungry. Besides, it was their obligation to feed me because I was the youngest and I was also their guest—and Armenians always feed their guests.

They talked as I ate, telling me how sorry they were that my poor father wound up in America instead of a paradise like Syria or France, where Armenians still spoke Armenian and ate lamb and bulgur instead of steak and potatoes, and where you could smoke anywhere you liked without being harassed by the government. In effect, they were telling me: Poor cousin! You are a fat and ignorant American, but it is not your fault, and we love you anyway. I thanked them profusely, then tried to excuse myself. They didn't even bother to argue, except with each other.

"Now I'll take him," Arsene said.

"No! I'll take him," Haygo replied.

"No!"

It was finally agreed that Arsene would drive, Haygo would come along, and I would become a mobile captive. Arsene ushered me into his black Mercedes C-Class sedan, a compact in America but a near limo in Paris. We immediately launched on a nighttime hypertour of Paris. Arsene was determined to show me every attraction from the Eiffel Tower to Sacré-Coeur in one supercondensed evening. He drove at fantastic speed, somehow managing to shift gears and steer his way around Paris traffic while gesturing to points of interest with both hands. Haygo remained impeccably coiffed and serene in the back seat. This was hardly an unusual experience for her.

The tour ended sometime after midnight, but my captivity did not. Arsene drove out of the city and deep into the suburbs, stopping on a dark street in front of a house that I could barely make out behind a tall fence in the moonlight. A dozen or more people were waiting for us inside, all family who had gathered at this late hour to meet their American cousin. After a round of hugs, I was led to the comfiest chair in the living room. Women brought trays of nuts and sweets from the kitchen, along with coffee and brandy. It was all for me. I was beyond full, but I could not turn it away, so I nibbled and sipped while being looked over. The inspection quickly turned into interrogation. The women arranged their chairs in a semicircle facing me and took turns asking questions. They were all smiles, but they were deadly serious. One of the women did her best to translate the questions into English, but I still had to do a lot of guesswork—and I worried about guessing wrong.

"You are married?" one asked.

"Yes," and there was no doubt what the next question would be.

"Is she Armenian?"

"Yes."

"Ahhh!" they all shouted, while nodding in approval. I felt certain I was passing the test, until the next question.

"Is her family Dashnak?"

This stunned me. No one would ask that question in America, even people who cared about the answer. I was less surprised by the boldness of someone's asking about my in-laws' politics than I was by their interest. Why would anyone care—and why would they assume I did? Why would they even suspect that our grandparents' politics would have some relevance to my life? I was too tired and too tongue-tied to even attempt to do more than simply answer the question.

"No, they aren't."

The reply was spontaneous.

"Ohhhhhhhh . . ."

Heads shook in disapproval. Luckily, the decisive question was yet to come.

"Is she Dikranagerdtsi?"

How strange again! Here I was in a foreign country in a roomful of people I'd never met before, and they wanted to know if I married a hometown girl, even though none of us had ever been to our hometown. Again, what really surprised me was that they seemed to have assumed this would be important to me, that I wouldn't have married a girl without at least asking what village her grandparents came from. What surprised me even more was the realization that it was indeed important to me, or at least interesting.

"Yes, she's Dikranagerdtsi," I said.

"Ahhhh!" they exclaimed approvingly.

There were big smiles all around as heads bobbed enthusiastically. I had passed the test and so had Robyn, even though she was an ocean away.

Even this successful examination did not end my captivity. Arsene took me home with him despite my insistence that I could not possibly leave my traveling companions alone all night. Throughout the few hours left until dawn, my mind replayed flashes of headlamp-illuminated Paris and the dim faces of deeply serious Armenian women scrutinizing my eating and marital habits. Even the next day, Arsene would not take me back to my hotel until I swore I'd return with Robyn for a proper visit. When I got back to Florida, I told Robyn to plan on a trip but not to bother checking out hotels.

"Are you sure your cousin really wants us to stay with him?" she asked.

"When you meet Arsene, you'll understand," I told her.

The meeting took place nine months later at Charles de Gaulle Airport, where Arsene was waiting for our plane as promised. He did indeed "kees" us. He communicated his joy by singing through much of the half-hour ride to his home. The demands of heavy traffic did not deter him from clapping to the music. He even danced with his upper body, his head bobbing and snaking. The music and the movements were clearly Armenian, as was a good deal of the conversation—at least on his end. The two typically monolingual Americans in the back seat were clearly not up to the challenge of responding, but this didn't stop Arsene nor anyone else we encountered in the next two weeks.

It is normal for Americans traveling abroad to constantly consult a foreign-phrase book while hoping to get by on a smile and a pitiable look, but we were not on a normal trip. Our time in France was spent almost exclusively with Armenians from the Middle East or from Armenia. Again and again, Arsene introduced me as the cousin who can't speak Armenian. "Amerikatzi," he always explained with a shrug. The reaction became familiar: frowns and finger wagging. This would have been easy to shrug off if it were simply anti-American sentiment. What made this painful is that it was personal. The onus was on us for allowing the stain of assimilation to blot out an essential part of our heritage. Assimilation of any sort turned out to be a touchy subject. It was easier for Arsene and Haygo to resist because they were born in a place where assimilation was neither expected nor encouraged.

In Syria, as in many other Arab countries, Armenian refugees were accepted without being absorbed. As Christians in a Muslim culture, they remained distinct; as exiles barely out of sight of their lost land, they remained fiercely determined to preserve their culture. Yet Arsene and others born in the region could not help becoming Arabized in many of the ways that my father became Americanized. They eat Arabic food. The Armenian music they listen to wouldn't raise an eyebrow in a Beirut discotheque. Although he has lived in France most of his adult life, Arsene watches Arab-language TV programs from the Middle East nightly through the wonder of satellite television.

But Arsene, who learned functional English while serving in the Syrian Army, insisted this was all superficial. "In Allepo, we say we are more Armenian than they are in Armenia," he informed me. I struggled to understand what he meant, and how this made him different from me. Except for my rudimentary conversational skills, I think I am as Armenian as any American could be. But I am, indeed, an American. That is the real difference, the one my father understood so well: Arsene will never really be French any more than he was ever Syrian.

Arsene moved to France in 1966 for the reason that propels so many immigrants: opportunity. He became an electrician and started a family. He married a French woman, not an Armenian. They had three daughters, who are now grown. When his first wife died, Arsene married Odile, who is Spanish. He said neither marriage diluted his identity. "She became Armenian when she married me," he said of Odile. It was hard to tell if she agreed because she speaks only French and Spanish, but it's clear that she adapted. She certainly cooks like an Armenian. They moved from Paris to a suburb called Bondy several years before so Marie-Luz could attend a full-time Armenian school nearby.

Arsene's house is as Armenian as he is, signaled by the containers of bright-red geraniums lining the tall front stairs. The rooms inside felt small, but there were more of them than I suspected when we entered, and Arsene

228

has made certain that no possibility of living space was ignored. He even expanded the garage out back to provide a bedroom and bath for Odile's daughter from a previous marriage, plus a spare bedroom that would have been perfect for us except that Arsene insisted we stay under one roof. He led us to a staircase that looked as if it had been pirated from a lighthouse, with curlicue railings barely wide enough for us to squeeze through as we cork-screwed our way up to the attic. It was unfinished to the American eye, with overhead truss supports presenting a constant navigational challenge that I failed more often than not, but there was a toilet and sink in a side room and a pair of mattresses on the floor. We were more than comfortable, and we were happy to be under Arsene's roof, if only by inches.

The home's kitchen was modest by American standards, with a fridge no bigger than a picnic cooler. Nothing larger proved necessary, as Odile smilingly set out on daily walks to the market and returned with arms loaded. We joined her several times and found ourselves huff-puffing well behind, getting a valuable lesson in how to eat more while gain-ing less. Much of what Odile carried home bypassed the minifridge and went straight down to a summer kitchen in the semibasement. Really, it was the Armenian kitchen, with no fridge or stove but just dark and cool enough for storing fruits and dried meats and all the other ingredients for an Armenian picnic.

The picnic grounds were just across the yard, where Arsene set a table and chairs under an awning alongside the garage. This is where we spent nearly all our time, enjoying that mysterious breeze as we ate and then rested until it was time to eat some more, which was never very long. Arsene and I passed the time between meals talking, sipping coffee, and playing backgam-mon, just as we would have in Dikranagerd.

This is where he told me a story that helped me fit one more piece into the puzzle my father left: Soon after arriving in Syria, his father recognized a man in a coffeehouse as a traitor from Dikranagerd. He greeted the man as a friend and pretended to know nothing about the betrayal. He left and returned with a knife. He greeted the man again, but this time told him he knew what had happened. The traitor had no time to flee: Arsene's father gutted him on the spot. Arsene illustrated by suddenly unsheathing a knife with a slightly curved, nearly black blade. "This is the knife," he said, offering me the yellowed bone handle. It was surprisingly light, but the blade was still sharp—and no doubt still deadly.

In Arsene's telling, the traitor was an Assyrian, not an Armenian, but he was clearly the man who recognized my grandfather's voice and told the Turks where to find him and his brother-in-law, Arsene's grandfather. My father told me one of his cousins killed the traitor. Now I knew who, where, and how. I told Arsene as best I could what my father told me about this man. Both of our stories lost details in the translation, but each of us understood the real point. "Dooglas, our fathers are happy we are here together."

Our visit lasted long enough for Robyn and me to attend the end-of-year program at Marie-Luz's school. It was an all-day, much-of-the-night affair that included recitations and skits in Armenian. The highlight for us was a costumed, musical version of *Snow White and the Seven Dwarfs*. Even "hi-ho, hi-ho" was translated into Armenian. It sounded like "heh-haw, heh-haw."

"I sent all my daughters to this school," Arsene said. "It cost a lot of money, but I don't care. They have to learn Armenian.." The older ones all did, but it's not clear how much they've retained. "It's very bad," Arsene said. "One of them marries a French man and lives in the mountains. One of them marries a Syrian man. The other one doesn't marry, but she doesn't stay with Armenians. I do all this for what?"

Still, he was doing it all again. Marie-Luz speaks French with her mother but Armenian with her father. "All we can do is try," Arsene said. "Maybe this time it works. We don't know what will happen in life."

While the schoolchildren took a break from performing, a recorded song played over the public address system. The words were French, but the voice was familiar, the French-Armenian singer and composer Charles Aznavour. Arsene closed his eyes and sang along. After a few verses, he translated for me.

"He says, 'They kill us. They make us go into the desert and we fall down. The Armenians fall down but they come up again. We are not dead. We are here.'"

I nodded to show that I understood. Arsene made certain.

"Dooglas!" he said. "We are here! We are alive! Our fathers are dead but we are here. We are Armenian."

Our visit to France ended two days later. On the way to the airport, Arsene made me promise to work on my Armenian when I got home. It is an obligation to our fathers, he said.

"You have to try."

"I will," I replied.

He said goodbye with a kees.

REFLECTIONS

After all this, I'm still suffering windburn from my ever-accelerating fall through Armenian history. I have been trying to get my fingers around that frayed cord all this time, but I can't quite get a grip.

I thumbed through many books and articles while writing this story, double-checking historical markers in my memory while placing new ones alongside them. It's a time-consuming process under normal circumstances, but reading or even just thinking about the Armenian experience causes me to stumble into one emotional trench after another, feeling trapped like my ancestors in the path of an invading horde.

The Genocide alone is gut-churning to contemplate. So is the continued struggle over its recognition. Why is history considered history except where Armenians are concerned? The world doesn't demand that anyone recognize the fall of Rome, or the Great Depression or the Civil War. What happened happened, and anyone who refuses to believe it is dimissed as an idiot. I don't see any reason to make an exception in the case of the Armenian Genocide.

There is no genuine debate, only verbal mud thrown mostly these days over the Internet. Feed the phrase "Armenian Genocide" into Google and you'll turn up endless, tiresome "exposes" by Turks and endless rebuttals by Armenians. Much of the back-and-forth is mean, angry, even vicious. I'm not interested in taking part. This mud, after all, is being thrown over the graves of our ancestors. Anyone who wants to be educated on the subject of the Armenian Genocide can read a book. As far as I'm concerned, anyone who doesn't can go to hell.

Dredging all this up is almost enough to make me hate Turks despite my father's example, except for this: I can't be sure who they are. As Bared Maronian shows in his documentary *Orphans of the Genocide*, many Armenian children were herded into state-run orphanages that were really Turkish-conversion camps. Those who resisted were killed. Those who survived—well, where did they go? How could I hate any Turk without being sure he wasn't the son or grandson or great-grandson of an Armenian who saved himself and perhaps also saved his family by taking a Turkish name and embracing Islam? Would he be less Armenian than I am? I know people who say yes, but they're wrong.

I'm also an optimist. I believe that Turks, like Americans, are smarter and more courageous than their government, which continues to deny reality. I'm encouraged by the intellectual vigor and sheer bravery of people who risk years in a Turkish prison simply for asking questions. I'm encouraged that Turkish novelist Orhan Pamuk, who was prosecuted after bravely acknowledging the slaughter of the Armenians, won the Nobel Prize for literature in 2006—-and that it was impossible for his government to keep that news from its people.

I think eventually freedom of speech and freedom of thought will be realities in Turkey because the Turkish people will demand them. When that happens, their history books will be rewritten and the arguments about the Genocide will be settled.

If only I were as optimistic about my own country.

As a senator, Barack Obama declared that "the Armenian Genocide is not an allegation, a personal opinion, or a point of view, but rather a widely documented fact supported by an overwhelming body of historical evidence. The facts are undeniable. An official policy that calls on diplomats to distort the historical facts is an untenable policy."

As a presidential candidate in 2008, Obama promised to correct that policy and recognize the Armenian Genocide. Armenians across the country responded with applause, votes and—most important—money.

Three months after his inauguration, President Obama broke his promise.

His "Armenian Remembrance Day" statement on April 24, 2009 omitted the word genocide. Instead of insisting that Turkey deal honestly with its past, Obama fashioned a false equivalency by encouraging "the Turkish and Armenian people to work through this painful history in a way that is honest, open and constructive." He added insult by asserting, "I have consistently stated my own view of what occurred in 1915, and my view of that history has not changed."

So much for his earlier insistence that the Armenian Genocide is factual and not "a point of view." The lessons I take from this have little to do with Obama, who is hardly the first Western politician to spurn Armenians after courting them. Politicians come and go, but the Armenians endure—yet so does our vulnerability to such perfidy. I wonder, and I worry, how long that can go on. Reading up on the Genocide and its aftermath only raised more doubts.

The intrigue and infighting across the Caucuses before and after the First World War is fascinating but hard to follow as alliances of convenience came and went. The strangest of all may have been the unlikely confederation of Armenians, Georgians and Azeris who briefly formed a Transcaucasian Republic amid the turmoil in 1917 before splintering apart and taking aim at each other. All around them, Turkish, Russian and German forces vied for position, as the oil fields of Baku in what is now Azerbaijan became the great prize of the Great War. Then Russia quit the battlefield after the Communists took power, and the Turks seized the opportunity to drive toward the Caucuses. Armenian troops marched into the breach and defeated Turkish armies in three decisive battles in the spring of 1918. The resurgent Armenians not only saved what was left of their clan, they helped seal victory for the Western powers, who dubbed Armenia their Little Ally.

Armenia declared its independence on May 28, 1918. It sounds like a happy ending but it ended nothing. The fighting continued and so did the jockeying and manipulation of greater forces. You can read very well-researched and carefully considered accounts but my own reading boils down to this: The Allies decided Armenia was a bad bet. To guarantee its survival would require a considerable investment of money, troops and probably lives. As always in the Western world, the pivotal question wasn't, "What will happen to these poor people if we don't help them?" Instead, it was, "What's the payoff for us if we do?"

In his book *The History of Armenia*, Simon Payaslian, a professor of modern Armenian history at Boston University, recounts the confusing choices faced by the leadership of the fragile republic. Almost all of those choices were bad. Payaslian writes that the Armenians expected the British to help in their continued territorial clashes with the Azeris, but the British were "concerned primarily with gaining access to oil supplies via the Baku-Batum pipeline, and they considered the Muslim leadership with Turkish support far more reliable as a political and military force in the region."

Armenia struggled along until August 1920, when the Great Powers seemed prepared at last to stand by their Little Ally. As penance for taking the losing side in the world war, Turkey signed the Treaty of Sevres with France and Great Britain. In doing so, it acknowledged the Republic of Armenia's sovereignty. It also accepted Armenia's borders, which took in much of historic Western Armenia and gave the country a vital port on the Black Sea. The following month, Turkish troops overran those borders. The French and British expressed disapproval but did nothing to stop the invasion. With its army surrounded, its supply lines blocked and the enemy closing in on the capital, Armenia's government pleaded for an armistice on Nov. 7, 1920.

While brushing up on the events of these gloomy days, I came across a dispatch in the *New York Times* by independent journalist Paxton Hibben dated exactly two weeks after Armenia sued for peace. Hibben portrayed a scene of utter hopelessness. Armenians living on what the international powers had certified as their own land were under siege by Turks as well as Soviet-backed Azeris. The Republic of Armenia had ceased to exist "except as a fugitive thing, a shadow government representing a scattered and fleeing people." Armenia's miraculous post-war resurrection had lasted just two years and six months. Because of my ingrained habit of reading even old news as news rather than history, I felt as though I were sitting at the breakfast table on Nov. 21, 1920, choking on my corn flakes as I read about the disintegration of free Armenia. Each time I read about it, I feel betrayed and that is a sickening feeling.

How can be it be that the victorious nations of Europe and America suddenly abandoned their Little Ally? Hibben's account shows that it wasn't sudden at all. The Republic of Armenia, born poor and weak, never had a chance to grow strong enough to survive. Among the examples Hibben gives of the Allies' treachery: The British stripped all the artillery from the Armenian fortress city of Kars in 1918 in order to supply their own army, then withdrew. The Armenian forces were driven out by Turks. The purloined armaments were never replaced when Kars returned to Armenian possession after the war; instead, the artillery wound up in the hands of the Russian Bolsheviks. Armenia raised $1.25 million to buy replacement artillery from the British, who took the money but never delivered the heavy guns. The

Italians, meanwhile, were selling artillery to the Turks. When Hibben asked an Italian source why, he got the answer: "Why not? They pay."

As a result, Armenians had only rifles for defense against Turkish cannons when the Turks laid siege to Kars in 1920. The outcome was disaster for the Armenians. It's impossible for me to read this and believe Europe ever had any serious intention of protecting Armenia, much less nurturing it. It is impossible for me to read this without tears.

Hibben was wrong about this: Armenia's government did still exist. It had enough life left on Dec. 2, 1920 to sign its own death warrant, the Treaty of Alexandropol. In return for the protection of Russian troops, the Republic agreed to self-destruct and make way for a Communist regime. Parliament never got a chance to ratify the treaty before being dissolved Soviet-style. Any debate among its former members had to be carried out in the gulags, or as sabers crashed down on their necks.

Unlike the Genocide, the fall of the Republic was a topic my father spoke to me about. He wanted me to know that the Armenians weren't blameless. He hated Communists, but he hated Armenian Communists most of all. He wanted me to understand that the republic was weakened from within by subversion and treachery. I've read plenty since to show that he was right, but the Armenian weakness for corrosive dissension didn't need encouragement from subversives. The chief political factions agreed on nothing from the beginning, not even whether to declare independence. Even the nation's most honored hero, General Antranik Ozanian, left the country in 1919 rather than continue to squabble with a government that spurned his advice. Because of this, the first Republic of Armenia faced its final struggle without its greatest general and most galvanizing leader.

Flash forward nearly a century to February 2013. I really am sitting at the breakfast table reading *The Times* when I spot a story about a group of entrepreneurs in Azerbaijan who want to build a dazzling resort city from scratch. They seem aware that Azerbaijan doesn't top most people's list of must-see destinations, but neither did Dubai until the oil sheiks discovered that a few judicious squirts of profit here and there could produce a desert wonderland of water parks, ski resorts and theme parks. The Azeris are confident they can out-do Dubai. Money is no object because Azerbaijan is now rich.

The *Times* explained it this way: "In 2006, Azerbaijan started pumping crude from its oil field under the Caspian Sea through the new Baku-Tbilisi-Ceyhan pipeline. Now, with the help of BP and other foreign energy companies, one million barrels of oil course through the pipeline daily, ending at a Turkish port on the northeastern corner of the Mediterranean Sea. This makes Azerbaijan a legitimate energy power (the world's leading oil producer, Saudi Arabia, produces 11 million barrels every day) with a great deal of potential."

The good news here is that the Baku gusher came in about 90 years too late to help Kaiser Wilhelm. Other than that, the contrast between Azerbaijan's prosperity and Armenia's struggles is stark, and the gap is likely to widen. Armenia has no oil and not much else that's easily turned into cash. Although Armenia regained its independence in 1991 after the collapse of the Soviet Union, it still suffers from its long-ago bargain with the devil at Alexandropol. After occupying the capital in 1920, the Soviets ceded nearly 80 percent of Armenia's territory to the Turks and Azeris, and what remains today is landlocked and blockaded by hostile neighbors—so hostile that soon after the Soviet withdrawal, Armenia and Azerbaijan plunged into war over the historically Armenian territory of Karabakh. Armenian forces won, but the issue is far from settled.

The *Times* story notes that in recent years, Azerbaijan has cleverly exploited its wealth and geopolitical position to elevate its international status. It is clearly seeking military as well as economic leverage. "These days, Azerbaijan, which is overwhelmingly Muslim, buys advanced weapons systems from Israel in return for oil," the paper reported. As the Italians would say, they pay—and apparently quite well. Reading the story propels me deeper into the digital clip files for more detail. I find that Israel sold $1.6 billion in missiles and drones to Azerbaijan in 2012. The conceit is that Israel wants a regional balance against Iran, but no one believes Azerbaijan is going to attack Iran. Azerbaijan is still at war with Armenia. The gun barrels are mostly cold these days but there's no peace treaty and plenty of violations of the cease fire. Azerbaijan clearly wants Karabakh back and is positioning itself to take it.

So what exactly has changed in a hundred years? There are many more Armenians in the West now and many have prospered. We are no longer the Starving Armenians, which is good any way you look at it. To Americans, we are real people who live next door, which means we may be less sympathetic than those rag-wrapped children on Near East Relief posters but we're harder to ignore. We're better organized politically, and our factions cooperate at least some of the time on some matters. We know a bit about politics and how to influence it, and we have money to cultivate a friendly ear or two in important places. We have a little more leverage, a better chance of being heard if not listened to.

Unfortunately, what hasn't changed—what may never change—is what matters most. The world's sympathy and support are still up for auction, and Armenia is being out-bid. It is all just too much to think about every day of my life, which is how often I'm reminded that I'm Armenian as I think about my father's half-finished stories. My digestion demands at least occasional diversion into more positive or at least neutral Armenian contemplation.

My wife and I share one such practice: We stay seated at the end of a movie while everyone else pushes past us to leave the theater. We sit through the credits, scanning the screen for Armenian names. You'd be surprised how often they turn up—sometimes an actor or director, sometimes the kid who fetched coffee for the actors and director. I know lots of other Armenians who do this. For us, it's fun; for our parents' generation, it was survivor's reflex. To see an Armenian name anywhere meant you were not alone. An Armenian name on an office directory or a newspaper masthead or in movie credits was an important sign of progress as well as acceptance.

One famous Armenian name overshadowed all others throughout my youth: William Saroyan. Never mind that so many people today, even literate people, know almost nothing about him. Saroyan was one of the great American writers of the 1930s and '40s, a time when very good writers were as plentiful as hobos and just as easily ignored. As a writer and as a personality, Saroyan was captivating. He was dashing, egotistical, bombastic, and profoundly talented. He stood shoulder to shoulder with the literary giants of the era: Steinbeck, Dos Pasos, Hemingway. They are all better-remembered and more highly regarded today. To me, the dishonor belongs to the critics. You can argue, but you'll be talking to yourself. I adopted Saroyan as my favorite writer when I was a kid, for the obvious reason. I read everything he wrote, even his later and lesser novels like *Rock Wagram*, about an Armenian waiter named Aram Vagramian who is discovered by Hollywood but has to change his name to get into the movies.

My favorite Saroyan story was *My Name Is Aram*. My best friend was named Aram, so I decided the story was about him. We all loved Saroyan because he wrote about characters with Armenian names and he had an Armenian name and he told everyone, every day of his life, that he was Armenian. He even went to Armenia and wrote about that, although by then only Armenians were paying attention. We loved him because that was OK with him. He continued to write for the *Hairenik Weekly* and other Armenian publications that paid him little or nothing even when he was a rich and famous man. We loved him most of all because he wrote this:

I should like to see any power of the world destroy this race, this small tribe of unimportant people, whose wars have all been fought and lost, whose structures have crumbled, literature is unread, music is unheard, and prayers are no more answered. Go ahead, destroy Armenia. See if you can do it. Send them into the desert without bread or water. Burn their homes and churches. Then see if they will not laugh, sing and pray again. For when two of them meet anywhere in the world, see if they will not create a New Armenia.

Saroyan really grabbed hold of me when I read an interview in which he said, "All Armenians are writers." What better recommendation could I get? I decided to follow Saroyan's example as well as his advice. I spent a good deal of my youth in my bedroom, typing short stories about Armenians. They were awful. I rarely managed to write more than a page or two before that dawned on me, but I didn't stop trying for a long time. I wrote plays, too, but they were no better than the stories. I couldn't understand why, since I was sure Saroyan had to be right. I finally spotted the loophole: He didn't say all Armenians could write fiction. I decided I was meant to be a journalist, which is easier because you don't have to make up the story.

After thirty-some years of mostly continuous employment, I had to concede it worked out. It doesn't bother me that I never won a Pulitzer Prize, because Saroyan did and he refused to accept it. Many people think of Pulitzers as newspaper awards, but they're given for all kinds of writing and photography as well as music and cartoon work. Saroyan won for his play *The Time of Your Life.* He explained that if you grant someone else the right to judge your work, you have to accept criticism as well as praise. He wasn't interested in either one. Saroyan's stubborn and principled insistence on being the sole judge of his own writing made a deep impression on me. In all my years in newspapers, I never entered a writing contest. It is the one quality of my career that I can confidently call Saroyanesque.

I felt such pride in my imagined connection to this great man that I felt truly crushed when I discovered that he wasn't necessarily a great man. He was a gambler who chiseled his friends out of money to pay his debts. He turned his back on his wife and his children. One by one, he alienated most of the people who'd loved, championed, and rewarded him. It was all completely at odds with his public persona, which was all high spirits and happy-go-lucky humor.

Even after I learned so much about Saroyan's faults I retained my admiration for the man and his writing. For all his style and wit, the trait I admired above all in Saroyan was his determination to keep going in whatever direction he chose, absolutely refusing to be slowed or sidetracked by anyone else. By the 1950s, the critics had soured on him, theater audiences followed the critics and readers let his books pile up in the discount bins. But Saroyan kept writing, and writing. He showed no hint of discouragement nor loss of confidence. No matter what setback Saroyan experienced, he announced that everything would be OK. His next book would be the greatest book ever written. His next play would make everyone forget every play written before. To me, this was the essence of being Armenian. I believed it was ingrained in the Armenian consciousness that if we quit, we are done for, in life as well as in battle. You fight even if you know you are going to lose; even if you've already lost. The Armenian revolutionaries, always outnumbered, were driven by the imperative: *Haratch!*—Forward! Retreat, no matter how seemingly sensible or even inevitable, was punishable by death.

The accomplishments of the inexhaustible Armenians forging ahead against all odds have grown more wondrous over the years as I've continued to read about them. I might have emptied my envelopes, spread the scraps across the dining room table, and written an unapologetic love story, except that I can still hear the voice of my father.

My father never finished his stories, but he told me the truth, which was the hardest part. The truth about our inherited sadness and anger is so painful that many Armenians are reluctant to explore it too deeply. It is much easier to be one of those casual Armenians who limits his involvement to shaking hands after church, playing backgammon once a year at the community picnic, and hanging a picture of Saroyan in the hall bath. It is easier still to be an Armenian-in-absentia like me, insisting you have no interest in politics or church feuds, conveniently unfamiliar with the language so you can just shrug and plead ignorance to escape all unwanted contact and conversation.

My steady retreat from Armenian affairs reveals the fault in my insistence that Armenians retreat from nothing. I also flattered myself and all the rest of us when I concluded that we are so tough that we cannot be eradicated. It is what we all want to believe—what we almost have to believe—because the truth about what we've done to ourselves is much harder to accept than the truth about what anyone else has done to us. We have failed each other many times by letting petty disagreements distract us from vital goals, abandoning our common cause.

Time and again we have chosen survival over freedom. King Dikran kept his crown only because he fell to his knees at the feet of his conqueror, and the generations who followed him followed his example. We bowed to Romans, Persians, Arabs, Greeks, Mongols, Russians, and Turks. We surrendered our independence, our dignity, and sometimes even our children. We survived through shrinkage, becoming so small and unthreatening that no enemy ever bothered to deliver the final blow.

There is an Armenian adage that admonishes us against these weaknesses: "Do not cross the coward's bridge, let the flood carry you; do not sleep in the fox's hole, let the lion devour you." I read this in a book my father gave me, the memoirs of Rouben Der Minasian, an Armenian patriot-turned-writer. The admonition is the lesson at the end of his account of the death of Serop Aghpiur. Serop was so fierce, so determined that the Turks called him pasha, a title of respect. The Armenians called him Aghpiur, meaning wellspring, because the spirit of Armenian resistance to Turkish oppression flowed from him to the nation.

Serop was so inspiring to Armenians that his enemies wanted him dead at any cost, but his death cost them nothing more than a cheap bribe to an Armenian traitor who put poison in Serop's tobacco. The enemy waited until Serop was nearly dead before invading his camp. Blinded by the poison, Serop ordered his men to prop him up so he could die emptying his rifle at the advancing Kurds.

I understand now why I cry when I read this. I'm not just sad, I'm embarrassed. I am embarrassed that the weak and frightened man who betrayed Serop is a familiar character from our history. I am embarrassed that King Dikran was betrayed to the Romans by his own son. I am embarrassed by the *nakharars*, our nobles, whose loyalty was so often to themselves first and then to whoever courted them. I am embarrassed by how often and how easily so many of our political leaders, our priests, and our intellectuals were bullied, bribed, or flattered into betraying their nation.

I wonder how many Armenians are bothered by these things? I wonder how many think about them, or know about them. I learned none of it reading Saroyan. His characters may speak Armenian or eat Armenian food or talk about the old country, but most seem to have been born at the beginning of each story, alive but without a past. They are not struggling with survivor's guilt or anger. They are not fighting about Armenian politics. They are not silenced by the burden of unbearable sadness. They are just heart-warming immigrants scraping by with a smile.

You could read hundreds of Saroyan tales and never come across a mention of the Genocide, the overarching event that shaped his life and all the lives of all the Armenians in the world. Saroyan's references to the tragedy were mostly oblique until his later years, when only a few Armenians still read him. His own daughter, Lucy, didn't know about the Armenians' haunting memory of their near extinction until she read the book *Passage to Ararat* as an adult.

Like Saroyan, the author's father was one of the first writers of Armenian descent to achieve success in the diaspora. Unlike Saroyan, he made no show of being Armenian. Born Dikran Kouyoumdjian in Bulgaria, he developed a most Anglo persona while growing up in England and he chose a name to suit: Michael Arlen. His son, whom he also named Michael, grew up with no real sense of his father's background. As a grown man in the 1960s, he made a journey of self-discovery to Soviet Armenia, where he was guided to a monument to the martyrs of 1915. "To be Armenian is to have this intolerable weight of sadness on one's soul," his guide told him, but Arlen could feel no such weight. He was urged to toss a flower into the eternal flame while thinking of all the victims who shared his blood, but Arlen hesitated. He felt no connection to those people.

Lucy Saroyan read this and immediately called her father. She interpreted Arlen's hesitation as shame, according to Saroyan biographers Lawrence Lee and Barry Gifford. She could not understand this talk about martyrs and sadness and intolerable weight, much less why anyone could fail to be happy to be Armenian. "All my life I've been proud of it and bragged to everybody that I was an Armenian, and I don't understand," she said. Her father replied: "It's time for you to know now. I wanted always to protect you from that. I wanted you to feel that it was a great and joyous experience, that it was full of laughter and love and fun."

It may be understandable and even admirable for a parent to shield his child from unpleasantness, but it is inexcusable for a writer of Saroyan's gifts. Great writers are supposed to explore great themes and great truths, no matter how ugly. They are supposed to be unafraid. Most of all, they are supposed to help the rest of us understand the world and deal with our pain, not hide it or hide from it.

This is what infuriates me about Saroyan now. I believe he failed me, even if I had no right to expect more. Why can't I be like other Armenians who love Saroyan for his flattery? We have every reason to demand adulation from our own writers after taking so much crap from the rest of the world. The failure, in that sense, is mine. I'll be reminded by every Armenian who reads this book that I am committing a shame by revealing the essential truth that in addition to being enduring, inventive, and ever faithful, we can be weak, quarrelsome, and so frightened that many of us will flee across the coward's bridge rather than face the flood.

This may be the truest source of my lingering anger. I have reached the same conclusion about Armenians that I have reached about all of our enemies through the ages.

We are merely human.

POSTSCRIPT

My favorite picture of my father was taken when he was about seventy years old. He is sitting on a couch, holding my baby daughter, Mandy, his only grandchild. They are both smiling. There is nothing anyone else would find remarkable about this family snapshot, carelessly composed and poorly lit, but it means the world to me.

Nishan and granddaughter Mandy.

I think about his father, who never smiled again from the day he left his family behind, and I think about his mother, murdered when she was so young. I think about my poor father as a boy, homeless and hungry. I think about him shivering from malarial fever in the tropics and shivering from the bone-chilling cold in the Ardennes. I think about all the people who tried so earnestly to kill him over so many years—Turks and Kurds and bandits and Nazis.

This is the greatest lesson my father taught me: After all that, he could still be happy. All it took was the love of his family.

Sources and acknowledgments

I am indebted to many wonderful friends and relatives who answered my tiresome queries about long-ago events and long-gone loved ones. At the risk of offense and omission, I must single out Alice and Azie Bakalian, Charlotte Ermoian, Ed and Mary Murachanian, and Gloria Allum. Especially generous were my mother-in-law, Mary Dabbakian, who sat patiently through my numerous interrogations, and Zabelle Dabbakian Keil, who lent me her written memoir.

My old friends Aram Aslanian, Greg Nedurian, and Sarkis Shirinian amended and amplified my imperfect memory of our shared childhoods. Ara Dinkjian was especially generous in contributing time and attention. He provided support at a critical time.

Also invaluable were my odar sounding boards, David Blasco and Bonnie Gross, and Kevin and Barbara Hall, who lent advice and encouragement. My friend and former colleague Ron Silverman helped immensely by asking the kind of wise-editor questions that too many young journalists today will never hear.

My wife Robyn, as always, proved to be my strongest champion and smartest adviser.

I must also thank the many contributors to the development of the Internet, which has made genealogical and historical research vastly more convenient. Census data once accessible only through hours of squinting at microfilm at a regional archive is now easily tapped through the website of the Palm Beach County Library system. The same portal allowed me to read histories of such disparate places as Chelsea, Massachusetts, and Visalia,

California. I also found a bonanza of other web data, including scans of wartime draft cards and immigrant passenger lists, at the subscription service Ancestry.com.

Also valuable were a number of online sources for Armenian history and culture, including the Armenian Research Center at the University of Michigan (http://www.umd.umich.edu/dept/armenian) and the electronic archive ArmenianHouse.org.

Historical editions of the *New York Times* are also available online, and I relied on them heavily as sources of contemporaneous reporting on the Armenian Genocide as well as such events as the assassination of Archbishop Levon Tourian. Other periodicals essential to my research were the *Armenian Weekly* and the *Armenian Review*, particularly the early volumes, from 1948 to 1960.

Because this is not an academic work, I've omitted footnotes. Instead, I've used the journalistic technique of attributing information to the source where I thought it was essential. I relied on the following books to deepen my meager knowledge of Armenian affairs, the military, and history in general. The list should be read with this caveat: All misinterpretations and faulty conclusions are my own and should not be charged to the authors of these generally excellent works:

The Armenians, by Sirarpie Der Nersessian

The Armenian Community, by Sarkis Atamian

Armenian Tigranakert/Diarbekir and Edessa/Urfa, edited by Richard G. Hovannisian

Armenia, Cradle of Civilization, by David Marshall Lang

Armenian Freedom Fighters: The Memoirs of Ruben Der Minasian

The Armenian Genocide: News Accounts from the American Press: 1915–1922, by Richard D. Kloian

Armenia, Travels and Studies, by H. F. B. Lynch

The Church of Armenia, by Patriarch Malchia Ormanian

Corregidor, by James H. Belote and William M. Belote

Corregidor: The End of the Line, by Eric Morris

59th Coast Artillery Soldier's Handbook

General Andranik and the Armenian Revolutionary Movement, by Antranig Chalabian

The History of Armenia, by Simon Payaslian

The History of the Armenian Genocide, by Vahakn N. Dadrian

The History of the Armenian People, by Jacques de Morgan

History of Lewond, the Eminent Vartapet of the Armenians, by the Reverend Zaven Arzoumanian

Last Rites: The death of William Saroyan, by Aram Saroyan

The Legacy: Memoirs of an Armenian Patriot, by Arshavir Shiragian

Paratrooper!, by Gerard M. Devlin

Passage to Ararat, by Michael J. Arlen

Saroyan, by Lawrence Lee and Barry Gifford

A Daring Young Man, by John Leggett

The Slaughterhouse Province, by Leslie A. Davis, edited by Susan K. Blair

The Splendid Blond Beast: Money, Law and Genocide in the Twentieth Century, by Christopher Simpson

Survivors: An Oral History of the Armenian Genocide, by Donald E. Miller and Lorna Touryan Miller

Tigranes II and Rome by H. Manandyan, translated by George A. Bournoutian

Turkish Armenia, by the Reverend H. F. Tozer

ABOUT THE AUTHOR

Douglas Kalajian is a retired journalist who worked for the *New York Daily News*, the *Miami Herald* and the *Palm Beach Post*. He is the author of the nonfiction book *Snow Blind* and co-author of *They Had No Voice: My Fight for Alabama's Forgotten Children*. He and his wife, Robyn, produce a website devoted to Armenian cooking (www.TheArmenianKitchen.com). They live in Boynton Beach, Florida.

19114772R00148

Made in the USA
Middletown, DE
04 April 2015